EUROPEAN *REVIEW* **OF** P...

Editorial Board
Manuel Garcia Carpintero
Roberto Casati
Eros Corazza
Jérôme Dokic
Petr Kotátko
Martin Rechenauer
Gianfranco Soldati
Tom Stoneham
Christine Tappolet

EUROPEAN *REVIEW* OF PHILOSOPHY

Response-Dependence
3

edited by
ROBERTO CASATI
AND CHRISTINE TAPPOLET

CSLI Publications
Center for the Study of Language and Information
Stanford, California

Copyright © 1998
CSLI Publications
Center for the Study of Language and Information
Leland Stanford Junior University

02 01 00 99 98   3 2 1
ISBN: 1-57586-105-4
ISBN: 1-57586-104-6 (pbk.)

CSLI Publications reports new developments in the study of language, information, and computation. In addition to lecture notes, our publications include monographs, working papers, revised dissertations, and conference proceedings. Our aim is to make new results, ideas, and approaches available as quickly as possible. Please visit our website at

http://csli-www.stanford.edu/publications/

for comments on this and other titles, as well as for changes and corrections by the author and publisher.

The text in this book was set by CSLI Publications in Minion, a typeface designed by Robert Slimbach. The display type is set in Stone Sans, designed by Sumner Stone. The book was printed and bound in the United States of America.

Contents

Realism or Response Dependence? / 7
    MARK POWELL

Euthyphronism and the Physicality of Colour: A Comment on Mark Powell's "Realism or Response-Dependence?" / 21
    CRISPIN WRIGHT

The Essence of Response-Dependence / 37
    RALPH WEDGWOOD

Terms, Things and Response-Dependence / 61
    PHILIP PETTIT

Red, Bitter, Good / 73
    PETER RAILTON

Response-Dependence Without Reduction / 91
    MICHAEL SMITH

Two Paths to Pragmatism II / 115
    HUW PRICE

Response-Dependence, Kripke and Minimal Truth / 155
    JIM EDWARDS

Rule-Following, Response-Dependence, and McDowell's Debate with Anti-Realism / 181
    ALEXANDER MILLER

Interpretivism / 205
    ALEX BYRNE

Metaphor and Judgements of Experience / 231
    ALISON DENHAM

Possibility and Conceivability: A Response-Dependent Account of Their Connections / 261
    PETER MENZIES

☞ MARK POWELL[1]
Realism or Response Dependence?

A central claim of various recent works by Philip Pettit (1990, 1991 and 1992) is that response dependence in a discourse is compatible with characteristically realist intuitions about its associated properties. This claim conflicts directly with a central theme in the work of Crispin Wright (see, inter alia, 1989, 1992 and forthcoming) who argues that response-dependence seriously undermines realist intuition about the associated properties by establishing a Euthyphronic rather than a Socratic conception of their metaphysical status. In this paper, I endorse Wright's view of the relationship between response dependence and realism. In that light, I suggest, Pettit's discussion of response dependence points up an instability in Euthyphronic anti-realism akin to that highlighted by Mark Johnston's "missing explanation" argument (1993). I indicate how the stability of Euthyphronic anti-realism may be defended in face of these challenges by generalizing the considerations that Davidson adduces in support of his thesis of anomolous monism.

1. Wright's Order of Determination Test and The Extremal Condition

Wright describes an 'order of determination' test for the predicates of a discourse and classifies those that fail the test—predicates whose extensions are determined rather than merely tracked by best opinions—as response-dependent.[2] According to Wright's order of determination test we

---

1. Edited by John Divers and Alexander Miller, 8th June 1995.
2. Or more precisely as *judgement* dependent. But nothing turns on this distinction in the arguments that follow.

can establish that the extension of a predicate Ø is determined, and not merely tracked, by the best opinions of relevant judging subjects only if we can construct an appropriate *provisoed biconditional* of the type:

(PB) $(\forall x)(\forall y)(C(x,y) \rightarrow (Øx \leftrightarrow y \text{ judges that } Øx))$

which is true and meets the following further conditions: that the truth of the biconditional can be established *a priori*; that the conditions of optimal or ideal cognition that are appropriate to the discourse (the C conditions) can be specified *substantially*; and that the C conditions can be specified *independently* of assumptions about the actual extension of Ø. Crucially, however, Wright argues that these conditions of a prioricity, substantiality and independence do not jointly suffice to establish the determination of the extension of Ø by best opinions—sufficiency in this respect requires further that an *extremal* condition be fulfilled. And a proper understanding of the relationship between realism and response dependence requires an understanding of what motivates Wright's deployment of the extremal condition in his order of determination test.

The key observation is that there is at least one kind of case in which we may construct a provisoed biconditional which satisfies the conditions of a prioricity, substantiality and independence while leaving unsettled the question of the order of determination which obtains between the extension of the predicate in question and best opinions—thus:

(PB1) $(\forall x)(C(x) \rightarrow (x \text{ is in pain} \leftrightarrow x \text{ judges that she herself is in pain}))$

Wright's subsequent thought is that one who accepts that (PB1) is true and that it meets the three aforementioned conditions might hold, quite consistently, that this is so on the grounds that we merely track, albeit *infallibly so* in our own case, the independently constituted extension of "pain". Consequently, a further condition on response dependence is proposed which is motivated by the need to exclude the general possibility that the initial appearance of response dependence (i.e. the availability of an appropriate provisoed biconditional that meets the conditions of a prioricity, substantiality and independence) might lead us to form the unwarranted conclusion that the discourse *is* response dependent. Such a conclusion would be unwarranted in the circumstances so long as a detectivist explanation of the appearances of response dependence had not been ruled out.

Hence the *extremal* condition: *it shall not be possible, without reference to human judgement or the conditions under which these will be best, either fully to analyse or at least to draw attention to general characteristics of the truth-conferring states of affairs in such a way that the obtaining of an appropriate provisoed biconditional (meeting the conditions of priority, substantiality and independence) is a consequence of this analysis or characterisation.*[3]

Thus the extremal condition is calculated to enforce a contrast between a genuinely response dependent and an apparently similar but nonetheless response independent conception of the discourse. The crucial, but surely uncontentious, point that remains to be added is this: the kind of conception of a discourse which is intended to be so contrasted with a response dependent conception captures an intuition of a kind that is naturally and effortlessly classified as realistic—i.e. that truth for the discourse in question is constituted independently of any function of human judgement. Consequently, in Wright's understanding—and in mine—we are quite justified in saying that if appropriate provisoed biconditionals of a disputed discourse have been established not to satisfy the extremal condition then, even though they satisfy the conditions of a priority, substantiality and independence, we have arrived at a situation in which the proponent of a recognizably realistic (response independent) conception of the discourse wins the dispute with the proponent of a recognizably anti-realistic (response dependent) conception of the discourse.

2. Pettit and the Missing Explanation Argument

Pettit's central thesis is that, apparently contra Wright, realism about a property is not challenged by the discovery that there is a concept Ø which is a response dependent concept of that property.

According to Pettit, realism about any discourse involves three theses—namely the descriptivist, objectivist and cosmocentric theses.

The *descriptivist thesis* (Pettit 1991, pp. 589–90) is the thesis that 'discourse D posits distinctive items' the existence of which is necessary if the characteristic expressions of D are to have truth values. That such entities are posited is a 'non-substantive' proposition of D: if one were to deny that, when true, the expressions of D are so in virtue of the obtaining of states of affairs involving these posited entities, one would thereby display misunder-

---

3. See Wright (1992) pp. 123–4.

standing of the expressions used—a mistake on a par with talking about a married bachelor. The *objectivist thesis* (*ibid*, p. 590) is the conjunction of the claims: (i) that the objects posited in D (as in the descriptivist thesis) exist; and (ii) neither the existence nor the character of the objects posited causally depends on, or is otherwise supervenient upon the epistemic states of participants in the discourse D. The *cosmocentric thesis* (*loc. cit.*) initially represents a clearly recognisable aspect of realist intuition, namely, that in an area of discourse D for which a realist construal is apt, avoiding ignorance and error amounts to making contact with the independent states of affairs posited by the objectivist thesis.

The crucial aspect of Pettit's characterization of realism is the deployment of the cosmocentric thesis—more specifically it is a consequence that Pettit takes to follow from that thesis, namely, that for any substantive proposition of D (the one's you needn't believe to understand D) it is *contingent* that the practitioners do manage to make contact with the independent states of affairs posited by the objectivist thesis. For it follows in turn from this view of matters, that it is incompatible with realist intuitions concerning epistemic access to the facts that it should be a *non-contingent* matter that the competent practitioners of D access the facts.

Let us turn now from realism to response dependence. Pettit articulates his conception of the latter as follows:

> ...on the traditional image the secondary quality concepts are certainly response-privileging. They are such that certain human responses, at least under suitable conditions, represent a privileged mode of access: a mode of access that rules out error and ignorance... I shall be concerned here with the allegedly response-privileging character of certain concepts and I shall have that sort of phenomena in mind when I speak of response dependence.[4]

Thus, according to Pettit, what is distinctive of response dependent concepts (of which secondary quality concepts are arguably paradigmatic) is that it is impossible in certain situations to be in ignorance or error as to their extension. On the basis of these explications of the notions of realism and response dependence Pettit raises the matter of their inter-relation:

> The question with which we are concerned is how far realism about any area of discourse is undermined by an admission of response dependence in this sense. (Pettit 1991 p. 599)

---

4. Composed from Pettit (1991) p. 597 and p.599.

and on the basis of Pettit's explications of the key notions the answer to the question raised will, of course be "not at all". However this answer follows on from an understanding of the key notions of realism and response dependence which, in light of Wright's discussion, we are entitled to regard as deficient. For Wright's crucial observation, it will be recalled, based on the pain case, was that the a priori and so (we may infer) non-contingent status of a true and appropriate provisoed biconditional—even when the specifications of the C conditions meet the requirements of substantiality and independence—is not inherently at odds with realism (hence the need for the extremal condition). In light of Wright's observation it would seem that Pettit has overlooked the possibility that the conception of best opinions as reflecting extensions to may co-exist with a conception of best opinions as infallible, and in so doing Pettit has misconceived the key notions of realism, response dependence and their inter-relation.[5]

Once the relationship of realism and response dependence is conceived in line with Wright's observation we may, however, find in Pettit the suggestion of a widely applicable strategy which may be adopted in order to defend a realistic, response independent conception of the *properties* intimated by a discourse.

Consider an a priori provisoed biconditional for redness:

(PB2) $(\forall x)(\forall y)(C(x,y) \rightarrow (x \text{ is red} \leftrightarrow y \text{ judges that } x \text{ is red}))$

in which, we will imagine, the specification of the C conditions (involving good daylight, x's having the visual equipment actually statistically normal for humans…etc.) satisfies both the requirements of substantiality and independence. If realism about the property of redness is to be maintained in light of the a priori status of (PB2) then a suitable explanation of that status must be forthcoming. Pettit has a simple story to offer. In short, (PB2) is a priori because it is via our responses in C conditions that we fix the reference of 'red'. This much ensures that the concept *red* is response dependent since it picks out a reference via a mode of presentation which involves some response of ours. But this much is compatible with a realist intuition about the property so presented, for the property picked out via a response depen-

---

5. To be clear, it is not the Cosmocentric Thesis which misrepresents the realist intuition but the further claim that "error or ignorance are always possible with regard to the substantive propositions of the discourse." (Pettit 1991 p. 592).

dent mode of presentation is not any less apt for realist construal than it would be were it presented via any other mode of presentation. Pettit puts matters thus:

> We essay thoughts and assertions involving a property that we identify on the basis of certain exemplars. What property do we manage to engage with? What property do we fix upon as the referent of our concept? ...According to the story developed, the property that we fix upon, the property that provides the referent for the concept of redness, is that property whose instances evoke red sensations in normal observers under normal circumstances... Take the world as populated, independently of us, by a great range of objective properties... With a concept like that of redness, the question arises as to what determines that the concept will hook onto this property rather than that: say on to this reflectance property, to take a plausible sort of candidate, rather than some other. In maintaining that the concept is response dependent... all we may mean is that that question is to be answered in a particular fashion: the concept hooks on to that property, whichever it is, that evokes red sensations under normal conditions. (Pettit 1991 p. 609)

These remarks fall short of addressing the letter of the extremal condition (as formulated above) since Pettit refers to our responses in C conditions in giving his 'genealogy' of the concept of redness. However Pettit may be read as contributing an important response to the challenge which the spirit of the extremal condition presents to the realist by providing an explanation, consistent with realism about the property in question, of the a priori status of a relevant provisoed biconditional. The importance of Pettit's contribution, further, is to increase the pressure on the Euthyphronic anti-realist to answer the missing explanation argument due to Johnston (1993, Appendix1). The argument, in outline, is as follows.

At a quite general level we are likely to have an intuition to the effect that, at least sometimes, when we arrive at a true opinion about some a posteriori claim P, the state of affairs P is actually causally implicated in our coming to hold the opinion that we do. That is, we judge on evidence that P, and if our evidence, call it E, is, as we would think, good evidence for the a posteriori claim that P, that must surely be because P is in some way causally implicated in its being the case that E was available to serve as evidence—it may even be that causal connectedness of an appropriate kind is constitutive of E's being good evidence for P. Now consider this intuition as applied to a correct judgement, in C, that x is red. The intuition tells us that, if we are correct, and are correct because we have good evidence, as opposed to mere guesswork or bad evidence, it must be that x's being red is causally implicated in the availability of that evidence. Therefore, the story continues, x's being red is, even in conditions C, causally implicated, at least sometimes, in our coming to judge that x is red. But causal connections are a posteriori connections, so if redness is indeed causally implicated in our judging that x is red, the claim, expressed by the provisoed biconditional—that if x is red in C then we will judge that it is red—cannot be a priori. Conclusion: contra the Euthyphronist best opinion must track, not determine, the extension of redness.

The connection between Pettit and Johnston, I believe, is that both draw attention to an instability felt across the following three claims:

(a) Redness is causally active in C conditions
(b) There is an a priori connection, via the provisoed biconditional, between a supposed cause and effect
(c) Redness is not a physical property

The Euthyphronist claims both (b) and (c), while we are apt to have intuitions along the lines of (a). Johnston uses (a) to ground the rejection of (b), and by implication also of (c). Pettit's line is apt to seem attractive insofar as it allows (a) to coexist with (b), but does only at the cost of rejecting (c). Thus Pettit and Johnston both use the apparent tension across the above claims to reject the very idea—upon which Wright's Euthyphronism is based—that an order of determination test which is considered as a descriptive claim about the concepts we actually work with is realism-relevant. So how might the apparent tension be resolved and the Euthyphronic position stabilized?

An initial response has it that it is open to the Euthyphronist to resist acceptance of (a). It may be argued that the option of resisting (a) is available since the claim is no inherent part of our practice with colour discourse—in Pettit's terms, (a) is a substantial proposition rather than a metaphysical commitment of our practice. This is in essence the defensive strategy adopted by Wright (1992, p. 129). The first move is to deny that the a priority of the provisoed biconditional conflicts with the notion that redness and opinions about redness are causally connected. The general consideration that supports this denial is that the same relata may appear under one mode of description as a priori connected, while appearing under another to be only causally connected. For the notion of causal connectedness does not require that there is no mode of description that sustains an a priori connection between relata, rather it requires that there is *a* mode of description under which the relata are presented as being related by causal laws. So, (b) is not in immediate conflict with (a). Nevertheless, Wright argues, the claim (a) has the status of a hypothesis. Given that our practice with colour predicates is governed by the a priority of the provisoed biconditional, which lies behind (b), the claim (a) is not an inherent part of the practice. Indeed the substantiation of (a) awaits the discovery that it is one, or perhaps a few, natural kinds which are invariably causally implicated in our judging that x is red in conditions C. So Wright concludes:

> were we to become convinced that there is only a multiple physical *heterogeneity* among e.g. same-coloured things, it ought to cease to seem sensible to ordinary thought to view colours as causally explanatory of best opinions about them. But so I think it would. (Wright, forthcoming, p. 21).

In short Wright will be willing to admit to (a) when it has been shown that (c) is false. And showing that (c) is false will involve producing an interesting physical type with which the colour in question is actually, invariably correlated. Fleshing out the notion of an 'interesting type' of states of affairs, he writes:

> we have to be able to think of these states of affairs as doing more in the world than would be consistent with their serving merely to answer the semantic demands—(where there is truth, there must be truth-conferers)—of the judgements in question [e.g.., colour judgements]. And this means, crudely, that other things must be so because of the obtaining of such states of affairs besides our having the appropriate responses under the appropriate conditions. But if that it is to be the case, then it looks as though there must be some other kind of unity in states of affairs of the sort: object so-and-so is red, than: being such as to be judged red by normal observers, etc. For if that was the extent of the unity, there would be no reason to expect that one was dealing with an explanatorily unified kind;—and surely then there *would* be a question about the propriety of the kind of claim [(a)]. (Wright, 1991, ms p. 4)

So, in advance of establishing an appropriate empirical correlation between redness and some otherwise unified physical type the claim (a) ought to be resisted, and claims (b) and (c) accepted.

Wright's response to the problematic has features which I incorporate in the response that I will shortly offer, but it also raises worries which I regard as substantial. Firstly, it offers to give the game away if it turns out that there is a natural kind in common among red things. However unlikely that outcome, it is not appropriate for the Euthyphronist to offer such a hostage to empirical fortune. As far as our practice goes, the Euthyphronist should insist it is a priori that redness just is not any physical property, and a fortiori redness is not a physical type, interesting or otherwise: I will back this up presently. Secondly, the condition imposed on the classification of redness as a physical type might already be seen to be met: if the redness of my jumper can be causally efficacious in the fact that my jumper appears as red in a photograph—and would we really want to deny that?—it would appear that there is a lawlike connection between the colours things are, that is the colour they appear in C conditions, and the physical effect they have on the chemicals which coat a film. But this seems too slender a basis on which to rest the problematic claim that redness is, after all, a physical property. And accordingly, I contend, Wright's response gives too much credence to realist intuition. While the a priority of the provisoed biconditional is perfectly at one with realist intuition, here as elsewhere realist intuition requires too much of the world. That is, as far as redness goes anyway, I believe that the realist cannot accord the a priori biconditional a salient role in our colour discourse without forfeiting the claim that redness is a physical property which we track. In this case at least, the a priori status of the biconditional ensures that the extremal condition cannot be met.

3. The Anomalousness of Response Dependent Properties

What no one seems to want to accept is that the problematic triad of claims (a)–(c) may be consistent, yet if this could be made out to be so, the threats to Euthyphronism from Pettit and Johnston would simultaneously be defused. The project envisaged, then, involves showing how it can be maintained that colours can feature in causal explanation despite being a priori connected to some of their effects (our judgements in C conditions), and, as an a priori matter, that colours are not physical properties. The form of the project is familiar since a set of exactly parallel claims, about intentional states rather than colours, is claimed by Davidson (1980) to hold consistently in accord with his thesis of anomalous monism.

Davidson's tactic, recall, is to argue that insofar as a belief, desire or other intentional state *token* is identical to some *token* brain state that intentional state token can be causally efficacious. On the other hand, the holism of the mental supports, while the (putative) radical incommensurability of criteria of application ensures, that there can be no law-like connections between mental and physical *types*. *Co-extensionality* may obtain so that all and only instances of belief type B are instances of brain state type S, but, the thought proceeds, while co-extensionality is necessary for property identity more—at least necessary co-extensionality—is required. But the different "contractual obligations" which govern use in the respective discourses—the different criteria of application that govern the linguistic practices of attributing mental states and brain states respectively—ensure that there is no necessary co-extension of belief type B and brain state type S. For the criteria which determine the application of concepts of these different kinds, and of which extensions are a function, are governed by wholly incommensurable and holistic systems of evidence, these systems being governed by incommensurate constitutive norms: reason in the case of mental state attribution, cause in the case of brain states.[6] This line of thought, then (if cogent) supports the view that (some) mental states are causally efficacious, even though they are related a priori to actions which are their effects and it can be established a priori that they are not physical states.

My suggestion is that the Euthyphronist may be able to replicate Davidson's neat track in order to deal with the problem he faces in the parallel case of colour by defending the consistency of the three claims (a)–(c). In order to do so the Euthyphronist must establish (on a priori grounds) that there is (an analogue of) token–token identity, though there can be no type-type identities between colours and physical states, and he must do so in a way that is compatible with the thesis of the a priori relation of best opinions and colours.

The most promising strategy by which the Euthyphronist may secure these objectives opens by arguing from a strong thesis about the status of the relation between best opinions and colours to the rejection of type-type identity. The strong thesis is that true a priori provisoed biconditionals for colours should be regarded as constitutive principles about colours each of which states an indefeasible criterion of application for a colour predicate in C-conditions. The crucial thought then is that the thesis of identity of a colour property and a physically specified property—say redness and Ø—entails a modal thesis:

---

6. David Wiggins (1993) argues in just this fashion against claims of moral/natural property identity. [Note added by JD and AM]

(M) $\Box\,[(\forall x)(\emptyset(x) \leftrightarrow \text{Red}(x))]$

which is incompatible with the indefeasability thesis. The argument, then, is as follows. If the (substantial and independent) specification of the C-conditions yields an indefeasible, best opinion, criterion for the application of "red" in those conditions, then any other putative criterion of application—such as the presence of ∅—is defeated in the event of a clash with the C criterion. Now if redness is ∅, and this entails (M), then as a matter of *necessity* the ∅ criterion does not clash with the (indefeasible) C criterion, for if a predicate ("red") has an indefeasible criterion of application, no other criterion of application for the same predicate can be indefeasible, unless it is necessary that the two criteria should never clash. The necessity of that claim in this case however requires the *necessity* of the claim that if x has ∅ then this will *cause* x to look red in C. But, such a causal claim and so cannot be (unrestrictedly) necessary and so the the putative identity of redness and ∅-ness is defeated by the demonstrated contingency. The conclusion is that colours are not physical properties—there is no identity of types between redness and any physical property ∅—and the diagnosis of the failure of the opposing realist intuition is that realism here demands too much of the world in requiring the unrestricted necessity of a causal relation.

The next stage in the Euthyphronist's strategy involves the accommodation of the familiar and compelling thesis of the supervenience of colours on physical states and the defence of an analogue of token-token identity. The claims I endorse here on behalf of the Euthyphronist are that colours supervene on physical properties and that this supervenience principle is a further constitutive principle for colours which yields an indefeasible criterion of application for colour predicates. This much will plausibly suffice for (an analogue of) token-token identity of colours and physical properties, and so allow the causal intuition captured in (a) to stand. For given that a token of red is identical to a token of some physical property, the colour token will, qua token of a physical property, be causally implicated in the production of the appropriate responses (and then judgements) in C conditions.

I contend, on behalf of the Euthyphronist, that the weak supervenience thesis (S):

(S) $\Box\,(\forall x)[\text{Red}(x) \to ((\exists\emptyset)\,(\emptyset(x) \land (\forall y)(\emptyset(y) \to \text{Red}(y))))]$

—in which Ø varies over physical properties—is true and that (S) is a non-substantive commitment, in Pettit's sense, of our colour discourse. Indeed, supervenience claims have a potentially crucial role in any account of our colour discourse which takes the role of provisoed biconditionals to be salient. For in such an account the role of (S) is to combine with the biconditionals in order to regulate colour judgements that are made outwith C conditions. Direct observation alone cannot afford us a judgement about what colour an object is in the dark, but if the total physical structure of the object that obtained in the dark could obtain in C conditions, and the object in question appeared red in those conditions, then the supervenience thesis (S) entitles us to infer that the object was or would be red in the dark. In the account of our regulation of colour judgements, then, the constitutive principle of supervenience plays a role which is indispensable, but subservient to the indefeasible C criterion of application. Moreover, by adhering to the supervenience principle (S) the Euthyphronist may appeal, in every case where an object is red—as determined by the C criterion—and appears red to a suitably placed and equipped subject, to the presence of some underlying physical state in which redness is realized and which may figure in a causal explanation of the perceptual event. It is in that sense that the Euthyphronist is entitled to maintain thesis (a) that redness is causally active in C-conditions just as the anomolous monist is entitled to claim that beliefs and desires are causally active in the genesis of actions. Finally, the Euthyphronist can save the intuition that redness is causally active in C conditions without conceiving redness as a physical property. The Euthyphronist avoids the latter commitment because he is not committed to there being a suitably homogeneous physical type $\prod$ which—as a matter of necessity—all red things instantiate. For (S) is understood and endorsed here so that many values of Ø may be specifiable only disjunctively and the values may form a class which is "uninteresting" in Wright's sense and, indeed, as heterogeneous as you like.

In conclusion, the Euthyphronist needs a line of response to the challenges raised by Pettit and Johnston in face of the apparent tension that obtains across the triad of claims (a), (b) and (c). I have suggested that such a line of response may be forthcoming if the Euthyphronist is prepared: (i) to clarify and strengthen the sense in which best opinions determine extensions by insisting on the indefeasability of the C criterion for the application of colour concepts, and; (ii) to maintain the incompatibility of response dependence about colour concepts with realistic and objectifying intuitions about colour properties.

Dept. of Logic and Metaphysics
University of St. Andrews

References

Davidson, D. 1980. "Mental Events" in his *Essays on Actions and Events*. Oxford: Clarendon Press, 207–227.

Haldane, J. and C.Wright, eds. 1993. *Reality, Representation and Projection*. Oxford: Oxford University Press.

Johnston, M. 1993. "Objectivity Refigured: Pragmatism Without Verificationism" in Haldane and Wright, eds. 85–130.

Pettit, P. 1990. "The Reality of Rule-Following". *Mind* 99, 1–21.

Pettit, P. 1991. "Realism and Response Dependence". *Mind* 100, 587–626.

Pettit, P. 1992. *The Common Mind*. Oxford: Oxford University Press.

Wiggins, D. 1993. "A Neglected Position?" in J. Haldane and C. Wright, eds. 329–338.

Wright, C. 1989. "Wittgenstein's Rule-Following Considerations and the Central Project of Theoretical Linguistics" in A. George, ed., *Reflections on Chomsky*, Oxford: Basil Blackwell. 233–264.

Wright, C. 1991. "Notes on Pettit" (Unpublished ms.).

Wright, C. 1992. *Truth and Objectivity*, London: Harvard University Press.

Wright, C. forthcoming. "Order of Determination, Response Dependence and the Euthyphro Contrast".

CRISPIN WRIGHT
Euthyphronism and the Physicality of Colour: A Comment on Mark Powell's "Realism or Response-Dependence?"

According to a Euthyphronist about colour, the extension of central colour concepts like **red**[1] is partially determined by our (phenomenological, or doxastic) reactions under certain ideal conditions (C-conditions). Mark Powell's paper engages the important questions whether such a view can be reconciled with physicalism about colour and—not necessarily the same thing—with the idea emphasised by philosophers such as Mark Johnston[2] that, even under the most ideal conditions, objects' colour properties are *explanatory*—so causal-explanatory, presumably—of the relevant reactions. Elsewhere[3] I have ventured positive if somewhat provisional answers on both points, suggesting (in effect—I did not exactly so express matters) that colour *concepts* may be Euthyphronic while in effect presenting

---

Mark Powell, "Realism or Response-Dependence?", *European Review of Philosophy*, vol. 3, pp. 1–13. Thanks to John Divers, Jim Edwards and Alex Miller for helpful comments.
1. I shall in general use bold-face when referring to concepts, plain-face when speaking of properties.
2. See his "Objectivity Refigured: Pragmatism without Verificationism" in J. Haldane and C. Wright. eds., *Reality, Representation and Projection*, Oxford: Oxford University Press 1993.
3. In *Truth and Objectivity*, Cambridge, Mass.: Harvard University Press 1993, at pp. 128–132.

(what turn out to be) physical *properties* and that—if such are indeed the properties they present—then that safeguards the explanatory intuitions in question.

Powell is dissatisfied with this moderate Euthyphronism for two reasons. First, he regards it as doing less than justice to the causal-explanatory intuitions in question to portray them as hostage in this way to physical (optical) science. Rather, they are already entrenched in our thinking. (For instance, objects' colours are—he believes we would want to say—among the causes of the way they appear in photographs; so presumably have effects on the chemicals which coat a film.) Second, he believes that Euthyphronism should unconditionally insist that red is no physical property—the moderate position gives "too much credence to realist intuition".

1.

In order to understand the (somewhat complex) dialectical situation here, we may focus, as Powell suggests, on the status of three claims (I depart slightly from the formulations of his paper):

(a) That even under optimal, substantially specified conditions of observation, C, an objects' colour—say, its being red—is among the *causes* of its appearance—its looking red.

(b) That it is *a priori* that under such C-conditions, all and only objects look red which are red (the Euthyphronist's "provisoed biconditional").

(c) That red is not a physical type.

The four positions under consideration are then as follows.

(1) A proponent of the "Missing Explanation" objection, such as Mark Johnston, regards (a) and (b) as incompatible.

(2) Philip Pettit's response[4]—at least as naturally interpreted[5]—is that there is no incompatibility if an acceptance of (b) is consistent with the denial of (c)—with affirming that red *is* a physical type; and he proposes that such a combination is indeed consistent, provided the a priority of (b) may be viewed as of a piece with the a priority generally attaching to the connection between the *reference-fixers* for a natural kind concept and its instances. The

---

4. Philip Pettit, "Realism and Response Dependence", *Mind* 100, 1991, 587–626.
5. Pettit *loc. cit.* p. 609.

concept **water**, for instance, if indeed a natural kind concept, is so set up that nothing counts as falling under it unless of a kind of stuff which is dominantly causally responsible for the co-instantiation of the features—tasteless, colourless liquid, occurring naturally in lakes and rivers, satisfying thirst, essential to life, solvent for many substances, etc., etc.—by reference to which we fix its extension. It is thus a priori that water is the stuff which, if anything does, generally produces co-instantiations of those features—the a priority claim is quite comfortable alongside the causal one. And so also it may be with (a) and (b) if we regard looking red under C-conditions as a reference-fixer for "red".

(3) In *Truth and Objectivity*, I observed, however, that no Euthyphronic concept comfortably fits the paradigm of a natural kind concept, since a priority for a suitable provisoed biconditional is inconsistent with the hostage to reference-failure which any prototypical natural kind concept must hold out. Nevertheless, I suggested that we might feel free to identify the property presented by a Euthyphronic concept with a suitable physical type if one—or a small number of such—presented itself—and that such intuitive sympathy as we have with (a) may be accounted for by optimism about this possibility, resulting in a rejection of (c). However should this optimism prove unfounded, then, I suggested, we would—and ought—to regard the intuitions underlying the Missing Explanation argument as compromised.

It is worth saying a little more about how this contrasts with the view taken by Pettit. The idea that many general pre-scientific concepts are in like case with **water**, taken as a paradigm of a natural kind concept, comes into prominence with Putnam and Kripke[6] and contrasts with an older model, associated (I believe wrongly) with the later Wittgenstein, according to which it would be a mistake to treat the types of features listed for water—tastelessness, colourlessness, etc.—as sustaining a merely contingent (causal) relation to the real determinant of the extension of the concept. Rather, they fix that extension themselves, after the fashion of a cluster of *criteria*—in the technical sense of that term that arose in the first generation of commentary on the *Philosophical Investigations*. On this model it would

---

6. *Loci classici*: Hilary Putnam, "The Meaning of 'Meaning'", in K. Gunderson, ed., *Language, Mind and Knowledge*, Minnesota Studies in the Philosophy of Science VII, Minneapolis: Minnesota University Press 1975; and Saul Kripke, *Naming and Necessity*, Oxford: Blackwell 1972.

suffice without further ado for a substance to be water that it displayed (some weighted majority of) the relevant surface features. There would be no further relevant question about its non-manifest essential character.

Now clearly there *could* be concepts—*criterially governed* concepts—for which this model was correct. Even if our actual concept of water is indeed a natural kind concept, we might have employed instead a concept, **schwater**, for which the water-indicators did play a criterial rather than reference-fixing role. Thus while **water** would fail of reference were it to turn out that there is no interesting or explanatorily unifying property underlying the presence of the water-indicators, no such conclusion would be warranted for **schwater**. If "water" expressed **schwater**, its use would be indefeasible by any purely scientific developments. And so will be the use of "red" if it is indeed constrained by an a priori true, provisoed biconditional meeting the four Euthyphronic conditions.[7]

Clearly, though, our working with a criterially governed concept would be still be consistent with the scientific disclosure of a natural property underlying the characteristic co-manifestations of the relevant criteria—so that a corresponding natural kind concept, had we employed it, would have been in good shape. That would have been the situation if the concept we express by "water" had been **schwater**. **Schwater** would still have picked out H_2O. What in that case would show that the concept *was* nevertheless criterially governed?

Kripke was perhaps the first to see clearly that their involvement of natural kind concepts has implications for the modal status of certain thoughts. If water is a natural kind—say H_2O—then it is *essentially* of that kind: something which manifested all the indicators but was not so constituted would not be water but some other kind of stuff. By contrast, if **water** were criterially governed—if it were **schwater**—then such a substance would fall under the concept whatever its essential constitution, and we ought to allow that while its instances are (mostly) made up of H_2O, there could be instances which are composed quite differently. So if **water** is a natural kind concept, and it is true that water is H_2O, it is *necessarily* true that water is H_2O. But if **water** were a criterially governed concept, it would be *contingent* what constitution its instances had—or indeed whether they had any uniform or typical

---

7. Summarised by Powell at p. 5 of his paper.

constitution. To determine the status of our actual concept, then, we should check our intuitions about claims such as:

> Water is H2O, but it might have been constituted differently,

or:

> Water might have had no normal physical constitution.

If the concept is indeed a natural kind concept, these should impress as solecisms.

So too with **red**. The Euthyphronic proposal about the concept is, in effect, that it is criterially governed, with looking red under C-conditions one dominant such criterion. That allows for it to be *flexible* with respect to whatever, if any, typical physical constitution red things have; so it leaves us free to regard "red" as a non-rigid potential designator of physical kinds, just as "water" would be if it expressed the concept, **schwater**. That, in essentials, was the view in *Truth and Objectivity*.

(4) Powell's view is that Euthyphronism lacks even this option since it is committed to (c). However, he maintains, (a)–(c) are nevertheless compatible. If he is right, then both Pettit and I are wrong to suppose that the Euthyphronist can do anything but reject the suggestion that colours are physical types; but a pure—genuinely anti-realist—Euthyphronism about colour will nevertheless, Powell thinks, be unqualifiedly consistent with the intuitions which underlie the Missing Explanation argument.

2.

Since the position I tried to reserve for the colour Euthyphronist depends on the referential flexibility of "red", a reader may be disconcerted to find that a key premise for the argument Powell develops for (c) is that the identity of red with any physical property—say Ø—must, like the identity of water with H2O, be a matter of (metaphysical, or essentialist) *necessity*. However I propose to defer consideration of this for a while. I'll return to the matter after reviewing Powell's argument.

The premise entails that the thesis, (M):

$(\forall x)(\emptyset(x) \leftrightarrow \text{Red}(x))$,

must also hold as a matter of necessity. But if **red** is Euthyphronic, we also have that it is a priori—so necessary[8]—that an appropriate provisoed biconditional holds:

(*Red*) $(\forall x)(C(x) \rightarrow (Red(x) \leftrightarrow Looks\ red(x)))$

We thus have distinct yet indefeasibly necessary and sufficient conditions for x's being red: under *all conditions*, that it be Ø, and under *C-conditions*, that it look red. It must thus somehow be a matter of necessity that these never clash. Powell's thought is now that, since the connection between x's being Ø—a matter of the microphysical constitution of its surface, presumably—and its looking red, can only be a *causal* one, the necessity—under C-conditions—that there be no clash must require the necessity of a causal connection between being Ø and looking red. But no—one would like to say "merely"—causal connection can hold of metaphysical necessity. So something is amiss with any premises which require otherwise. The Euthyphronist, in particular, must therefore reject the necessity of the thesis M, irrespective of what physical type is chosen for Ø.

Again: the nerve of the thought is that if an object's being Ø gives a *metaphysical* guarantee—albeit in a restricted class of circumstances—of its having a certain appearance, the relation between guarantor and guaranteed cannot be merely causal. Euthyphronism about colour, coupled with the belief that colours are physical types, forces us to regard an object's being of such a type as providing such a metaphysical guarantee. But the connection—between an object's being of any particular physical type and its manifest appearance— *ought* to be at most a causal connection. So the Euthyphronist should jettison any supposition of type-type identity between colours and physical properties.

This line of argument is arresting. But there may seem to be an immediate line of response, deploying materials to which Powell himself is sympathetic. Briefly, it is by no means obvious that there has to be the tension between the notions of metaphysical and causal sufficiency which it assumes. Powell is hospitable to the idea that an account of response- or

---

8. Like Powell, I am taking it that metaphysical necessities of e.g. identity, origin and constitution can harmlessly commingle in inferential contexts with conceptual necessities. My own view is that they are actually the very same kind of—absolute—necessity, albeit (perhaps) originating in different ways.

judgement-dependence running along the lines I have proposed must incorporate something to the effect of my fourth *Extremal Condition* if a contrast is to be drawn between cases where ideal responses *partially determine* the extension of a concept and a case where they merely *infallibly track* an independently determined extension. If that is right, then—unless the idea of tracking is somehow not to be construed *causally* in any such case—there can be no solecism inherent just in the idea that it can be a matter of absolute necessity that, under certain substantially specified conditions, an object's possession of a certain property will be tracked by—hence causally implicated in the production of—a thinker's opinion or other form of response.

In sum: If (M) and (*Red*) are each necessary, then so is

(P) $(\forall x)(C(x) \rightarrow (\emptyset(x) \leftrightarrow \text{looks red}(x)))$.

Powell's thought is that, no matter what the background circumstances, the connection between an object's microphysical properties and its appearance can only be a causal one, and thus cannot be metaphysically guaranteed, even conditionally. The response is that if it is ever possible to have a conceptual guarantee that subjects who meet certain substantially specified conditions are infallible over a certain subject matter, a structurally similar provisoed biconditional will hold of necessity, even though their opinions be thought of as *produced by*—rather than determinative of—the subject matter in question. There is no obvious absurdity in the idea that while our opinions about some range of facts are in part caused by those very facts, we can nevertheless circumscribe in substantial terms all possible ways in which we might go astray and so—by hypothesising that none of them applies—generate a necessarily true provisoed biconditional.

It might be rejoined on Powell's behalf that there is still an unresolved tension. If the *only* way of reconciling the necessity of (M) and (*Red*) is by, in effect, construing the necessity of the latter as a reflection of subjects' *infallibility* about red under C-conditions, then that is precisely not to effect a reconciliation which the Euthyphronist about colour can accept. However this rejoinder misses the point. Powell's problem concerned the necessity not of (*Red*) but of (P): it is in (P) that the embedded biconditional must surely be agreed on all hands to call for a causal relation. To invoke the idea of infallibility in order to accommodate the necessity of (P) is *not*, however, a commitment to an infallibilist construal of the necessity of (*Red*). It is about the extension of the concept, Ø, that, according the suggestion, the satisfaction of the C-conditions brings infallibility. That is not a commitment to the idea that under C-conditions we are similarly (merely) infallible about the extension of **red**; for **red** is not Ø. The infallibility, or otherwise, of a class of judgements will be a function of the *concepts* they configure. There is no contradiction in the idea that while (*Red*) satisfies the Euthyphronist's extremal clause, (P) does not.

There will be more to say. However I now wish to canvass a different argument which, without involving any contention about causation, can deploy essentially Powell's materials—but with one additional presupposition—to reach the same conclusion: that for the Euthyphronist about colour, red cannot be a physical type.

Any claim that a certain truth is *conceptually* necessary is, of course, hostage to what we can, coherently and lucidly, conceive.[9] The needed additional presupposition just advertised is that *metaphysical* necessities generally are likewise defeasible by a successful attempt to conceive of their not holding. Thus no absolute necessity is genuinely counter-conceivable. It is just that when a necessity is claimed to originate in the essence or origin, e.g., of an object or substance, and is hence a posteriori, attempts at counter-conceiving are open to a certain kind of obstacle. For example, the alleged metaphysical necessity of water's being H2O is not defeated merely by lucidly conceiving of stuff in all manifest respects like water which turns out, microphysically, to be other than H2O, since it is question-begging to suppose that, in conceiving of stuff which is (merely) in all *manifest* respects like water, we thereby conceive of water. If water does indeed have a non-manifest essence, then those conceivings are different. In brief: when an alleged necessity is *de re*, any purported counter-conceiving must, if it is to work, be able to defend the claim that its content reaches right out to embrace the *res* in question, as it were, rather than stopping short at a surface of characteristic properties.

Now for the Euthyphronist about colour there can be, under the relevant C-conditions, no difference between being red and being in all *manifest* respects as a red thing would be—what the necessity of the provisoed biconditional ensures is, in effect, precisely that in this restricted class of circum-

---

9. Compare Hume: "...*whatever the mind clearly conceives, includes the idea of possible existence,* or in other words, *that nothing we imagine is absolutely impossible.*" *Treatise* Bk I, pt. II, section II.

stances, the essence of red is wholly open to view. And in that case the supposed metaphysically necessary identity of red with Ø *can be* put under pressure from a thought experiment, since it appears readily conceivable that conditions be C, that an object look red in them, and yet microphysical investigation discloses that the object is in some condition other than Ø.

It will strike readers familiar with Saul Kripke's *Naming and Necessity* that this line of thought is, nearly enough, an exact parallel to the famous argument there developed against physicalism about pain. To be sure, Kripke's argument exploits the fact that there is simply no provision for a phenomenal distinction between feeling pain and being in pain, whereas the argument just adumbrated runs from the premise that, under a restricted range of circumstances, there is no corresponding distinction between being red and looking so. But that difference is of no consequence, so long as the circumstances in question are ones which we can properly claim to be able to conceive as obtaining. And if the C-conditions are substantially specified, then surely we can.

This reconstruction of Powell's argument is worth a more detailed exploration than is possible here, and I hope to return to it on another occasion. The premise on which it depends, that all absolute necessities, metaphysical ones included, are subject to constraints of conceivability is a substantial item of modal epistemology and needs a substantial defence. Note, however how naturally it seems to have come to Kripke at least to assume this. It never seemed to occur to him to respond to the hypothetical objector, who thinks she can conceive of Hesperus turning out to be other than Phosphorus, or of heat being something other than molecular motion, or of water turning out not to be H_2O, by saying: "So what? What has conceivability to do with it? I didn't claim these things were *conceptually* necessary." Rather the validity of the prima facie conceptions, and their prima facie relevance, are straightaway conceded. The defence is rather that they are not of what they appear to be—that what is actually conceived in these cases goes no further than *qualitative* similarity to what was intended.

3.

Back now to the concern I bracketed earlier. It remains that the most that is in prospect from the foregoing considerations is a proof that colours are not physical types on the assumption that if they were so, it would be a matter of necessity that they were. That in effect is what is denied if we think, as in *Truth and Objectivity*, of colour concepts as criterially governed. Nothing has yet been said against that view.

However there is something which can be said. Where Ø is a specific physical property, the necessity—if true—of the proposition that red is Ø, would be carried by the rigidity of the term, "red". Now ordinary intuition would perhaps anyway support the claim that "red" *is* rigid—that in speaking of an object's redness in hypothetical circumstances, we would always intend to speak of the very same property which, in calling an actual object "red", we would intend to ascribe to it. If Euthyphronism about **red** is correct, however, then this intuition may be reinforced by a suggestive argument. *Do red things have a property in common?* Ordinary thought surely has it that they do: that, just in virtue of being red, samples of red—though of course they may differ in shade—always share a common determinable condition. (Contrast, say, samples of jade.) But if they do, then it is an inescapable consequence of the necessity of the provisoed biconditional, (*Red*), that the property in question must be conceived as one of which it is a necessary feature that it is possessed by any object with looks red under C-conditions.[10] Since if **red** were criterially governed, there *would be* no property which is *necessarily* possessed by all instances of the concept under C-conditions—for the whole point about criterially governed concepts is that they allow of variable modes of instantiation—it follows that Euthyphronism about colour, if it is to be consistent with our ordinary thinking, is a commitment against the idea that **red** is criterially governed. In that case the *Truth and Objectivity* proposal, that **red** is both Euthyphronic and criterially governed, is out of court and there is no extant obstacle to Powell's assumption that any identification of red with a physical type must purport to hold of necessity. So Powell's claim that no such identification is consistent with Euthyphronism remains to be rebutted.

4.

One common response to Kripke's original argument about pain is that it has no power against *token-by-token* identifications.[11] Any particu-

---

10. If (*Red*) is necessary, we have:
 Necessarily: $(\forall x)(C(x) \,\&\, \text{looks red}(x) \rightarrow \text{red}(x))$
 So a seemingly unexceptionable property-abstraction yields that red is that property F such that necessarily: $(\forall x)(C(x) \,\&\, \text{looks red}(x) \rightarrow F(x))$.

lar pain can still be a particular *token* physical state even if—assuming the argument is good—our concept of pain precludes identifying pain with a physical *type*. Powell's suggestion is that such a recourse is available to the Euthyphronist about colour too: indeed, that response-dependent concepts as a class will exemplify something akin to the anomalousness for which Davidson has made a case in connection with the intentional, and that just as Davidson's view is consistent with the physicality of token intentional states, so a physicalist conception is available of the instances, token by token, of response- or judgement-dependent concepts. Since any physical items may be unproblematically regarded as causally active, a way is thereby provided to reconcile Euthyphronism with the causal-explanatory intuitions invoked by proposition (a) and appealed to in the Missing Explanation argument.

A proper discussion of this proposal would have to engage transpositions of many of the hard issues which are raised by Davidson's anomalous monism. I will close by commenting on just two of them.

First, a point about Powell's invocation of the idea of *supervenience*. Powell suggests that, once identifications of colours with physical types are debarred, the fall-back position of token-by-token identification is actually *imposed* by the kind of supervenience which holds between colour and the physical. The supervenience which, he suggests, is a constitutive principle for colour issues in the necessity that any red thing, for instance, will exemplify some physical property (or range of properties) Ø such that anything which has Ø is likewise red. This would, of course be a trivial consequence if colours were (necessarily) physical types. Why does Powell think it is imposed if they are not?

He is less than fully explicit, but a natural line of thought would run as follows. The supervenience requires that, as a matter of necessity, any change in an item's colour must be attended by a change in its physical condition. This would be utterly mysterious if the properties in question were simply of quite different kinds: how could change in an object's physical condition absolutely *necessitate* change in other, non-physical respects? Unless an object's colour properties are *somehow* constituted in its physical constitution, it seems impossible to understand how the two could be linked

---

11. See Colin McGinn, "Anomalous Monism and Kripke's Cartesian Intuitions", *Analysis* 37, 2, 1977, pp. 78–80.

as a matter of necessity. Thus only physicalism, of however attenuated a form, can make sense of the supervenience.

I think this line of thought is wholly illusory. It is not clear how token-by-token physicalism actually helps to explain the relevant form of supervenience at all. To be sure, if we are given merely that the redness of a particular tomato actually *is* some token physical condition of it, then we may infer that had it not been red, it would have been in a different physical condition—that is, a different *token* physical condition. But the mooted form of colour-on-physical supervenience requires that a change in the colour predicates truly applicable to an object requires change in its physical description at the level of the *types* of physical state it is in— "Ø", in the above formulation of supervenience, is a variable for physical types.[12] Mere token-by-token physicalism cannot explain the validity of *that* principle. For it is silent on whether, if the tomato had not been red, the different token physical state which it would then have been in could not still have been of a physical type it is actually in, so is consistent with the idea—preposterous as it may seem—that its then physical state could have been in every way *indistinguishable* from its actual physical state. Colour-on-physical supervenience, as ordinarily understood, proscribes that.

The matter needs further discussion but I offer the conjecture that *only* type–type physicalism about colour can explain the form of colour-on-physical supervenience to which Powell is, surely rightly, sympathetic. That is *not* to suppose that Euthyphronism actually clashes with such colour-on-physical supervenience. But it would pre-empt any *explanation* of the latter if Euthyphronism does indeed preclude type–type identities. So if the conjecture is right, then there will be a clash if the supervenience may not legitimately be taken as a *primitive* principle but is viewed as requiring explanation by appeal to more basic features of colour properties.[13]

---

12. If it were not, the stated supervenience principle would not justify our projecting colour properties on the basis of an object's physical states under (near) C-conditions onto objects in like physical states under non-C-conditions. But Powell, rightly as it seems to me, lays emphasis upon the centrality of this form of projection in the explanation of our conception of e.g. things' colours when in darkness.
13. Token–token physicalism, as a response to Kripke's argument (but see note 14), will be correspondingly insufficient to explain the normally accepted form of

5.

Finally, a suggested correction to the way Powell, and many others, have portrayed the kind of position which he advocates for the special case of colour. I have in mind the play with *anomalousness*.

Let's ask, can the token-by-token proposal really save the causal-explanatory intuitions which fuel the Missing Explanation argument? A seemingly powerful line of objection argues, to the contrary, that such a form of colour physicalism would actually prove—under readily conceivable empirically possible circumstances—a serious obstacle to our ever doing so.

Imagine—of course, this is not the actual empirical story—that the aetiology of our colour responses proves to be physically relatively straightforward. Take the simplest possible case: when some single type of surface reflectance property, say XYZ, seems to be invariably involved in causing the appearance of red. If Powell's argument works, the objection runs, then surely we would be metaphysically *debarred* from identifying red with that property! But then it looks as though anyone who held that it is their token-by-token identity with physical states which explains the causality of objects' colours, would be forced in this scenario *either* to reject the best candidate for a physical explanation—that in terms of XYZ—*or* to view an object's appearance as red as being physically overdetermined, caused both by its being XYZ and by its being in whatever *other* token physical state constituted its particular redness (though, of course, it would be difficult to know what token state that was, since the seemingly invariable cause of a red appearance would be, by hypothesis, the object's being XYZ).

An analogue of this objection, which may appear devastating, would apply in any case where a merely token-by-token physicalism was defended and where the relevant physical science might coherently be envisaged nevertheless as proceeding relatively smoothly at the level of physical types.

However the objection makes a crucial assumption. It assumes that if we may not identify redness with a physical type, then we are barred with identifying tokens of redness with tokens of a single physical type. That may be questioned. Consistently with rejecting the identity of redness, as a type of state, with the state of being XYZ, we might in the described scenario retain

---

supervenience of sensations upon brain-states, so that the latter principle too will be in jeopardy if it cannot be taken as primitive and if Kripke's argument succeeds.

the explanatory advantages of that identification by identifying each object's *individual redness* with *its particular state of being XYZ*. Then, if best science were to find that being XYZ is indeed the normal cause of an object's appearing red, the fact that XYZ could not legitimately be *identified* with redness would be no obstacle to adapting this finding to Powell's purpose in hand—that of sustaining the idea that objects' colours cause their colour appearances. It would be enough that justification for regarding the state of being XYZ as a normal cause of a red appearance would suffice to justify taking *this* object's being in *this* XYZ state as a cause of *its* red appearance. If we then proposed that its particular XYZ state *is* its redness, that would be to take its redness as a cause of its red appearance, just as Powell wants.

If this is right, it points up something important, namely how merely token-by-token identifications with the physical can always tap into the explanatory advantages that would have been secured by corresponding type–type identifications. Thus token-by-token theories need not, per se, involve any consequences about *anomalousness*. Sure, physical laws are essentially general, so naturally formulated in terms of types of property, event and state. Thus in order to harness such laws to the explanation of what we presume to be the effects of objects' colours, it might seem that we have to find types of physical state for the colours to be. And then, if such identifications are proscribed, it may seem as though some form of anomalousness, or scientific opacity, of colour must be the upshot. But not so fast: the simple countervailing thought is that if a law connects one type of state with another, it thereby connects their tokens. So to treat of colour in a fully intelligible but physical-scientific way, we do not need type–type identifications: it would be enough that token colour states be token physical states of (some manageable number of) types that are tractable at the level of physical law.

These considerations may seem to speak for the coherence of Powell's ingenious strategy—once purified of the play with anomalousness—for reconciling the triad (a), (b) and (c). However I had better remind the reader that the Powellian argument against type–type identity (in both its original causal and suggested Kripkean forms) depended on the premise that "red" is rigid. This premise and the intuition, that red things necessarily share a property, by which it was supported are both presumably inconsistent with the token-by-token proposal in any case, since the latter must allow that no single property need be shared by red things. It would therefore appear that no argument that colours are not physical types which depends on the rigidity of colour predicates can allow of an accommodation involving token-by-token identification instead.[14] If that is right, then Powell's token-by-token physicalism is necessarily unmotivated by his argument, and one may feel that the proposal of *Truth and Objectivity*, allowing for contingent type–type identity of colours and physical states, remains fundamentally unchallenged.[15]

University of St. Andrews
Fife KY16 9AL
Scotland
cjgw@st-andrews.ac.uk

---

14. The same consideration, if good, must defeat McGinn's response to Kripke's original argument: it cannot be coherent to accept an argument against the identification of pain with C-fibre stimulation which depends upon the rigidity of pain yet simultaneously to canvass the identifiability of particular pains with particular token physical states.

15. To be sure, Powell voiced a supplementary concern: that our intuitions about the causal efficacy of colours are entrenched in a way the *Truth and Objectivity* proposal cannot safeguard. He quotes this passage:

> ... were we to become convinced that there is only a multiple physical *heterogeneity* among... same-coloured things, it ought to cease to seem sensible to ordinary thought to view colours as causally explanatory of best opinions about them. But so I think it would. (*Truth and Objectivity*, p. 132).

Powell disagrees, both with the normative and with the sociological claims in that passage. The matter would bear a lot more discussion, but I'll say very briefly why I think the objection is misconceived. Consider a situation in which the hostage held out by the *Truth and Objectivity* proposal is not redeemed: no underlying physical similarity, nor even a manageable range of physical similarities, holds between items correctly described as red. Compare the situation if no underlying physical similarity, nor even a manageable range of such similarities, had proved to overlap correct predications of water. Now **water** was associated with any number of intuitive causal beliefs—about thirst, dissolution, rust, cleanliness, etc., etc.—long before Dalton. Suppose such beliefs apparently proved robust in the scenario just envisaged. So people went on describing themselves as believing e.g. that water assuages thirst despite knowing that water was of no one physical type nor even any manageable range of physical types. Would that have to be irrational? We need a distinction. What would be irrational in the circumstances would be the belief that *being water* was a causal-explanatory property. But retaining beliefs about the causal powers of samples of water would be no commitment to that. (Compare the difference between believing that being a red toadstool is a causally explanatory property and believing that red toadstools typically have certain causal powers.) Granting, then, for the sake of argument that the kind of intuitive belief to which Powell calls attention—for instance, about the effects of coloured objects on the chemicals which coat a film—would indeed, as a matter of sociology, be robust in the face of disenchantingly heterogeneous findings in the physics of colour, it would be a further question whether such robust beliefs would require interpretation as commitments to the causal powers of colours. It would only be if they did that the *Truth and Objectivity* account would call them into question. And if they were correctly so interpreted, then I stick to it that they *would* be irrational. However we would have to be alive to the less demanding interpretative possibility which would view such beliefs as ascribing certain causal powers to coloured things, not to their colours. My suspicion is that Powell, and those for whom his remarks on this may strike an intuitive chord, are probably making too little of that contrast.

Ralph Wedgwood
The Essence of Response-Dependence

Long ago, Democritus proclaimed: 'by convention colour, by convention bitter, by convention sweet: in reality atoms and the void' (Barnes 1987, p. 254). Ever since, philosophers have been tempted by the view that colours, flavours, values, and the like, are less objective than shape or mass or motion. It can be true that certain objects are square, or that they have a certain mass, purely in virtue of how those objects are in themselves; but it is not true, purely in virtue of how the objects are in themselves, that they are red, or bitter, or good.

In this rough and intuitive form, this thought has always seemed attractive to philosophers. However, it has proved difficult to develop the thought into a more precise theory without incorporating other, less attractive elements. In this paper, I shall explore a relatively new approach to capturing the thought that colours, or flavours, or values, are less objective than shape or mass or motion—the approach based on the idea of 'response-dependence'. In the first section, I try to indicate an intuitive distinction, between the more objective and the less objective, which I believe that this approach should capture. In the second section, I examine the conceptions of response-dependence that have been developed by Mark Johnston, Philip

---

An earlier version of this paper was presented to the University of St. Andrews Philosophy Club, and to my former colleagues in the Department of Philosophy at the University of Stirling. I am grateful to both groups, and also to Alex Byrne, Timothy Williamson, Crispin Wright, and two anonymous referees, for helpful comments. I should especially like to record my gratitude to the late Murray MacBeath.

Pettit and Crispin Wright, and I argue that they fail to capture this intuitive distinction. Then, in the following three sections, I propose an alternative conception that succeeds in capturing the intuitive distinction.

1. Response-Dependence: The Intuitive Distinction

Among analytic philosophers, there have been three main approaches for developing the intuitive thought, that colours and values and the like are less objective than shape or mass, into a more precise theory: non-cognitivism, eliminativism, and various broadly subjectivist forms of reductionism. Recently, each of these three approaches has come to seem deeply unattractive. In this paper, I shall not rehearse the objections that have been directed against these approaches over the years. But it is important to explain why the response-dependence approach is distinct from those older, more familiar approaches.

If colours or values are less than fully objective, then statements describing objects as red, or good, cannot be true purely in virtue of how those objects are in themselves. Non-cognitivists and eliminativists both maintain that such statements are not true at all: according to non-cognitivism, such statements, though meaningful, are neither true or false; according to eliminativism, such statements are all either false or meaningless. According to the response-dependence approach, on the other hand, some such statements are actually true. So this approach is incompatible with both non-cognitivism and eliminativism.

This approach accepts then that some statements describing objects as red or good are true. If it is to claim that colours or values are less objective than shape or mass, it must deny that these statements are true independently of us, purely in virtue of how those objects are in themselves. So this approach is committed to holding that these statements are true, not independently of us, but in virtue of those objects' relations to us.

More specifically, this approach claims that, when an object is red or good, it is red or good in virtue of some relation to our subjective responses. However, it is not committed to giving strictly non-circular necessary and sufficient conditions for an object's being red or good, in terms of the subjective responses that such objects evoke in us. Since the approach does not insist on such non-circular necessary and sufficient conditions, it is distinct from reductionism (including all broadly subjectivist forms of reductionism).

Although the response-dependence approach is distinct from reductive subjectivism, it too involves giving necessary and sufficient conditions, for what it is for something to be red, or good, in terms of the subjective responses that red or good objects sometimes evoke. Many philosophers have suggested that such accounts might take the following form:

> x is F if, and only if, x is disposed to evoke subjective response R in subjects S in circumstances C.

In this paper, however, I shall not assume that all such accounts must employ the notion of a *disposition* in this way. There are numerous controversies surrounding the notion of a disposition (see Blackburn 1993 and Johnston 1992, pp. 228–34). For example, if x is disposed to φ in circumstances C, does this mean merely that, if x were in C, it would φ? Or does it mean that x has the 'higher-order property' of having some intrinsic natural properties that would typically cause objects to φ in C? A general characterization of response-dependence need take no position on these controversies. Moreover, we should not rule out the possibility that there is some other sort of account of what it is for things to be F, in terms of some other sort of relation between objects that are F and some type of subjective response to such objects, that would also support the conclusion that being F is response-dependent. In this paper then, I shall merely assume that a response-dependence account, of what it is for things to be F, involves a claim of the following, more general form:

> x is F if, and only if, $A(x, R)$

> —where R is a type of response, on the part of thinking subjects, that essentially involves some sort of representation or recognition of something's being F.

What has this to do with subjectivity? Gideon Rosen has objected that it is a perfectly objective matter what subjective response an object is disposed to evoke in certain circumstances (1994, pp. 289–297). For example, it is a perfectly objective matter whether a certain object is disposed to evoke some mental response, such as annoyance or nausea, in normal dogs: it is a purely objective question of canine psychology. So how does a biconditional of this form show that there is anything less than fully objective about being F?

To respond to this objection, we should remember two points. First, the response-dependence approach claims that objects are red, or good (or whatever), at least partly *in virtue of* some relation to some type of mental response on the part of thinking subjects; and, second, the type of mental response in question involves some sort of recognition or representation of something's being red or good. (So, for example, if nausea does not essentially involve any sort of recognition or representation of something's being nauseating, then nausea is not a response of the appropriate kind.)

Because of these two points, the response-dependence approach captures an intuitive thought that is suggested by the line from *Hamlet* (2.2.247–8): 'There is nothing either good or bad but thinking makes it so'. According to Hamlet, it is being thought good that makes something good, and being thought bad that makes something bad: if I think that racism is bad, then my thought cannot be detecting any fact of the matter that is constituted independently of my thought; on the contrary, my thought is part of what makes it the case that racism is bad in the first place. In this way then, this view does seem to imply that goodness and badness are less than fully objective.[1]

There are many areas in which the idea of response-dependence might prove fruitful. Johnston suggests that for a law to be constitutional within the United States just is for the Supreme Court not to be disposed ultimately to regard the law as unconstitutional (1993, p. 104). To take another example, there has been a vigorous debate in gay and lesbian studies, about whether or not sexuality is 'socially constructed' (Halperin 1990 and Stein 1993). This may be interpreted as the question whether it is part of what it is to be, for example, a homosexual, that one identifies oneself as a homosex-

---

1. Rosen argues that the response-dependence theorist must accept that, if one side of any such biconditional is objective, then so is the other side; indeed, it is plausible that both sides of the biconditional state exactly the same fact. So he would respond to my claim about Hamlet's view of goodness by claiming that it is an entirely objective (psychological) matter whether racism is thought bad; hence it must be an equally objective matter whether racism actually is bad. But, if x's being thought bad is exactly the same fact as x's being bad, then it is a fact with a very curious feature: it essentially involves a representation of itself. For the fact to obtain it must be thought to obtain. So, even accepting Rosen's assumptions, it seems plausible to me to deny that this fact (that x is thought bad) is quite as objective as it first appears.

ual, or at least is a person of a type which is actually classified in that way in one's society. However, the most familiar examples are the secondary qualities, such as colours. According to this sort of view, it is at least part of what it is for something to be red that it has a certain relation to human visual experience. Consider for example this account of what it is to be red:

> x is red if, and only if, x has some of the intrinsic natural properties which would typically cause objects to look red when seen in suitable conditions.

This account is compatible with red things' being extraordinarily heterogeneous with respect to the 'intrinsic natural properties' that cause them to look red. So it is tempting to read this account as making this relation to human visual experience, rather than any physical property, the fundamental feature that all red things have in common, in virtue of which they all count as red; and on this reading the account seems to imply that redness is response-dependent.

According to this view, redness is capable of cutting sharply across the lines of intrinsic natural dissimilarities. Plato suggests that in classifying things we should not be like clumsy butchers, who hack their way through bone; instead, we should try to carve through the joints (*Phaedrus* 265e). Intuitively, it seems, if redness is dependent in this way on some type of human subjective response, it would not mark any joint that the world has independently of us; this is why it is less objective than properties (such as primary qualities or natural kinds perhaps) that do mark such independent joints in the structure of the world.

So the idea of response-dependence seems to capture an important distinction, between the objective and the subjective, in an intuitively appealing way. As we shall see, however, the idea is still in need of clarification.

2. Johnston, Pettit, and Wright

The easiest way to give a general characterization of response-dependence is by means of a schema: A response-dependence account, of what it is for things to be F, accepts that it is true that some objects are F, but claims that objects are F at least partly in virtue of some relation to some type of subjective response to such objects.

This schema shows that a response-dependence account is an *ontological* or *metaphysical* account, of what it is for things to be F. It is stated entirely at the level of reference, not at the level of sense. It is not a semantical account, of the meaning of the term 'F'; nor is it an epistemological or psychological account, of the way in which we think about, or achieve epistemic access to, an object's being F. In that sense, it is not an account of the concept *F*—at least not if the concept is the meaning of the term 'F', or a way of thinking about the property of being F. Of course, an account of the concept *F* may sometimes imply an account of what it is for things to be F. Nonetheless, in the first instance, they are about two different things: one is an account of a certain way of *thinking* of things' being F; the other is an account of what it is for things to *be* F.

If we want to regard the latter account as an account of some entity, then it is an account of the *property* of being F, not of the concept *F*. So, to characterize response-dependence by means of an explicit statement, rather than just a schema, we must quantify over properties: A property counts as response-dependent if, and only if, it is part of what it is for something to have the property that it stands in a certain relation to a certain mental response to that property. For the rest of this paper I shall speak in terms of *response-dependent properties*. (For the purposes of this paper, I shall prescind from nominalist qualms about the existence of properties.[2])

To defend the intuitive idea that colours or flavours or values are less objective than primary qualities or natural kinds, we must argue that the *properties* of being red, or bitter, or good, are response-dependent. It is not enough to show that the concepts *red* or *good* are response-dependent in some way. Even if these concepts are response-dependent in some way, it needs to be shown that the properties that these concepts stand for are also response-dependent. If those properties are not response-dependent, it would be true that some objects have those properties purely in virtue of

---

2. We should also note that a response-dependence account of what it is for things to be F is not an account of what it is for the property of F-ness—conceived as a universal, or as an abstract object of a certain sort—to exist. A response-dependence account of what it is for things to be F need take no stand on the ontological status of properties. Suppose that we believed that the existence of the property of F-ness, conceived as an abstract object of a certain kind, was dependent on the concept or concepts that can be used to ascribe this property. This does not commit us to any particular view of what it is for something to be F; in particular, it does not commit us to the view that nothing can be F completely independently of our concepts.

how those objects are in themselves: those properties (redness, goodness, and so on) would be perfectly objective. Hence the core of any adequate conception of response-dependence must be an account of *response-dependent properties*, not of response-dependent concepts. This, I shall argue, is the basic problem with the conceptions of response-dependence that have been developed by Mark Johnston, Philip Pettit, and Crispin Wright: they are accounts of response-dependent concepts, not of response-dependent properties.

Thus, Johnston focuses on what he calls 'response-dispositional concepts' (Johnston 1993, pp. 103–11). Assuming, for example, that our concept *red* is a response-dispositional concept, then the concept just is the concept of the disposition to produce experiences of the relevant type. In general, a response-dispositional concept just is the concept of a disposition to evoke responses of some specific kind. (A 'response-dependent concept' is a response-dispositional concept or a truth-functional combination essentially involving a response-dispositional concept.)

There are at least two reasons why this account does not provide what I am looking for. First, as I have already suggested, it is not clear why all response-dependent properties must be definable in terms of *dispositions* to evoke responses in suitable conditions. Perhaps an account of a property in terms of some other sort of relation, between instances of the property and some type of mental response to it, would also reveal the property in question to be response-dependent.

Second, Johnston's distinction is a distinction between two types of *concept*, not between two types of *property*. It is possible for two different concepts to stand for the same property: for example, the concept *water* and the concept *H₂O* plausibly both stand for the same property. Even if a property is in fact a disposition to evoke certain responses, there could be a concept standing for that property which is not itself a concept of such a disposition. (For example, consider the concept *the property of the flag that explains why the bull got angry.*) So it could be that some, but not all, of the concepts standing for a given property were response-dispositional concepts. But what I am looking for is a metaphysical distinction between two types of property—not a distinction between two types of concept.

Of course, we could base such a distinction between types of properties on a parallel distinction between types of concepts. Suppose that we had an account of what it is for a concept to present the property that it stands for as response-dependent (where, contrary to Johnston's account, this is not limited to presenting the property as a *disposition* to evoke the relevant responses). Then we could define a response-dependent property as a property that can be thought of by means of any such concept. But it is not clear that anything is gained by this indirect route. Why should it be easier to give an account of what it is to *think of* a property as response-dependent than to give an account of what it is for a property to *be* response-dependent? Of course response-dependent properties are correctly thought of as response-dependent. This does not show that an account of what it is for a property to be response-dependent must be based on an account of what it is for a concept to present the property as response-dependent.

A still stronger point applies to what Pettit used to call 'response-dependent concepts' (1991) and now calls 'response-privileging' or 'response-authorizing' concepts (1993). According to his conception, a concept is response-authorizing if there is an a priori guarantee that (given certain suitable conditions) an object falls under the concept if, and only if, we are disposed to respond to the object in a certain way. There is, however, no reason to think that the properties that Pettit's response-authorizing concepts stand for cannot be entirely objective in every way. He suggests that even natural kind concepts, such as our ordinary concept of *water*, may be response-authorizing concepts (1991, pp. 598 and 615). And he explicitly rejects the suggestion that the objects or properties that response-authorizing concepts stand for need be in any way dependent on our responses (1993, pp. 202–3):

> the assertion that a concept is response-authorizing is, precisely, an assertion about the concept, not an assertion about that of which it is a concept: not an assertion about the property or object or operation in question. It is to say that the reference of the concept is determined in such a way that our responses are privileged under certain conditions: they are not capable of leading us into ignorance or error. It is not to say anything about the property or object or operation in itself, and so a fortiori it is not to say that that entity is dependent on us…

Clearly, Pettit's conception of response-authorizing concepts does not provide an account of the metaphysical distinction, between objective and subjective properties, that interests me here.

Wright's ideas also centre around a distinction between two types of concept: concepts for which our 'best opinions' are involved in determining the concept's extension, and concepts for which these best opinions merely reflect an independently determined extension (see his 1988, 1989, and 1992). This is supposed to be exemplified by the way in which Euthyphro's definition of the pious, as that which the gods love, reveals the extension of 'pious' to be determined by the best opinions about piety—that is, by the opinions of the gods.

According to Wright, the view that our best opinions are involved in determining a concept's extension is a denial of one sort of metaphysical realism about the property that that concept stands for. Offhand, however, his ideas seem, like Pettit's, to have more to do with concepts, and with the way in which it is determined which property a given concept stands for, than with the nature of that property itself. Nonetheless, his ideas are at least a refinement of Pettit's. He too considers a priori 'provisoed biconditionals' or 'provisional equations' of the form:

> If subject S is in circumstances C, then: x is F if and only if S judges that x is F.

But he imposes a few more conditions on these provisional equations than Pettit does. So we should consider whether these additional conditions ensure that the property of being F really is a response-dependent property.

Wright suggests that 'best opinions' play this 'extension-determining' role if such a provisional equation meets the following four conditions. First, the equation must be *a priori*. Second, circumstances C must be *substantially specified*: they must not be specified in a trivializing fashion, as circumstances that have 'whatever it takes' for S to be right about whether or not x is F. Third, whether circumstances C obtain must be *independent* of the detail of the extension of the concept *F*: to ensure this, circumstances C should be specified without using the term 'F', except perhaps within intentional contexts attributing propositional attitudes to S. Finally (the '*Extremal*' condition), there should no rival explanation of why the provisional explanation is true, other than the explanation in terms of the role played by best judgments in determining the extension of the concept.

It seems to me that there are provisional equations involving natural kind concepts that meet these conditions. Suppose for example that S's circumstances are as follows. Every sample of a natural kind in S's environment presents the type of appearance that samples of that natural kind actually typically present; and, for every type of appearance that S would regard as the typical appearance of some natural kind, nothing in S's environment is presenting that appearance other than samples of the unique natural kind that has actually typically presented that appearance in the past. Moreover, S assumes that her perceptual circumstances are typical in this way and generally favourable; she perceives all the samples of natural kinds in her environment, registers the appearance that they present, and forms all the non-inferential judgments that it is rational for her to form on the basis of registering these appearances; and she forms no other judgments in the circumstances. Finally, S perceives x; and S possesses the concept *water*. Let us refer to circumstances of this kind as 'circumstances C'. Then, plausibly, this provisional biconditional holds:

> If S is in circumstances C, then S judges that x is a sample of water if and only if x is a sample of water.[3]

This provisional biconditional appears to meet Wright's four conditions. (i) According to a plausible story, the reference of the concept *water* is fixed as that natural kind (if any) that actually typically presents the type of appearance that those who possess the concept treat as their primary means of recognizing water. This story implies that the provisional biconditional is a priori. (ii) Circumstances C are clearly substantially specified: the provisional biconditional as a whole is far from trivial, since it implies various non-trivial theses—such as that, if water is a natural kind, then anyone who possesses the concept *water* will be able to recognize water when it presents its actually typical appearance. (iii) Circumstances C are also independently specified, since the specification does not use the term 'water' except to say that S possesses the concept *water*; and that is equivalent to using the term

---

3. For example, consider some unusual artifact that presents exactly the type of appearance that S would regard as the typical appearance for water. This is obviously liable to prompt S to form false judgments of the form: x is a sample of water. But circumstances C will not contain any such thing. If anything in S's environment is presenting that type of appearance, then it is a sample of the unique natural kind that has typically presented that type of appearance in the past—viz. water itself. (If there is no unique natural kind that has typically presented that appearance in the past, then nothing in S's environment will present that type of appearance.) Because S assumes that her circumstances are typical in this way, and forms only rational, non-inferential judgments on the basis of her registering these appearances, there is also no chance that she will think that x is some unusual sample of water that presents an appearance other than that which water typically presents.

within the scope of propositional attitude ascriptions. (iv) Finally, the best explanation of why this provisional biconditional holds is by appeal to the role that our 'best judgments' play in fixing the reference, or determining the extension, of our concept *water*—best judgments here being judgments that are caused by the natural kind that actually typically causes the experiences that form our primary basis for perceptual judgments involving the concept.

This is a problem for Wright's account because, as Wright himself recognizes (1992, p. 131), it is intuitively plausible that natural kinds are not response-dependent properties. If any properties mark joints that the world has independently of us, then natural kinds do. So Wright does not give an adequate account of the metaphysical distinction that interests me any more than Johnston or Pettit do.

3. 'Constitutive Accounts': What Are They?

I propose that a property is response-dependent just in case any adequate constitutive account of what it is for something to have the property must mention some type of mental response to that property. The relevant sort of dependence then is what might be called 'constitutive' dependence. But what is a 'constitutive account' of a property?

The idea of a constitutive account of some object or property is expressed by many phrases that are commonly used by philosophers, though their meaning is rarely adequately explained. For instance, if we take as our example the property of value or being valuable, then one way to express this idea is to speak of an account of what *constitutes* a thing's value, or of what its being valuable *consists in*. As with almost all phrases that express this idea, this way of speaking can be transposed into the formal mode; we can speak of what the truth of the statement that a thing is valuable consists in, or of what constitutes the truth of that statement. Another phrase that expresses the same idea is a special non-causal use of '*makes it the case that...*'. Thus, we speak of what makes it the case that a thing is valuable, or simply of what makes it valuable, or (in the formal mode) what makes it true that the thing is valuable. In a similar way, we also speak of the 'truth-maker' for statements about value. Other explanatory idioms can also express this idea. We can speak of that *in virtue of which* a thing is valuable, or of what the statement that it is valuable is *true in virtue of*. More simply, we can just ask *why* a thing is valuable, or why it counts as valuable, or what *explains* why it is valuable, so long as it is clear that 'why' and 'explanation' are not to be given a specifically causal interpretation. Finally, we may also speak of *what it is* for a thing to be valuable, or simply of what value fundamentally *is*. A statement of what value is, in this sense, may be called a *constitutive account* or *explanation* of value, and perhaps also an *analysis* or *definition* of value.

Though commonly used in philosophy, these phrases are hard to understand; and we need to understand them better if my proposal is to shed any light on the nature of response-dependence. I shall continue to assume here that constitutive accounts can be stated in the form of necessary, universally quantified biconditionals. I shall also assume that these biconditionals do not have to be non-circular; that is, the right-hand side of the biconditional need not avoid using any simple term that stands for the property that is being accounted for (nor need it avoid using any simple term that stands for some other entity a full constitutive account of which would have to speak of the property that is being accounted for). If a constitutive account of a property is fully non-circular in this way, then it amounts to a *reduction* of the property in question. Indeed, we could even define reductions in this way, as completely non-circular constitutive accounts: if a necessary biconditional is to give a reduction of the property ascribed on its left-hand side, then it must not only be non-circular, but the right-hand side must also give a constitutive account of what it is for the left-hand side to be true.[4]

These biconditionals then do not have to be reductive or non-circular in order to be genuine constitutive accounts. But clearly not all necessary biconditionals are genuine constitutive accounts: otherwise, there would never be any reason to read such a biconditional as giving a constitutive account of the property ascribed by the left-hand side of the biconditional, rather than the property ascribed by the right-hand side. The biconditional would simply reveal its two sides to be necessarily equivalent: we would have

---

4. This is the view of Michael Dummett (1993, p. 57), who states that a reduction must give an account of what the reduced sentence is true in virtue of, if it is true. (An alternative understanding of reductions is simply as property identities, involving the identification of the property ascribed by a 'suspect' concept, with the property ascribed by some 'kosher' concept. If one is sceptical of the coherence or interest of this distinction between 'suspect' and 'kosher' concepts, then one should be equally sceptical of the coherence or interest of this conception of reductions.)

no reason to regard it as a constitutive account of the property ascribed by one side rather than the other. In many cases of constitutive accounts, however, we do have a reason to treat the two sides of the biconditional in this asymmetric fashion.

Someone might propose that such a biconditional is a constitutive account of the property ascribed by its left-hand side just in case it is a *conceptual* truth, guaranteed to be true by the nature of the concept that is used to ascribe the property in question. But this proposal can be shown to be inadequate by appeal to the example of water that we considered earlier. The following seems to be a conceptual truth, guaranteed to be true by the nature of the concept *water*:

> x is a sample of water if and only if x is a sample of the underlying natural kind that actually typically causes the sort of experience that we use as our primary means of recognizing water.

But intuitively this is not a constitutive account of the nature of water. This connection to human experience is not part of what water is; it is incidental to what makes something water.

This point has an important consequence for the theory of response-dependence. The fact that there is a biconditional conceptual truth, where the left-hand side ascribes a property to some arbitrary object, and the right-hand side speaks of some relation between the object and some type of mental response to the property, is not enough to show that the property in question is response-dependent. Otherwise, the property of being made of water would be response-dependent. We must impose a further condition: the biconditional must also be a *constitutive* account of the property in question. But we have still made no progress towards understanding what a constitutive account of a property is.

Moreover, it seems that being a conceptual truth is not always even necessary to make a biconditional into a constitutive account. Consider the following biconditional:

> x is a sample of water if and only if x is a sample of H_2O.

This is obviously not a conceptual truth. Still, it seems to me to give a constitutive account of water: it explains what it is about something that makes it a bit of water; it tells us what water fundamentally is. Admittedly, it may be that all the constitutive accounts that reveal properties to be response-dependent are conceptual truths: the accounts of what it is to be red, or constitutional, that I considered above would seem to be conceptual truths, if they are truths at all. But the general point still holds: constitutive accounts are not always conceptual truths, and conceptually true biconditionals are not always constitutive accounts.

As the example of water makes clear, a constitutive account of a property tells us something about the property itself, and need not elucidate or give the meaning of the concepts that may be used to think about that property. Of course, we could give a constitutive account of a concept too: we could grapple, not with the question 'What is water?', but with the question 'What is the concept *water*?'—that is, 'What is it to think about water?' But that would be an account of something entirely different: it would not be an account of water, of a type of material stuff; it would be an account of a concept or type of thought.[5] Perhaps our concept *water*—the way in which we typically think of water—depends on our perceptual experiences of water; it does not follow that water itself has any such dependence on our experiences.

In exploring the nature of response-dependence then, we must bear in mind this vital distinction between a constitutive account of a property and a constitutive account of a concept that can be used to ascribe that property. We must understand what 'constitutive accounts' are in general, regardless of whether they are accounts of concepts in human thought or language, or accounts of properties that are real features of external things.

Once it is clear that we are considering constitutive accounts of properties themselves, not just constitutive accounts of the concepts that we use to ascribe those properties, then we may well wonder how the biconditional linking water with H_2O can be a constitutive account of water. It is highly plausible that the property of being made of water is exactly the same property as the property of being made of H_2O. So why should we take one side of the biconditional as giving an account or analysis of the other, rather than

---

5. Many philosophers assume that an account of the concept *water* will be of the form: x is a sample of water iff A(x). But that is the form of an account of water itself, not an account of the concept *water*. An account of the concept *water* should take the form: A concept C is the concept *water* iff A(C). Compare Peacocke (1992), chapter 1.

vice versa? We simply have the same property twice over, once on each side of the biconditional.

Part of the answer to this challenge must be that, even if the property ascribed on each side of the biconditional is the same, the analysing side speaks of certain other objects or properties that are not spoken of on the analysed side. Obviously, if we analyse water as H_2O, we speak, not only of the property being analysed—namely, water or H_2O—but also of hydrogen and oxygen, which are not spoken of on the analysed side of our biconditional. This is why the analysing side of these biconditionals is usually more complex than the analysed side.

This, however, is only part of the answer. If we assume that any two necessarily equivalent predicates stand for the same property, then it is quite trivial to generate biconditionals where both sides ascribe the same property to some arbitrary object, but where one side also speaks of certain further objects or properties that the other side does not. For example:

> x is red iff x is red and a member of the set that contains x and all the natural numbers.

But obviously this does not count as a proper constitutive account of what it is to be red.

The point must be that, even if a given property can be 'constructed' (by means of operations that are analogues of conjunction, negation, existential generalization, and so on)[6] out of various other objects or properties, it does not follow that (to put the point crudely) the property itself involves those objects or properties as constituents. For example, even if the property of being red can be constructed out of various arithmetical and set-theoretical objects in this way, it need not itself involve any of them as constituents. On the other hand, if any adequate constitutive account of what it is for something to be red must mention some type of visual response, then the property of being red would involve that type of visual response as a constituent. However, we still need to understand what exactly a 'constitutive' account amounts to. I shall attempt to develop such an understanding in what follows.

---

6. The fundamental ontological conception that I shall be assuming, at least in order to fix ideas, is the theory outlined in George Bealer (1982), chapters 1–4. (I shall not be assuming the views that Bealer defends in later chapters.)

4. The Essentialist Interpretation of Constitutive Accounts

Aristotle clearly believed that when Socrates asked Euthyphro 'What is piety?', he was seeking a *real definition* of piety.[7] A real definition of some object (whether a particular or a universal) is a formula that states the essence of that object. Perhaps then the feature that makes a necessary biconditional into a constitutive account is that it should be a real definition, or state the essence, of a particular or universal that is spoken of on the left-hand side. This proposal seems the more plausible since Aristotle's favourite formula for essence—phrases of the form 'what it is for something to be a human being'—is also, as we have seen, one of the phrases that contemporary philosophers employ to indicate that they are giving a constitutive account. It is also plausible that it is essential to redness that something is red if and only if it has one of the intrinsic natural properties that would typically cause objects to look red in suitable conditions.

As I claimed in the previous section, there is no reason to demand that all constitutive accounts should be both non-circular and individuating. To impose this demand is to insist that these accounts should be reductive. But real definitions do not have to be reductive or non-circular. Assuming that one object 'constitutively depends' on another if the second object must be mentioned in a real definition of the first, then we can make the same point by saying that constitutive dependence is not asymmetric: it is possible for two objects each to depend constitutively on the other. This, anyway, is the proposal that I shall try to develop here: that the distinctive feature of constitutive accounts is that they are real definitions or statements of essence.

This proposal faces a serious obstacle, however. This obstacle is the widespread belief that the notions of real definition and of essence, if they are intelligible at all, are reducible to more simple modal terms. Those contemporary philosophers who tolerate the notion of essence simply define the essence of an object as those properties which it is impossible for the object to exist without. But then the distinction between a necessary biconditional, and one that states the essence, or gives a real definition, of something spoken of on the left-hand side, will simply collapse. It is impossible for water to exist without being the basic kind of stuff that is actually dominantly caus-

---

7. See Irwin (1995, §15, pp. 25–6). Irwin refers there to Aristotle's *Metaphysics* 987b1–4 and 1078b23–30.

ally responsible for the experiences that we use as our primary means of recognizing water. So it would follow that this connection to our experience is an essential feature of water, according to this modal view of essence.

There are however strong reasons against this modal conception of essence: as Kit Fine has pointed out, it has several quite unacceptable consequences. It is impossible for Socrates to exist without being a member of the set that includes Socrates and all the natural numbers. So according to the modal conception of essence, it is part of the essence of Socrates that he is a member of this set. But intuitively, this is not part of Socrates' essence or nature. As Fine puts it (1994, p. 5): 'Strange as the literature on personal identity may be, it has never been suggested that in order to understand the nature of a person one must know which sets he belongs to.'[8]

Rather than repeating Fine's attack on the modal conception of essence, I shall simply assume that we need a new conception of essence. But I shall not attempt any reductive definition of essentialist notions in other, non-essentialist terms. It seems plausible to me that Fine is right: these essentialist notions are fundamental metaphysical concepts, which are incapable of any non-circular definition. Still, these essentialist notions can be explicated by characterizing their logical properties, and their connections to other metaphysical concepts. Indeed, I suspect that these essentialist notions are of the greatest importance in clarifying many other metaphysical concepts—including the concepts of supervenience and ontological dependence, of the relations of part to whole, and of determinate to determinable, of the way in which a belief (for example) can be 'realized' by a certain neurophysiological state, and so on. However, I cannot pursue these questions here. The only way in which I will try to explicate the concept of essence is by giving a rough sketch of what is arguably its most fundamental connection—that is, its connection to *modality*.

Even if we reject the idea that essence can be defined in purely modal terms, there is clearly a strong link between essentialist and modal notions.

---

8. See also Fine (1995a). Fine's two other main objections are as follows. (i) Where 'p' can be replaced by any necessary proposition, then, for any object x, it is necessary that if x exists then p; so the essence of anything involves all modal facts (which is absurd). (ii) It seems possible for two philosophers to agree on all the modal facts while disagreeing about essence: e.g. the philosopher who thinks that persons are embodied minds, so ontologically dependent on minds, versus the one who thinks that minds are abstractions from persons.

Fine proposes that we should reverse the order of priority between the concepts of essence and modality. Instead of defining essence in terms of modality, we should define modality in terms of essence, in something like the following way.

We may think of the essence of an object (whether an individual or a universal) as given by the *real definition* of that object—that is, by the basic necessary principle which, together with the essences of other things, is the source of all the object's modal properties. If the object is an individual, then this basic necessary principle will concern what it is for something to be that individual; it will be the principle that determines which individual (if any), in any possible world, is identical to the individual in question. In this way then, the essence of an individual is what explains its identity: it is its *principium individuationis*, what individuates it, or makes it different from all other things.

On the other hand, if we are concerned, not with an individual, but with a property or relation, then the basic necessary principle about the property or relation will concern what it is for a sequence of objects to exemplify this property or relation: it will be the principle that determines which sequences of objects (if any), in any possible world, are instances of that property or relation. In this way, the principle will reveal what 'unifies' the property, or constitutes the 'real similarity' shared by all its instances, both actual and counterfactual.

Suppose for example that the essence of being red is to have some intrinsic natural property that would typically cause objects to look red when seen in suitable conditions. This then would be the source of various modal properties of redness, such as the impossibility of 'fool's red', or the possibility of red objects that are never seen, or of red objects that are physically quite unlike the red things of the actual world. Redness has an essence because these modal truths involving redness are not chaotic: they all have their source in, and are explained by, the fundamental necessary principle concerning what it is for something to be red—that is, the essence of redness.

But what is meant by saying that these principles are the *source* of the modal properties of objects? I can only suggest the rough outline of an answer to the question; and I will not be able to defend this answer in detail. But very roughly, we may say that a proposition is necessary if it is a logical consequence of these fundamental necessary principles concerning things;

and a proposition is possible if it is logically consistent with these fundamental necessary principles.[9] But what sort of 'logical consequence' is in question here?

Just as I am treating properties as real features of things, and not just as predicates or concepts in human thought or language, so, in the same way, I shall assume that propositions are conditions, or possible states of affairs; that is, they are real ways the world might be, or real conditions that the world might be in, not just thoughts or sentences in any human thought or language. Many of these conditions or propositions will be conditions that actually obtain—that is, ways the world actually is, or *facts*. So it is important here that we do not interpret 'logical consequence' in metalinguistic terms; we need a conception of logical consequence that applies directly to propositions, conceived purely as ways the world might be, not as sentences in any language. Equally, however, we should not understand logical consequence simply as 'necessary consequence', conceived in purely modal terms; we should avoid presupposing the modal notions that we are trying to explain.

I have assumed that propositions and properties (more precisely, universals of any kind) can be constructed out of objects (whether individuals or universals) by means of various operations, which are analogues of predication, negation, conjunction, and so on. The required conception of logical consequence can be defined in terms of these operations. Just as there will be some fundamental necessity concerning each individual or universal, so too there will be a fundamental necessity concerning each of these operations. We may assume that the fundamental necessity associated with each of the operations will in effect be a familiar logical principle, such as: 'Neces-

---

9. Fine holds that the essence of an object consists of those propositions that are 'true in virtue of the object's identity', and that necessary propositions are ones which are 'true in virtue of the identity of all objects' (see Fine 1994, p. 9, or 1995b, p. 56). Fine also distinguishes between 'constitutive essence'—the properties of an object that are strictly definitive of its nature—and 'consequential essence'—the essential properties of the object closed under logical consequence. When he says that necessary propositions are 'true in virtue of the identity of all objects' he is referring to the *consequential* sense of 'true in virtue of *x*'s identity'. When I speak of essence I shall always mean *constitutive* essence: this is why I say that a necessary proposition is one that *follows* from the essences of objects.

sarily, for any conditions (or propositions) *A* and *B*, any condition that can be constructed by conjunction out of *A* and *B* obtains iff *A* and *B* both obtain.' This principle defines the nature of the conjunction operation; and principles of this kind enable the required notion of logical consequence to be defined in a familiar way. Roughly, we can imagine these principles as constraining the construction of sets of propositions: for example, if such a set of propositions contains a proposition that can be constructed by conjunction out of *A* and *B*, then it must also contain *A* and *B* as well. Then we can say that one proposition is a logical consequence of a second if any of these sets that contains the second proposition also contains the first as well.[10] My tentative suggestion then is that it is in this sense that all necessary propositions are logical consequences of the essences of things; and this is how it is that the essences of things constitute the source from which all metaphysical necessity and possibility flow.

5. Response-Dependent Essences

This then is the essentialist conception of 'constitutive' accounts that I propose to appeal to in elucidating the idea of response-dependence. A property is response-dependent just in case it is an essential part of something's being an instance of the property that it stands in some relation to

---

10. This conception of logical consequence between propositions (conceived simply as ways the world might be) need not rely on the assumption that propositions have a unique intrinsic structure: a proposition has consequences, not in virtue of its intrinsic structure, but in virtue of *all* the ways in which it can be 'constructed', by means of various operations (analogous to predication, negation, conjunction, existential generalization, etc.), out of objects such as individuals, properties, relations, and propositions. It is the nature of these operations that is the source of this relation of logical consequence. (Of course, if we assume that each proposition has a unique intrinsic metaphysical structure, then the notion of consequence is more straightforward: it could simply parallel the metalinguistic notion for an ideal language that mirrors this basic structure of reality.)

    Kit Fine writes, 'we should think of the nature of the logical concepts …as being given, not by certain logical truths, but by certain logical inferences.… The concept of consequence is not presupposed but is already built into the rules' (1995b, p. 58). But what is an inference if not a linguistic structure or a psychological process? So I doubt whether Fine's understanding of logical consequence is ideal for elucidating the ideas of essence and modality. Let me stress however that I have no objections to Fine's formal 'logic of essence', which is developed in detail in his (1995c).

some sort of mental response to that property. If redness is response-dependent, then it must be essential to something's being red that it stands in some relation to a certain type of visual response to redness. If ethical qualities, such as the property of being morally wrong, are response-dependent, then it must be essential to something's being morally wrong that it stands in some relation to some type of disapproval or opposition that is a response to such moral wrongness.

According to this proposal, such statements of essence, or real definitions, provide the most fundamental constitutive explanations that can be found. There is no room for any further question about *why* ethical qualities are response-dependent while primary qualities and natural kinds are not. That is simply a basic constitutive fact about these various types of property. However, although this fundamental metaphysical fact neither requires nor admits of further explanation, we can certainly still ask the epistemological or methodological question: What *justifies* us in *believing* that ethical qualities are unlike primary qualities and natural kinds in this respect?

The answer to this question, I believe, is that such beliefs can be justified by reflection on the nature of the *concepts* that we use to ascribe these qualities. In some cases, for example, we can simply introduce a concept by the stipulation that it is to stand for a property that has a certain essence. In other cases, analysis of some concept that we already possess may reveal that the concept can only stand for a property that has a certain sort of essence. In yet other cases, conceptual analysis may reveal that some concept in our repertoire does not determinately stand for any unique property; and one may propose a conceptual reform determining that the concept is to stand for a property that has a certain essence.

What I am proposing now is quite compatible with my earlier claim, that it is a mistake to explain what it is for a property to be response-dependent in terms of the nature of the concepts that can be used to ascribe that property. I am now suggesting that we must appeal to the nature of our concepts to explain how we can *know* that a property is response-dependent. That is, I am proposing, not that essentialist notions can be reduced to the idea of conceptual truths, but that such essentialist notions actually figure in the *content* of certain conceptual truths.

Why should we expect that reflection on the nature of a concept should tell us anything about the essence of the property that the concept stands for? The key point is that a concept cannot succeed in determinately singling out any unique property unless the concept, along with the thinker's circumstances, also singles out the essence of that property as well. To single out a unique property, out of all the countless properties that there are, a concept must not only have the right extension in the actual world: it must also have the right extension in all other possible worlds as well; and I have suggested above that it is precisely the essence of a property that determines which objects (if any), in any possible world, are instances of that property. So singling out the essence of a property is an essential part of singling out the property itself; and there must be something about the nature of the concept that enables the concept, together with the thinker's circumstances, to fix on the essence of the property that the concept is to stand for.

For example, it seems somehow built into the concept *water* that, if the concept stands for anything at all, then it stands for a kind of stuff whose essence consists in its underlying nature, rather than its superficial appearances. So the nature of the concept *water* determines that the concept must stand for a natural kind, not a response-dependent property. On the other hand, the nature of the concept *red* determines that it must stand for a response-dependent property: it is built into the concept *red* that the concept stands for a property that essentially consists in having any feature that will present the right sort of superficial appearance in appropriate conditions.

I cannot undertake an investigation of the nature of concepts here, or of what it is for a certain truth to be 'built into a concept'. But the claim that an essentialist truth is built into the concept *red* need not imply that everyone who possesses the concept *red* must possess the concept of *essence*. On the part of the thinker himself, there need be no more than a vague grasp of what makes conditions for perceiving red things unfavourable, and of what it is for an unperceived object to be red. Even here there is a sharp contrast between the concepts *water* and *red*. Conditions are unfavourable for perceiving water wherever there is anything superficially resembling water whose underlying nature is different from that of most samples of water; whereas conditions are unfavourable for perceiving redness only if there is some abnormality in one's perceptual function, or if the lighting and atmospheric conditions differ too much from a certain familiar paradigm. It is plausible that these differences between the concepts *red* and *water* support the claim that there is an important metaphysical difference between redness and water. The superficial appearances familiar to those who possess the concept *water* are merely involved in 'fixing the reference' of the concept; whereas the superficial appearances familiar to those who possess the concept *red* are involved, not merely in fixing the reference of the concept, but in the essence of the property that the concept stands for.

In several respects, I concede, my proposed conception of response-dependence remains programmatic. In particular, it relies on a concept of essence that many philosophers will regard as dubiously intelligible. I am confident that further investigation will dispel many of these suspicions. But until such further investigation is carried out, we will not know whether there is anything behind the intuitive distinction, between more and less objective properties, that the response-dependence approach attempts to clarify.

Department of Linguistics and Philosophy
Massachusetts Institute of Technology
77 Massachusetts Avenue
Cambridge, MA 02139-4307
USA
wedgwood@mit.edu

References

Barnes, J. 1987 *Early Greek Philosophy*, Harmondsworth: Penguin.

Bealer, G. 1982 *Quality and Concept*, Oxford: Clarendon Press.

Blackburn, S. 1993 "Circles, Smells, Finks and Biconditionals", *Philosophical Perspectives*, 7, 259–79.

Dummett, M. 1993 *The Seas of Language*, Oxford: Clarendon Press.

Fine, K. 1994 "Essence and Modality", *Philosophical Perspectives*, 8, 1–16.

Fine, K. 1995a "Ontological Dependence", *Proceedings of the Aristotelian Society* 95, 269–90.

Fine, K. 1995b "Senses of Essence", in W. Sinnott-Armstrong, ed., *Modality, Morality, and Belief*, New York: Cambridge University Press.

Fine, K. 1995c "The Logic of Essence", *Journal of Philosophical Logic*, 24, 241–73.

Halperin, D. 1990 *A Hundred Years of Homosexuality*, New York: Routledge.

Irwin, T. 1995 *Plato's Ethics*, Oxford: Clarendon Press.

Johnston, M. 1992 "How to Speak of the Colors", *Philosophical Studies*, 68, 221-63.

Johnston, M. 1993 "Objectivity Refigured: Pragmatism without Verificationism", in J. Haldane and C. Wright, eds., *Reality, Representation and Projection*, New York: Oxford University Press.

Peacocke, C. 1992 *A Study of Concepts*, Cambridge, Mass.: MIT Press.

Pettit, P. 1991 "Realism and Response-Dependence", *Mind*, 100, 587–626.

Pettit, P. 1993 *The Common Mind: An Essay on Psychology, Society and Politics*, New York: Oxford University Press.

Rosen, G. 1994 "Objectivity and Modern Idealism: What is the Question?", in Michaelis Michel and J. O'Leary-Hawthorne, eds., *Philosophy in Mind*, Dordrecht: Kluwer Academic Publishers.

Stein, E. 1993 *Forms of Desire*, New York: Routledge.

Wright, C. 1988 "Moral Values, Projection and Secondary Qualities", *Proceedings of the Aristotelian Society* Supplementary Volume, 62, 1–26.

Wright, C. 1989 "Wittgenstein's Rule-Following Considerations and the Central Project of Theoretical Linguistics", in A. George, ed., *Reflections on Chomsky*, Oxford: Oxford University Press.

Wright, C. 1992 *Truth and Objectivity*, Cambridge, Mass.: Harvard University Press.

Philip Pettit
Terms, Things and Response-Dependence

The word 'response-dependent' was introduced by Mark Johnston (1989) to pick out those terms and concepts that are biconditionally connected, as an *a priori* matter, with certain more or less primitive responses: in particular, with responses of a perceptual or affective character. Colour terms provide the least contentious examples, for it is agreed on many sides that something is red, as an *a priori* matter, just in case it is disposed to look red to normal observers in normal circumstances. While there are different accounts on offer as to what normality involves, and while there are different explanations available of why the biconditional holds true, many people will agree that colour concepts and colour terms satisfy Johnston's requirement for response-dependence.

The questions I wish to discuss here bear on what response-dependence in this sense entails; in particular on what, if anything, it entails for issues of philosophical interest. I argue against two apparent lessons, one relating to how we apply response-dependent terms and concepts, the other relating to the nature of the properties and other entities to which they refer. While rejecting these apparent lessons, however, I defend a third; this concerns the reference-fixing significance of response-dependence as distinct from the application or reference of response-dependent terms. In arguing along these lines I remain broadly faithful to an approach that I have already presented elsewhere (Pettit 1991, 1993).

1. The application of response-dependent terms: a negative lesson

The claim that it is *a priori* that something is red just in case it is disposed to look red to normal observers in normal circumstances is reminiscent of the sorts of claims offered in analysis of explicitly dispositional terms. It parallels the claim, for example, that something is fragile just in case it is disposed to break under this or that sort of pressure or that it is soluble just in case it is disposed to dissolve on immersion in this or that liquid.

Now with terms for properties like fragility it usually goes without saying that the analysis teaches us an important lesson about how we usually judge, or at least about how we usually check, that something has the property. We ask ourselves whether or not the object is likely to break under the pressure in question; at the limit we may even test for whether it breaks under that pressure. The question, then, is whether the same goes for how we usually judge or check that something is red. Do we ask ourselves about how it is likely to look, or do we test for how it looks, to normal observers in normal conditions?

This question bears on how we think of the property of redness. Does the dispositional character of the biconditional for redness mean that we ordinary folk conceive of redness as an explicitly dispositional property? Does it mean that we treat the term 'red' as a term whose application is to be guided by considerations about the sorts of sensations realised in normal observers in normal conditions? Does it mean that the biconditional gives what I have elsewhere described as the application conditions for the term (Pettit 1991)? Does it mean, in Mark Johnston's (1993, pp. 106–07) phrase, that the concept is response-dispositional?

To all of these questions I believe that the answer should be, no. There are accounts of how the biconditional for redness can hold, and hold as an *a priori* truth, without serving to give the application conditions for the term. Under these accounts we do not think of the property of redness as a disposition, in the way that we think of fragility as a disposition, and yet the *a priori* linkage between redness and the disposition to produce certain sensations of redness is firmly established.

The account that I myself prefer as to how we think of the property of redness is one such story (Pettit 1993, p. 199). I call it an 'ethocentric' account, because it gives a central role to habits of sensation and practices of correction and the Greek work 'ethos' covers both habit and practice. It goes like this.

1. People have sensations of redness in the presence of red things.
2. Although they may not be aware of those sensations as such, or have a term in which to describe them, redness-sensations lead people to link together those things that elicit the sensations; the things look the same.
3. People typically go by how things look in determining what else belongs to this kind; the presumption is that if something looks similar to established examples of the class, then it belongs to the class.
4. Given the salience of the class of red things, people learn the use of the words 'red' and 'redness' in a more or less ostensive way: from their point of view, redness is that property, the one present here in this object, there in that, and so on.
5. They are sensitive, however, to interpersonal and intertemporal discrepancies between their sensations or judgments, baulking at any discrepancy between times or perhaps individuals in how something looks; they assume that other things being equal redness itself is constant across times and individuals.
6. Thus people are ready to discount how something looks as evidence of its being red or non-red: they display a disposition to discount various discrepant appearances in the course of restoring congruence: the light was bad, it may be surmised, the person was wearing funny glasses, the object was revolving rapidly, or whatever.

This ethocentric account of how we learn and use terms like 'red' and 'redness' is opposed to any suggestion that we are guided in the application of such terms by the biconditional for redness. It has us think of redness in an ostensive manner as a property available to be picked out in perception, not as a property of the dispositional kind exemplified by fragility. It is consistent with our not even being able to understand the biconditional, let alone apply it; for all the account says, for example, we may not have any understanding of what it is for observers and conditions to be normal.

But though the ethocentric account suggests that we think about redness as an ostensive property, not a dispositional one, it still gives us ground for defending something close to the biconditional for redness, and as an *a pri-*

ori matter. Thus it suggests that even if we do not think about redness as dispositional, that property does indeed have a dispositional aspect: if they can name the property, then its presence in something goes *a priori* with the thing's being disposed to look red to normal observers in normal conditions.

The ethocentric account supports the *a priori* truth of the biconditional, so far as normal observers and normal conditions are understood on an independently attractive pattern (Pettit 1991; 1993, pp. 92–97; 1998 cf Wright 1988). Let 'normal' be defined, not by reference to a list of normal observers and conditions, and not by reference to the effect of normality in enabling people to get things right—not in a whatever-it-takes-way—but rather by reference to ethocentric practices. Let normality be the property pertaining to those individuals and circumstances that are not of a kind with those that are discounted—discounted as unreliable—in the course of resolving discrepancies; let normality be the property, in this sense, of being fit to survive practices of resolving discrepancies.

The notion of normality, so defined, need not be available to people themselves but it is introduced on the basis of their spontaneous practices; it is not an alien imposition. And yet it enables us to say with justification that, assuming they can name the property, something is red just in case it looks red to normal observers in normal circumstances; in saying this, we merely articulate a principle that is implied in the way people trust their habits of sensations and authorise their practices of revision in making judgments of redness. Moreover, it enables us to say that this qualified biconditional is true *a priori*. Anyone who is party to the way people follow their sensations and adjust in face of discrepancies will be in a position to know of the truth of the biconditional; it does not require empirical confirmation.

The upshot, then, is clear. The admission that a term or concept is response-dependent in the sense given by Mark Johnston to that description does not entail that we are guided in our use of it by the biconditional governing the term. It says little or nothing on how we are supposed to think about the property to which the term applies.

2. The reference of response-dependent terms: a negative lesson

In a recent paper Ralph Wedgwood (1996) maintains a similar position on the application of response-dependent terms, arguing that we need not think of them in the explicitly dipositional way. He defends an uncongenial view, however, on the reference of such terms. He argues that response-dependence gives us a way of characterising the lesser objectivity of some properties. So far I need not be opposed. But in the course of that argument he suggests, perhaps incautiously—incautiously because unnecessarily—that response-dependent predicates cannot stand for properties that objects exemplify 'independently of our mental responses'. Here I differ. I think that the property to which a response-dependent predicate refers—or, more generally, the entity to which a response-dependent term refers—need not be mentally dependent in this sense.

What would it be for the property of redness to be mentally dependent in a relevant way? I shall assume that redness will be dependent if it is the higher-order property of being such that—of having such lower-order properties that—the bearer would look red to normal observers in normal conditions. Such a property is a disposition, not just the ground of a disposition, and its very realisation presupposes that the category of normal obervers and normal conditions is well-defined; it presupposes that there is at least a possible world where the term 'normal', as we have defined it here, refers to determinate observers and conditions.

Why is it necessary for the realisation of the property in question—dispositional redness, as we may call it—that there are normal obervers and conditions, not in the actual world, but only in a possible world: that is, in the actual world or in some other possible world? The reason will be evident from an analogy. In order to be soluble an object must be such that it would dissolve in liquids, or at least in certain liquids. But an object would remain soluble in the actual world even if everything here froze up and there were no actual liquids available; it would remain soluble so far as it remains the case that it would dissolve in liquids: it dissolves in liquids at the nearest possible world where liquids are available.

It is worth noticing that though the reality of dispositional redness only requires the possibility of normal observers and normal conditions—though its mental independence is only compromised to that limited extent—the reality of a rigidified cousin of dispositional redness requires the actuality of such observers and conditions. Suppose the biconditional for redness, as some may think appropriate, requires that the red object is disposed actually to look red to normal observers in normal conditions; suppose that redness is taken to be that dispositional property that involves looking red to such normal observers, and in such normal conditions, as materialise in the actual world. In that case the reality of dispositional redness—rigidified dispositional redness—presupposes that such obervers and such conditions are available in the actual world, not just in some possible world.

Not only would the mental independence of dispositional redness be further compromised if that property is assumed to be rigidified. It is also worth noting that the independence would be compromised along a different dimension—and perhaps in a more significant way—in the event of a second sort of assumption. We characterised dispositional redness as that higher-order property of being such that the bearer would look red to normal observers in normal conditions and we added, parenthetically, that being such that it would look that way involves having suitable lower-order properties. But suppose it is assumed that this parenthetical addition is misleading. Suppose it is assumed that as between something that would look red in suitable circumstances and something that wouldn't there need be no difference in categorical lower-order properties. Suppose it is assumed, in other words, that dispositional redness is a bare or empty disposition with no categorical grounding. Such bare dispositional redness, whether rigidified or not, would be lacking mental independence along a very important dimension. It would be such that having the property comes to nothing more or less than normally seeming to have the property, whether normally seeming to have it in the actual world or in some possible world.

We have seen that redness would be dependent on our mental responses in the event of being identical with dispositional redness, and particularly in the event of being identicial with rigidified or bare dispositional redness. But I want to show now that the truth of the *a priori* biconditional for redness—or, strictly, of the qualified version—does not entail that redness is dispositional redness. We can see how that *a priori* biconditional might remain true even in the event of redness being non-dispositional.

We can see how it would remain true, specifically, in the event of redness being identified not with the higher-order property of being such as to look red but with the suchness in question. Under the possibility I have in mind, redness is the lower-order property—no doubt, the lower-order disjunctive property—that makes things look red in suitable circumstances. If you prefer, it is the property that discharges the role that is characteristic of redness, making things look red in suitable circumstances. It is the realiser property, as we might say, not the role or dispositional property (Jackson and Pettit 1988).

If redness is the realiser property in this sense then it should be clear that it is not particularly dependent for its exemplification on our mental responses. If a certain molecular structure—perhaps we should say a certain disjunction of structures—realises the fragility role, making things break under appropriate pressures, that does not mean that it depends in any way for its exemplification on such breaking. And if a certain property realises the redness role, making things look red in suitable circumstances, that does not mean that it depends in any way for its exemplification on such looking. The connection between the molecular structure and the breaking is contingent, not necessary; and similarly the connection between the realiser property for redness and the looking will be contingent too.

Is there any problem in continuing to defend the ethocentric story, and in particular the qualified biconditional for redness, if redness is the realiser property rather than the role or dispositional property? No, for pretty straightforward reasons.[1] Even if redness is identified with a mentally independent, perfectly objective property, there remains a question, in David Lewis's phrasing, as to why this property and not some other gets to deserve the name of 'red'. Any story that sustains the *a priori* biconditional for redness, and in particular the ethocentric story presented, can be seen as providing an answer to that question.

Why does a certain molecular structure deserve the name of 'fragile', if indeed we identify fragility with the property that realises fragility, and not with the dispositional property itself? Obviously the answer is that it is that structure, and not any other, which leads things to break under certain circumstances. The linkage with breaking does not go to the heart of the property in question, as we have noticed; the property does not depend for its realisation on that relationship. But the linkage does go to the heart of explaining why the word 'fragile' is used with reference to the presence of that property and not any other.

---

1. If the reasons seem straightforward to me, that is probably because I have enjoyed the great benefit, over many years, of talking about these matters with Frank Jackson. His John Locke lectures are a source of illumination on relevant questions; see Jackson 1998.

Why does a certain realiser property deserve the name of 'red', if indeed we identify redness with the realiser property and not with the dispositional one? By analogy, the answer must be that it is that property, and not any other, which leads things to look red under suitable circumstances. The linkage with looking red will not compromise the ontology of the property, making it depend for its exemplification on such looking. But under any plausible story it will explain why the word 'red' is used with reference to the presence of that property and not any other.

Why is it *a priori*, then, that if they can name the property, something is red if and only if it looks red to normal observers in normal conditions? Not because the property of redness is necessarily tied up with looking red in such circumstances. Rather, because the property in question—the lower-order realiser property, as we are taking it to be—happens to be that property which causes things to look red to us under suitable circumstances. We are guided by how things look in determining what is red and what is not; this is borne out by the ethocentric story and by every plausible rival. And so it is *a priori*—it is knowable from a knowledge of how we are guided—that a certain mind-independent property will count as redness if and only if it engenders appropriate looks.

3. Fixing the reference of response-dependent terms: a positive lesson

I argued in the last section that a response-dependent term like 'red' may refer to a perfectly mind-independent property: specifically, to the property that realises the redness role, rather than to the dispositional or role property. I argued, in particular, that consistently with having such a reference we can still understand why the term should be response-dependent: why it should be governed by an appropriate *a priori* biconditional. Consistently with 'red' referring to a mind-independent property, there will still be a question as to why that property gets to be identified as redness. And the answer to that question must be that given how we use the word 'red', it is *a priori* knowable that it will refer to a property that causes things to look red. I now want to generalise this line of argument, defending a positive position on the significance of response-dependence.

For all that I have said so far, it might be that as we vary our views on the ontology of redness we will find different reasons for why the term should be response-dependent: different reasons for why it should be *a priori* that something is red if and only if it looks red to normal observers in normal conditions. If redness is identified with a mind-independent property, the reason will relate to how that property gets to deserve the name of 'red'. If redness is identified with any mind-dependent property—say, with dispositional redness, whether or not in rigidified or bare versions—other reasons will apply.

What I now wish to point out, however, is that no matter how redness is construed ontologically, one single reason is going to be available to explain why the term 'red' is response-dependent. It remains the case under each available ontology that we have to explain why the property in question gets to deserve the name of 'red'. And under each ontology the most plausible explanation—say, the explanation implicit in the ethocentric story—will entail that something is red if and only if it looks red to normal observers in normal conditions. The mode in which the reference of 'red' is fixed explains the response-dependence of the term under all ontological theories of redness. It does not serve in that explanatory role just for the case where redness is taken as a mind-independent property.

No matter what terms or what things are in question, there is always an issue as to why this or that term—this or that term in our mouths—refers to this or that thing. The question bears on what it is about that thing which makes it the right referent for the term. It concerns, not the matter of what the referent is, but the way in which it is fixed that that is entitled to be the referent.

Consider the term 'water'. Those of us schooled in the intuitions of direct reference will have little doubt about what it is that this term refers to, and refers to in all possible worlds as well as in the actual world: it rigidly refers to the natural kind that is chemically designated as H_2O. But even with a term like this there is a question as to how it is fixed that H_2O is the referent.

Suppose we inhabited and interpreted the word 'water' in a different actual world: in a world, let us say, where the stuff inhabitants drink and the stuff in which they wash, the stuff that occupies the seas and falls from the skies, is not H_2O but XYZ; a world, as we can put it, in which XYZ plays the watery role that H_2O plays in the familiar actual world. What would the word 'water' refer to in our mouths in such a world? Clearly XYZ. Clearly XYZ, because the referent of 'water' is determined in any world—in any world that is given the place of the actual world—by appeal to the watery role. Whereas that role picks out H_2O here, it would pick out XYZ if the world imagined occupied the place of the actual world.

The term 'water' is a rigid designator, as we mentioned, so that starting from a particular world as actual, the referent is the same at other possible worlds as it is at that world; it is always H_2O, if the starting point is our actual world; it is always XYZ, if the starting point is the other world. But even with a term like water, so we can now see, there is a difference between the question as to what the referent of the term is and the question as to what it is that makes that referent appropriate: what it is that entitles the thing in question to be described in that term.

As it is with water, so it is with other terms. There is always a question, not just about what the referents are, but also about what fixes those referents as appropriate. And we show that we have a fair sense of the answer to that question so far as we are able to say, not just what the terms actually refer to, but also what they would refer to in the event of a different world occupying the place of the actual world.

Let us go back now to response-dependent terms, in particular to the predicate 'red'. No matter what redness is, there is always going to be a question as to what makes the property in question the appropriate referent for the term. And no matter what redness is, we are surely all going to say that what makes that property appropriate as a referent is the fact that it co-varies with things looking red, at least when observers and conditions are normal. Suppose we inhabited and interpreted the word 'red' in a world that was different from the actual one in this or that respect. What would the word 'red' refer to in that case? No matter what ontology we espouse, we will identify the referent on the basis of what would look red to normal observers in normal conditions in such a world.

Let redness be a mind-independent property and the reason something is red if and only if it looks red in suitable circumstances has to do with why that property deserves to be called 'red'. But let redness be a mind-dependent property and the same consideration applies. What fixes it that the higher-order property of being such as to look red in suitable circumstances deserves to be called by the name of 'redness', if indeed it is what we call by that name? The fact, clearly, that our use of the term 'red' is guided by how things look in such circumstances. Quite independently of other considerations, that fact and that fact alone is sufficient to explain why it is *a priori* that something is red if and only if it looks red to normal observers in normal conditions.

The emerging lesson is that quite independently of ontological considerations, it is possible to understand why a certain term is response-dependent, being governed by a suitable *a priori* biconditional. To the extent that our use of the term in question is answerable to suitable looks or to things like looks—to the extent that an ethocentric style of story holds true—the referent of the term is going to deserve that name by virtue of involving suitable looks. And to that extent there will be grounds for a corresponding *a priori* biconditional; this will serve to express the answerability of the term to the way things look, not to communicate anything about the ontology of the item in question.

I have argued that the response-dependence of certain terms—their connection with a suitable *a priori* biconditional—is fully explained by the way their referents are fixed as appropriate and I have laboured the point that this is so whether those referents be taken to be mind-independent or mind-dependent in character. But what does remain true, of course, is that under the sort of ontology that presents redness, for example, as a mind-dependent property, the biconditional may have dual or multiple significance. It may serve, not just as a way of marking how reference is fixed for the corresponding term, but also as a way of giving the essence of the property in question. Thus if redness is the higher-order property of being such as to look red in suitable circumstances, the biconditional has ontological significance as well as significance in the explanation of reference-fixing. This is what gives Wedgwood an opening for his project of using response-dependence in the attempt to characterise the lesser objectivity of some properties.

In conclusion, a commitment. I have remained studiously neutral here and in earlier publications on precisely which property should be identifed with redness. But I should just mention that the view that redness is a realiser property, not a role or dispositional property, fits most comfortably with the ethocentric story. Under that story redness is picked out ostensively as that property which is present here in this object, there in that, where its salience for ostension depends on our enjoying certain sensations in the presence of the objects in question. But the property picked out ostensively in that way is quite naturally cast as the lower-order property that lies at the causal origin of the sensations rather than with the higher-order property that consists in having a suitable lower-order producer of sensations. It is that property which makes an impact on us in the first place, not the higher-order property that is defined by reference to it.

Research School of Social Sciences,
Australian National University,
Canberra, ACT 0200
pnp@coombs.anu.edu.au

References

Jackson, F. 1998. *From Metaphysics to Ethics.* Oxford: Oxford University Press.

Jackson, F. and P. Pettit. 1988. "Functionalism and Broad Content", *Mind*, Vol. 97, 381–400.

Johnston, M. 1989. "Dispositional Theories of Value", *Proceedings of the Aristotelian Society,* Supplementary Volume 63, 139–74.

Johnston, M. 1993. "Objectivity Refigured: Pragmatism without Verificationism", in J. Haldane and C. Wright, eds, *Reality, Representation and Projection,* New York: Oxford University Press

Pettit, P. 1991. "Realism and Response-dependence", *Mind*, Vol. 100, 587–626.

Pettit, P. 1993. *The Common Mind: An Essay on Psychology, Society and Politics,* New York: Oxford University Press.

Pettit, P. 1998. "A Theory of Normal and Ideal Conditions", *Philosophical Studies,* Vol 65.

Wedgwood, R. 1996. "The Essence of Response-dependence", *European Review of Philosophy,* vol. 3, pp. 31–54.

Wright, C. 1988. "Moral Values, Projection and Secondary Qualities", *Proceedings of the Aristotelian Society,* Supplementary Volume 63, 1–26.

PETER RAILTON
Red, Bitter, Good

1.

Valuing and evaluation are pervasive features of our lives, yet their purported object, value, has proven puzzling. Many philosophers have concluded that we do best to explain it away—to develop an understanding of valuing and evaluation without objectifying value. A principal motive for such "anti-reificationism" has been the belief that attributions of value are essentially expressions of subjective responses to the non-evaluative features of the world. No evaluative objects are needed to answer to these judgments: value is projected upon the world, not discovered in it.

Recently, however, interest has grown in philosophical approaches to value that seek to explain it as involving a subjective response without thereby explaining it away. Value might be akin to a secondary quality, such as color. Of course color attribution is linked to a sensibility on our part, but this need not in itself impugn our familiar ways of talking about color—that objects indeed are colored, that their colors can (and often do) guide our color judgments, and so on. Perhaps we could be led to question these familiar ways of talking about color if we could be convinced that color perception or color discourse somehow systematically misrepresents the world. But such claims would require substantial further argument and do not follow simply from the observation that rationally-optional sensibilities are implicated in color perception.

How good is the analogy between color and value? An adequate answer

---

I am grateful to Alex Byrne, Jonathan Dancy, James Griffin, Alex Miller, James Pryor, Robert Stalnaker, and Stephen Yablo, among others, for helpful discussion. They are plainly not responsible for whatever confusions remain.

would involve giving an account of both, and that clearly is too large a project for this paper. But there might nonetheless be room to discuss one important set of issues concerning the analogy, roughly, those connected with *relativism*. One line of objection to the analogy between color and value has been that color, precisely because of its involvement with subjectivity, is relativistic in a way that moral value in particular purportedly is not.[1] Simon Blackburn has written:

> It is not altogether simple to characterize the 'mind-dependence' of secondary qualities. But it is plausible to say that these are relative to our perceptions of them in this way: if we were to change so that everything in the world which had appeared blue came to appear red to us, this is what it is for the world to cease to contain blue things, and come to contain only red things. The analogue with moral qualities fails dramatically: if everyone comes to think of it as permissible to maltreat animals, this does nothing at all to make it permissible: it just means that everybody has deteriorated.[2]

Other writers have, however, defended the analogy between value and color at just this point. They share Blackburn's anti-relativism about moral qualities, but take issue with what he says about the sense in which color is "relative to our perceptions". They argue as follows.

It is agreed on all sides that the extension of color terms is partly determined by reference to subjective human perceptual experience. Disagreement sets in when defenders of the analogy insist—against Blackburn—that the extension is *rigidly* fixed by *actual* human perceptual experience. That is, many philosophers would reject the following equation:

(1) x is red = x is such as to elicit in normal humans (and in normal circumstances) the visual impression of redness.

Imagining a thought experiment similar to Blackburn's, these philoso-

---

1. To say that moral value 'purportedly' is not relativistic is to say that moral relativism is viewed by most as a strongly *revisionary* thesis in ethics.
2. Simon Blackburn, "Errors and the Phenomenology of Value", in Ted Honderich (ed.), *Morality and Objectivity: A Tribute to J.L. Mackie* (London: Routledge and Kegan Paul, 1985), p. 14. Blackburn here speaks of moral permissibility, which is not itself a value term in the strict sense. Some slippage will be needed between deontic and evaluative categories if we are to weave together the words of various discussants into a single debate. I do not believe, however, that the point Blackburn wishes to make turns on whether we see him as speaking of moral permissibility or moral goodness.

phers argue that changing human physiology in such a way as to make blue things look red to (then) normal humans would *not* change their color. As Sidney Shoemaker puts it:

> I don't think that if overnight massive surgery produces intrasubjective spectrum inversion in everyone, grass will have become red and daffodils will have become blue; instead, it will have become the case that green things look the way red things used to, yellow things look the way blue things used to, and so on. I think that our color concepts are, for good reasons, more "objective" [than certain other sensory qualities]....[3]

Typically, intuitions such as Shoemaker's are captured by moving from an equivalence like (1), above, to something closer to (2):

(2)   x is red = x is such as to elicit in normal humans as they *actually* are (and in *actually* normal circumstances) the visual impression of redness.[4]

Let us grant that Shoemaker's intuition about color change is more plausible than Blackburn's, so that (2) is a better candidate for truth than (1). Color concepts, we will suppose, enjoy the sort of non-relativism or "objectivity" (which here means in part: independence from certain changes in our attitudes or sensibilities) that (2) confers.

The rigidification in (2) may remove the disanalogy Blackburn had in mind between color and value.[5] Might we even deploy this notion of "objectivity" to understand the purported non-relativism of moral value? Here is one approach to moral value, modelled on (2):

(3)   x is morally good = x is such as to elicit in normal humans as they *actually* are (and in *actually* normal circumstances) a sentiment of moral approbation.

---

3. Sidney Shoemaker, "Self-Knowledge and 'Inner Sense'", *Philosophy and Phenomenological Research* 54 (1994): 249–314, p. 302.
4. See for example Mark Johnston, "Dispositional Theories of Value", *Proceedings of the Aristotelian Society*, suppl. vol. 63 (1989): 139–174, esp. pp. 140–141. The original inspiration for this rigidification is found in Martin Davies and Lloyd Humberstone, "Two Notions of Necessity", *Philosophical Studies* 38 (1980): 1–30, esp. pp. 22–25.
5. Blackburn lists five other "significant differences between secondary properties and those involved in value and obligation". See his "Errors and the Phenomenology of Value", pp. 13–15.

If (3) were correct, then the mere fact of humans changing their moral attitudes concerning the treatment of animals would not in itself alter the moral quality of gratuitously tormenting animals. *Actual* humans, we suppose, do in fact morally disapprove of this sort of thing.[6]

Equation (3) would secure a certain non-relativism or "objectivity" (again: independence from fluctuating attitudes or sensibilities) for moral value in a manner that closely parallels what we have said about color. Too closely, I will argue. For there are, I believe, serious obstacles to an approach to moral non-relativism through fixing reference by actual moral responses. An alternative explanation of moral non-relativism or "objectivity"—meant

---

6. Though equation (3) is consilient with Blackburn's intuition, it faces an immediate difficulty: the gap between any actual human response, even if normal and even if the response has the phenomenology of moral approbation, and any genuinely *normative* conclusion. It would appear that (3)—which presumably would be deemed *a priori* true—enables us to bridge the fact/value gap effortlessly.

What if, for example, actual human approbation settles upon a certain kind of act or practice owing in part to a *factual misunderstanding* on our part of its nature or consequences? One remedy might be to shift (3) into an idealized, subjunctive form: what actual humans *would* morally approve were they fully informed, vividly aware, and so on.

Yet there remains a logical gap (it seems) between idealized moral approbation (a psychological phenomenon) and moral goodness (which has normative purport).

Many advocates of the analogy between color and moral value therefore have insisted that (4), rather than (3), is the proper *a priori* equation:

(4) x is morally good = x is such as to *make appropriate* in normal humans as they actually are (and in actually normal circumstances) a sentiment of moral approbation.

Equation (4) preserves the rigidification that allowed (3) to escape relativism arising from changes in moral attitudes, but it is normative on both right- and left-hand side, and so bridges no fact/value gap.

This certainly removes one obstacle to the acceptance of (4) as an account of moral value. But the manifest disparity between our revised equation for color, (2), with its causal talk of eliciting a response, and our revised equation for moral value, (4), with its overtly normative talk of making a response appropriate, has disenchanted some philosophers with the claim that the analogy with color runs deep.

In what follows, I will attempt to take the analogy to color more nearly at face value, and thus will rely upon formulation (3).

to account for intuitions like Blackburn's—will be suggested. As we will see, this alternative account may not spoil the analogy between moral value and secondary qualities, but it does suggest that the secondary qualities in question are not those of color, despite their paradigmatic status.

2.

Consider the following science-fictive case, which may afford an analogy of sorts with Shoemaker's science fiction about color.

Let us suppose that a widespread change in human circumstances and ontogeny results in a decisive shift in our intrinsic, informed preferences or tendencies toward approbation. Actual normal humans, it is often claimed, take an *intrinsic* interest in kin relationships. For example, we are said to intrinsically prefer, other things equal, bestowing a benefit on a biological relative—a parent, offspring, next-of-kin—rather than on an unrelated individual whom we happen to know equally well and who is otherwise equally deserving. The preference in question is not only *that a relative be benefited* (rather than a non-relative), but also *that we do the bestowing*. Some measure of value would be lost were the benefit not bestowed in accord with the line of kin connection.

This preference is thought to be independent of whatever other values might be realized in conveying the benefit. For example, it does not depend on whether greater happiness is produced in aiding a relative—indeed, it does not depend on whether one is aware that the benefited individual is a relative. If one were approached for aid by two nearly identical individuals in nearly identical circumstances, *except* that one is long-lost (and no longer recognized) kin—say, a brother or parent from whom one had been separated at birth—then this particular value would be realized if one's aid went to the individual who happened to be kin, knowingly or not. Such an outcome would, on this view, simply be more fitting. Kinship, flesh and blood, is thought to matter in its own right, and not solely because of the extrinsic gains to welfare that would arise from such special connections.

Now for the science fiction. Imagine that advances in medical technology, combined with a growing sense of the inconveniences of caring for infants (not to mention the special challenges of living through adolescence!), lead adult humans to devise a form of reproduction through automated, full-scale replication of themselves. Happily, one might say, the process does not produce exact replicas. The replica individuals bear a strong resemblance to the originals, but, for reasons that are not well understood, they tend to look somewhat different from, and to lack the individual memories of, their "parents". They emerge from the automated process tongue-tied and awkward, but surprisingly soon most become fully fluent in word and motion. Indeed, their initial, confused condition and subsequent (usually rapid) progress are reminiscent of nothing so much as the recovery of young adults who have undergone strong shocks in accidents.

Imagine, too, that (again for reasons not well understood) replica individuals also lack a special, intrinsic interest in those from whom they are replicated or who are otherwise genetically close to them. Biological relatedness does not seem to matter in its own right to them, even after they have fully "matured" and are successfully integrated into the community, and even when they are well informed and reflective. In virtually all other respects, they are emotionally and affectively our replicas. They are, for example, perfectly capable of developing strong and lasting affections, and they, like us, tend to take an especially strong interest in those with whom they share interests and daily life. A new human who has been helped through the initial, post-replicative stages by his or her biological "parent" typically forms a special, long-term attachment to that individual. But this sort of attachment is only contingently related to actual kinship—replicas can be, and often are, "raised" by someone biologically unrelated to them. So this "filial affection" is more like the special gratitude and affection old humans would feel toward those who acted as one's parents during a challenging year as a foreign exchange student. For the new humans, it would not matter intrinsically whether their "host family", as we might call it, was in fact genetically related to them.

We may suppose that, although the two groups, old and new humans, mutually recognize their differences on this score, such recognition does not change either group's intrinsic preferences. Precisely because the preferences in question are intrinsic, neither group feels it can satisfactorily explain itself to the other. Older humans find it hard not to think that (in one respect, at least) new humans are missing something in life; new humans find it hard not to think that (in one respect, at least) old humans are incorrigibly prejudiced in thinking that biological relatedness, over and above the stuff of actual human interactions, is a special value-making feature.

Let us pursue a bit further our fictive narration. Despite the initial oddness of this reproductive arrangement—and some of its counter-intuitive results in the eyes of old humans—it soon proves so satisfactory overall that it fully replaces other forms of reproduction. Diaper manufacturers and publishers of books with titles like *Raise Your Newborn Right*, *The Two-Career Family: How to Win Back Your Life*, *Why Teens Won't Listen*, and *Juvenile Delinquency* (3 vols.), switch to other lines of business. Only new humans exist.

Suppose now that we actual humans are contemplating such a time. We are asked to imagine the following course of events. One new human, Ed, underwent replication some years ago to create another, Ethan, but became separated immediately afterward owing to a medical problem that required that Ed be taken to a distant city. Ethan thus was "raised" during the early months of life not by biological kin, but by unrelated new humans. This is not a rare or painful thing. Many replicas are raised by unrelated individuals, and sufficiently many new humans enjoy this process—which comes to be called "awakening" and to be mildly subsidized for related and unrelated host families alike—that there was, at the time of Ethan's arrival, a waiting list of those eager to host replicas. Social scientific research shows no interesting difference between individuals awakened by related vs. non-related hosts.

As typical new humans, neither Ed nor Ethan has a special interest in biological relatedness as such. Ed undergoes a protracted recovery, and when he finally leaves the hospital his deep gratitude to his doctors and nurses is uppermost in his mind, not Ethan. He resettles in his new city, knowing there are excellent arrangements for the awakening of replicas in the absence of biological kin. Ethan, for his part, does not pine to meet or learn of his biological "parent". He has a relatively untroubled awakening, and forms a warm bond to his host family. He gives the idea of "reconnecting" with his biological "parent" no more thought than we old humans would give "reconnecting" with the attending physician present at our birth.

Years go by. Though Ethan and Ed plainly resemble one another, differences in eating habits, manner, grooming, accent, and dress give them fairly distinct appearances and personas. One might meet them both at a party and not immediately conclude that they are kin. Ed prospers in his new location; Ethan takes a job involving extensive travel. One day he travels to a city which happens to be the one to which Ed moved, though Ethan is unaware of that. We find Ethan boarding the airport limousine to travel to his hotel. He's normally chatty and sociable in this sort of setting, quick to strike up a conversation with whoever happens to be next to him. As it happens, the person who sits on his left is his Ed himself; on his right, an unrelated stranger. Were Ethan to enter into a conversation with either, it would be somewhat enjoyable for both parties—Ethan really is pleasant to chat with for the span of a twenty- or thirty-minute ride, even if he does dwell a bit too much on himself. Let us suppose that the unrelated stranger would enjoy such a conversation a bit more than Ed, and that Ed and Ethan wouldn't recognize one another as related in any event. It remains true that if Ethan were to engage Ed in conversation, then a biological "parent" would make a connection with his offspring. He'd meet his "son", and come to learn from Ethan himself something of what has become of him in life (though not, of course, under that description). Ethan seldom gets twenty minutes into a pick-up conversation without having touched on the high points of his professional life. Ed, we will suppose, would never otherwise "reconnect" with Ethan. Indeed, were Ethan instead to have initiated a conversation with the man seated on his right, Ed would simply have taken no notice of him. Ethan's conversation with the other man would also touch on life highlights, but they'd all escape Ed—he'd soon have donned his Walkman headset and absorbed himself in an airport news-shop novel. Ed would get off at his downtown office without so much as exchanging a word or a glance with Ethan.

An actual human contemplating these two possible scenarios among new humans might find an intrinsic preference that Ethan turn and talk to Ed, his "parent", rather than the man on the right. It is better or more fitting, we might think, that his own flesh and blood make this acquaintance and hear something of the story of his life. (We will assume that, from the standpoint of morality, there is no independent issue about the permissibility of his speaking to either.) From our old-human perspective, we would deem that some measure of value would be lost if the opportunity afforded by this chance re-encounter were altogether squandered and the two men were to remain utter strangers to each other. "Too bad," we'd think.

But would this response on our part really make sense? How would we justify the view that greater value would be realized if Ethan were to speak to Ed—or that this would be a morally better outcome? Extrinsically, more good would be done if Ethan were to speak to the stranger, who would enjoy his company more. And intrinsically, no one present in the limousine—or even alive at the time—prefers giving consideration to kin connections as such. Of course, *we* may find that we intrinsically prefer that Ethan talk to Ed—just as, in this world, we favor kin connections even when the agents involved are indifferent. But we and our ilk will be long gone by the time Ed and Ethan are seated side by side, and no more good could come to us. Could our intrinsic preference, which has no echo in their preferences or indeed any in anyone's preferences from then onward, be a ground for some good coming about through their actions, or for a moral directive as to how they should act?[7]

If the extension of 'intrinsic value' is *rigidified* in the manner of talk of color (recall equation (2), above), then it seems we are committed to saying that there is indeed some intrinsic good in Ethan talking to Ed rather than the stranger, a good which could in principle offset the greater enjoyment of the stranger in Ethan's company. Recall that according to the rigidified view of color, a widespread shift in the human physiology of color perception would not change the color of grass—it would remain green even though it came to look red to humans, and humans who judged it red *tout simple* would be making a mistake. If we considered intrinsic value to be likewise rigidified, then the particular change in human intrinsic preferences imagined above would not alter the intrinsic value of relations effected among biological kin—it would mean only that humans had become insensitive to this value. When we ask ourselves what is good in relations among new humans, on this view, we always advert to what is intrinsically motivating for actual humans in actual circumstances. That is, we would have to say that even if making a connection to one's genetic kin ceased to hold any intrinsic interest for humans, and even if humans did not seem to be suffering any sort of anomie or dysfunction as a result, still, such connections would make things intrinsically better—and perhaps also morally better.

Such an assessment does not seem terribly plausible. John Stuart Mill offers a famous (notorious?) principle that might help explain why:

---

7. This concern does not depend upon any premise to the effect that a person's good can only be advanced by something that makes a difference to the course of her experience. At least insofar as intrinsic preferences are concerned, reflection on examples involving experience machines, systematic deception, and the like, may convince us that we have robust intrinsic preferences concerning the course of our *lives* that are not necessarily reflected in differences in our *experiences*.

(M)   …the sole evidence it is possible to produce that anything is desirable is that people do actually desire it.[8]

Mill's 'actually', I would suggest, is not the rigidifying 'actually'—it can be replaced by a contextual 'in fact'. Indeed, he goes on to write:

> If the end which the utilitarian doctrine proposes to itself were not, in theory and in practice, acknowledged to be an end, nothing could ever convince any person that it was so.[9]

Now once there are no more old humans, there is no longer anyone who is—in theory or in practice—intrinsically interested in kin relationships. So, just as it would not advance my good in the present to satisfy a desire I once had but have long since lost—to use an example of Richard Brandt's, a childhood desire to celebrate each and every birthday for the rest of my life with a ride on the Gravity Monster roller-coaster[10]—it would not advance anyone's good for kin connections to be made after intrinsic motivation in favor of such relations had disappeared from the planet.[11] And it is perhaps equally difficult to see any moral purpose advanced thereby.

3.

If value—at least in the case of intrinsic, and perhaps also moral, value—is not rigidified in the manner of color, does this mean that there cannot be a useful analogy between value and secondary qualities? Perhaps not. For, as Sidney Shoemaker has argued, not all secondary quality predicates appear to be rigidified, either:

Consider Jonathan Bennett's example of phenol-thio-uria, which

> tastes bitter to three-quarters of the population and is tsteless to the rest. If as the result of selective breeding, or surgical tampering, it becomes tasteless to everyone, I say it has become tasteless. And if more drastic surgical tampering makes it

---

8. J.S. Mill, "Utilitarianism", ch. 5; p. 288 as reprinted in Mary Warnock (ed.), *John Stuart Mill: Utilitarianism [and other essays]* (New York: New American Library, 1962).
9. *Ibid.*
10. Richard B. Brandt, *A Theory of the Good and the Right* (Oxford: Oxford University Press, 1979), pp. 249–50. The example has been slightly altered.
11. We are assuming that this intrinsic preference has disappeared not only from actual preferences, but even from reflective, informed preferences. It has lost its motivational ground in the human population altogether.

taste sweet to everyone, I say it has become sweet.[12]

Shoemaker's remark may not apply to the whole range of gustatory terms, but his intuition does seem quite plausible for 'sweet' and 'bitter'. And these terms, one might think, are very much closer to "Pleasing/not pleasing to the tongue" than 'red' or 'green' is to "pleasing/not pleasing to the eye".[13] That might help us to understand their lack of rigidification. Shoemaker writes:

> Our dominant interest in classifying things by flavor is our interest in having certain taste experiences and avoiding others, and not our interest in what such experiences tell us about other matters. With color it is the other way around ....[14]

It seems to me plausible that our vocabulary of intrinsic value is likewise primarily geared to the task of asking what to seek and what to avoid, depending upon whether it would be (in some sense) a positive or negative thing intrinsically to lead a given life.[15] It is, then, unsurprising that the domain of what is intrinsically good for humans is not rigidly fixed by actual human responses, but reflects instead potentially evolving or changing human responses.

Does this make judgments of intrinsic good *relativistic*? Not if that means something like "observer dependent". What matters is not who is making the judgment, but *of whom* the judgment is being made, which can be constant across differences in observers. It would be better to say that intrinsic good is *relational*—what is intrinsically good for an individual *I* of kind *K* depends upon the nature of *I* and *K*. Likewise, one might say, for

---

12. Shoemaker, "Self-Knowledge and 'Inner Sense'", p. 302. Shoemaker refers the reader to Jonathan Bennett's "Substance, Reality, and Primary Qualities", in C.B. Martin and D.M Armstrong (eds.), *Locke and Berkeley* (New York: Anchor Books, 1968). I am grateful to James Pryor for calling my attention to Shoemaker's claim and to Mark Crimmins for helping me to locate it.
13. My dictionary gives "Having or being of a taste that is sharp, acrid, and unpleasant" as the first definition of 'bitter'; and it gives "Pleasing to the senses, feelings, or the mind; gratifying" as the second definition of 'sweet'. Neither its definition of 'red' nor of 'green' makes any mention of such positive or negative experiential features. See *The American Heritage Dictionary of the English Language* (Boston: Houghton-Mifflin: 1979).
14. Shoemaker, "Self-Knowledge and 'Inner Sense'", pp. 302–3.
15. We can, I think, expand Shoemaker's point to include our intrinsic concern that our lives possess certain non-experiential features as well.

sweetness. Phenol-thio-uria is "relationally sweet"—whether it is, for x, sweet does not depend upon the identity or nature of the person asking this question, but upon the identity and nature of x.[16]

Would this mean that there is no answer to the question "Is sugar sweet?", when asked not of some particular person but simply in general? No more than there is no answer to the question "Is Michael Jordan tall?" Sugar is sweet because it is a physiological *match* for the sweetness-sensing capacities of almost everyone; Michael Jordan is tall because he is taller than the vast majority of humans. Ordinary contexts assume ordinary comparison classes. But there are special contexts. We might be comparing Michael Jordan to other high-scoring greats in the history of basketball (among whom he is not particularly tall), and we might be talking about sugar and the gustatory propensities of those with damaged nerves in the tongue. "Sugar isn't *always* sweet," a researcher might tell us.[17]

The image of sugar as a match for normal human sweetness-sensing capacities can now be deployed in describing the fictive example of the old vs. new human ways of life and reproduction. There is, we have assumed, a match between the realization of special connections with genetic kin and something in the intrinsic motivational structure of old, i.e., actual, humans. Actual humans exhibit a fascination with ancestry and a commitment to progeny that go well beyond evident gains in other sorts of value. There would, however, be no corresponding match between the realization of such special connections and the intrinsic motivational structure of new humans. Genetic relatedness would persist, but no corresponding intrinsic motivation. It would therefore be quite unclear how realizing such special connections could be "more fitting" in a world exclusively populated by new humans, or how it could make their lives (or anyone's life) intrinsically better or more worthwhile.

---

16. A relational approach differs from a relativistic, indexical approach in much the same way that equation (1) (which makes explicit a relation to *normal human* responses) differs from (2) (which makes explicit an indexical *actually*). For a relativistic, indexical approach to statements of value that contrasts with the relationalism discussed here, see James Dreier, "Internalism and Speaker Relativism", *Ethics* 101 (1990), 6–26.
17. To my ear, "Sugar isn't *always* sweet" suggests initially something about changing sensation, while "Grass isn't *always* green" suggests initially something about changing grass (e.g., in the dry season). Context, of course, affects these initial readings.

4.

Hume argued that justice is an "artificial virtue", arising from conditions of moderate scarcity and confined sympathy. It depends, on his view, upon a contingent mutuality of interests, "education", and "human conventions".[18]

"Artifice" here is not the same thing as arbitrariness, he emphasizes, since the interests justice serves are of central importance to us as things now stand. Still, were scarcity much less, or generalized human sympathies much greater, then we would find no vice at all in the behavior of a hungry child who takes an apple—which otherwise would remain unpicked, fall to the ground, and rot—from a tree on the vast estate of a distant lord. Indeed, the very notion of an "estate" would seem to us without moral standing. Hume contrasts the artifice of justice and property with "natural virtue", such as special concern for one's genetic kin:

> In like manner we always consider the *natural* and *usual* force of the passions, when we determine concerning vice and virtue.... A man naturally loves his children better than his nephews, his nephews better than his cousins, his cousins better than strangers, where everything else is equal. Hence arise our common measures of duty, in preferring the one to the other. Our sense of duty always follows the common and natural course of our passions.[19]

But what if these "natural" passions themselves depend upon certain patterns of reproduction and child-rearing? Evolution may well predispose us to form special attachments to those who raise us and whom we raise,[20] but new humans would not undergo the usual developmental period of prolonged infancy and they might frequently be "raised" primarily by biologically-unrelated individuals. Special love of nephews and a preference for nephews over cousins may have seemed perfectly natural and virtuous in eighteenth-century Scotland, but may come to seem more of a social artifact even from the perspective of the highly mobile society of the United States

---

18. *A Treatise of Human Nature*, Book III, Part II, Section I. In the edition by L.A. Selby-Bigge (Oxford: Clarendon, 1888), p. 483. Hume elsewhere notes other factors, including the "ravishability" of many goods and the importance of rules.
19. *Treatise*, ibid., pp. 483–4.
20. This might be "inclusively fit", since we cannot ordinarily identify genetic kin by observation, and since (we suppose) "those who raise us" has typically correlated well in the evolutionary past with those more closely genetically related than the human population at large.

in the twentieth century, where these "natural duties" and their distinctive emphases in concern seem attenuated.[21] The seeming intelligibility of the example of new humans, however, suggests that "human nature" could persist without this particular intrinsic motivator. New humans might lack altogether our current genetic preoccupations and base their recognizably human sympathies instead upon other forms of mutual interest and personal loyalty familiar to us. These concerns would occur "naturally" to them, and would help form the foundation for their individual and social flourishing. If taking up the moral point of view involves (at least) non-partial, intrinsic concern for the well-being of those affected, it would seem untenable for us to insist that new humans would exhibit a moral deficiency in showing greater loyalty and devotion to friends, lovers, colleagues, and to their "hosts" and replicas they have "awakened"—those, in sum, with whom they share formative experiences—rather than those with whom they share DNA.

Moral thought is sometimes labeled *projective*, and there are disputes about the aptness of this characterization and about whether the label is in some way pejorative. Moral thought *would*, I think, be projective in a pejorative sense if by its very nature it committed us to referring moral judgments about a world of new humans and their norms to the responses of actual humans in actual circumstances. Before we project norms garnering the approbation of actual humans onto relations among non-actual humans we must ask whether the sorts of lives from which we and they derive meaning and intrinsic value are the same. In posing this question we need not appeal to a utilitarian principle as such. Rather, a much more general principle is at stake, one which (for example) Rawls has used to criticize utilitarianism: "the correct regulative principle for anything depends on the nature of that thing."[22]

---

21. Of course, an intrinsic interest in closer kin connections survives in this country even so. History affords another interesting example of a related sort of change. When political rule was personal or familial, it was typically thought appropriate for leaders to give special preference to kin. In the modern period, the rise of (in principle) impersonal forms of government has made favoritism toward family members a paradigmatic vice.
22. John Rawls, *A Theory of Justice* (Cambridge: Harvard University Press, 1971), p. 29. Rawls invokes this principle in arguing that utilitarianism is unacceptable because it does not take into account the separateness of persons.

5.

Rigidification, then, seems to this extent inappropriate as a way of capturing the objectivity of moral assessment. In asking whether new humans would still bathe in water we may wish to keep the extension of 'water' rigidly fixed by actual human usage and actual circumstances. In asking whether ripe bananas would still be yellow in the new-human world we may wish to rigidify on our actual color responses. But in asking whether it would be intrinsically or morally good for new humans to give special weight to kin connections we may not want the reference of 'intrinsically good' or 'morally good' to be fixed by what elicits the positive responses of actual humans in actual circumstances.[23]

Does giving up on this sort of rigidification lead to the moral relativism Blackburn decried? That would appear unacceptable. David Wiggins begins his own discussion of a rigidified subjectivism by invoking a remark of Bertrand Russell's:

> I cannot see how to refute the arguments for the subjectivity of ethical values, but I find myself incapable of believing that all that is wrong with wanton cruelty is that I don't like it.[24]

---

23. Plainly, I do appeal to *some* principles of ours in asking how we'd assess the new human example: that morality is impartial and concerned with (perhaps among other things) the goodness of lives, that satisfying someone's intrinsic, reflective desires is *prima facie* a contribution to the goodness of her life, or that the proper regulative principle for a thing regulates in accord with the nature of that thing. These principles are, however, (something like) necessary or constitutive truths of the moral or evaluative domain rather than substantive moral or evaluative judgments. Holding these constant as we consider which more substantive judgments would be made concerning acts or persons in another world is thus akin to holding constant our notions of color or taste or water when asking what color grass has, or whether phenol-thio-uria is sweet, or whether XYZ is water, in another world.
24. Quoted in Wiggins' essay "A Sensible Subjectivism?", in his *Needs, Values, Truth* (Oxford: Blackwell, 1987), p. 185. Once again, we need to slide between the vocabulary of "ethical values" and the vocabulary of rightness and wrongness. I take it, however, that Russell's point could equally be expressed as: "I find myself incapable of believing that all that is morally bad about wanton cruelty is that I don't like it." To the extent that Russell has in mind *expressivism* as a subjectivist view, it can be replied that no clear-headed expressivist need regard his or her likes and dislikes as the right- and wrong-making features of the world.

Rigidified subjectivism—along the lines of equation (3), above—does indeed yield the result that even if humans were to undergo some change that would make them approve wanton cruelty, this would not make it morally good. It is the moral approvals and disapprovals of actual humans—including their disapproval of wanton cruelty—that would fix the extension of 'morally good'.

In rejecting equation (3), it may seem that we have lost the capacity to respond to Russell's concern, or to accommodate Blackburn's telling intuition about the treatment of animals.[25] What if, for example, the new humans not only had decidedly different attitudes toward parent/child relations, but also no longer disapproved of wanton cruelty toward animals? Would such conduct thus become morally unobjectionable?

Relationalism about intrinsic value, along with the (relatively uncontroversial) view that moral evaluation is non-partial, has no such implication. Pain, we believe, is intrinsically bad for whoever—or whatever—experiences it. Wanton cruelty toward animals involves the unrestrained infliction of pain upon them without any commensurate benefit to their well-being, a condition that would not be changed if we were to change *our* attitude toward its permissibility. Human approbation of its torment would not in the least improve the experience of a dog being kicked or a horse being whipped. Russell is certainly correct in saying that what is wrong with wanton cruelty is not that we dislike it. Rather, it is the intrinsically unliked character of the torment such conduct would cause its recipients—a torment which is unaffected by our attitude—that makes the behavior wrong.

This is an alternative explanation of the "objectivity"—in the sense of "independence from our particular attitudes"—of our judgments about wanton cruelty or maltreating animals, an explanation which does not involve either non-relational intrinsic value (it is enough if pain is a harm to

---

25. There is at least one difficulty about both Russell's and Blackburn's examples that we will ignore here. One might argue that 'wanton cruelty' and 'maltreatment' are both *by definition* prima facie morally questionable. Substantive moral theory is not needed to show that we could not, by any possible change in attitude, make such conduct right—a dictionary would suffice. We must imagine that the examples have been stated in less tendentious language: e.g., instead of 'wanton cruelty', substitute 'the deliberate infliction of significant pain on others for the sole purpose of satisfying one's desire to do so'.

the beings experiencing it) or rigidification of our moral response to kickings and whippings.

Is this a sufficient explanation of Russell's and Blackburn's observations about objectivity? How far can we appeal to such notions to capture other forms of objectivity in moral judgment? Might there be some higher-order level of evaluative or normative language at which rigidity re-emerges? These questions take us beyond the scope of the present paper.

6.

The question whether intrinsic value or moral value is analogous to secondary qualities is overly broad. One might do better to ask: analogous to *which* secondary qualities and in *what* respects? Color has been the natural stand-in for 'secondary quality' in most philosophical discussions of the analogy, reflecting perhaps the predominance of vision in human sensory life. But perhaps taste—or rather, the gustatory vocabulary of bitterness and sweetness—is a more plausible candidate. To be sure, value talk is full of visual imagery, but perceptual models of value judgment are only partly convincing, and even there gustatory imagery is also common—one is, I suppose, about as likely to say that one "savors" value as that one "sees" it. But even this is too hasty. 'Intrinsic' value is indeed rather like 'sweet' and 'bitter'—and unlike 'red' and 'green'—in its relational, functional character and its relation to guiding choice toward the desirable and away from the undesirable. But moral value has a more complex character, which in certain cases leads it to mimic the rigidification of color. Intuitively, Shoemaker notes, we use color terms to assemble information about the world around us for input into deliberation, not to steer choice more directly. Thus, changing human color reception would not change colors. We would not want people to *misread* the change in the appearance of grass as a change in its physical constitution and environment. Similarly, changing human sensibilities toward animals would not change the moral badness of wanton cruelty toward them. We would not want people to misread the change in their own attitudes as a change in what happens to the beasts themselves. Thus color and moral value seem to run in parallel.

The parallel breaks down on the moral side, however, once we consider cases in which the sensibilities that change are those partially *constitutive* of a moral good, such as special concern for genetic kin. If these change, then what was held to be morally better—e.g., a special connection with kin—

can become morally indifferent. The point here is that subjectivity can enter in various ways into the making and perceiving of value, some of which may have no parallel at all with the involvement of subjectivity in secondary qualities.

In thinking about value it is altogether too easy to project, conflating the familiar and conventional with the natural and inevitable. One could write a pocket history of progress in moral sensibility in terms of the successive unmasking of such conflations—with respect to slavery, inherited rule, the status of women, and the borders of tribe, "people", or nation. Objectivity about intrinsic and moral good alike calls for us to gain critical perspective on our own actual responses, not to project their objects rigidly.

Department of Philosophy
University of Michigan
2215 Angell Hall
Ann Arbor, Michigan, 48109-1003
USA
prailton@umich.edu

MICHAEL SMITH
Response-Dependence Without Reduction

1. Blackburn's dilemma for response-dependence

Many think that the mark of evaluative judgements of the form 'It is right to φ' and 'It is desirable to φ' lies in the internal or necessary connection between such judgements and the will (Hare 1952, Blackburn 1984, Korsgaard 1986, Lewis 1989, Gibbard 1990, Smith 1994). A judgement to the effect that φ-ing is right, or desirable, counts as evaluative only because, *inter alia*, absent weakness of will and the like, the person making the judgement has some motivation to φ.

Non-cognitivists famously argue from this internalist premise to the conclusion that such evaluative judgements express motivations, or dispositions to be motivated, rather than beliefs (Hare 1952, Blackburn 1984, Gibbard 1990). Their argument is that, since belief and desire are distinct existences, it is possible to combine believing that the world is a certain way, for any of the various ways it could be, with a pro-attitude towards its being that way, or indifference towards its being that way, or even a con-attitude towards its being that way. The attraction of non-cognitivism is then supposed to be that it alone tells us that the state expressed by an agent's evaluative judgement and that expressed by her motivations or dispositions to be motivated are not distinct existences, but are rather one and the same: there is simply the motivation, no belief at all.

Against this background many philosophers began to take an interest in response-dependent analyses of value in the 1980s (McDowell 1985, Smith 1986b, Wright 1988, Smith 1989, Lewis 1989, Johnston 1989). According to these theorists, the non-cognitivist's argument contains a crucial flaw. For even if we do think of evaluative judgements as expressions of beliefs they argued that there would still be a necessary connection of sorts between evaluative judgement and the will if the beliefs in question were beliefs about the judge's own motivational responses to the world. There was therefore a scurry of activity as different theorists each tried to come up with a plausible response-dependent analysis of value, one which guaranteed the right sort of connection between evaluative judgement and the will but without, in the process, generating any counter-intuitive consequences of its own.[1] Before this work was all out, however, and before the work that was out had been properly assimilated, one very prominent non-cognitivist, Simon Blackburn, launched a potentially devastating attack on response-dependent analyses of value (1993).

In 'Circles, Finks, Smells and Biconditionals' Blackburn argued that, whatever their differences, those who favour response-dependent analyses of some concept, C, must believe that there is an *a priori* true biconditional of the form:

> X is C iff X tends to elicit [reaction] from [persons] under [circumstances]

Moreover, notwithstanding the fact that many response-dependent theorists explicitly rejected the claim to be providing an analytic reduction of value, he argued that if such a biconditional is to do its job, its status as an *a priori* truth must in turn reflect a certain sort of dependency between the left hand side and the right hand side. An understanding of X's being C must consist, in some sense, in an understanding of X's having a tendency to elicit [reaction] from [persons] under [circumstances].

With just this much agreed about the project of analysing concepts in a response-dependent style Blackburn raised what he thinks is an unavoidable dilemma for response-dependence.

> Suppose we stay with the goal of understanding the judgement that X is C. The... problem we meet is... one of navigating between two disasters, that I shall call Scylla and Charybdis. Scylla is that we falsify the kind of judgement that 'X is C' actually makes. Charybdis is that we get this right but at the cost of making the same kind of judgement at some place within the right hand side... This structure is familiar in the case of value. Scylla is that we go naturalistic or empirical;

---

1. Response-dependent theorists disagreed among themselves whether it would be counter-intuitive to suppose that belief and desire are not distinct existences. Contrast, for example, Smith (1987) and Lewis (1988) with McDowell (1978).

Charybdis that we make an ethical judgement on the right hand side. (Blackburn 1993, p. 272)

Let's consider the two horns in turn.

On the first horn, Scylla, [reaction], [persons] and [circumstances] are all specified in non-evaluative terms. Blackburn's own example is:

> X is good if and only if X is such as to elicit desires from us as we actually are when we come across it (Blackburn 1993, p. 272)

But this biconditional is evidently false because we know that, as a matter of fact, we have all sorts of desires for things that are not good, and that there are all sorts of good things that we do not desire. Moreover, even if it did just so happen to be true that the good things are all and only those we, as we actually are, desire when we come across them, it would still be at best an *a posteriori* truth, not an *a priori* truth.

Nor is Scylla made tractable by coming up with more complicated formulations of the biconditional. Consider, for example, David Lewis's (1989) suggestion that:

> X is a value if and only if X is what we would desire to desire under conditions of full imaginative acquaintance with X

The same sorts of problems arise. Whether the things we would desire to desire are or are not good is supposed to depend on the causal consequences of our imaginings. But, to the contrary, there is good reason to believe that our imaginations can distort our reactions in unjustifiable ways, a point well made by Mark Johnston.

> Even if one is initially benevolent, complete awareness of the suffering of the mass of sentient beings would be horrifically depressing, and hardness of heart rather than valuing their release might well be the causal upshot. (Johnston 1989, p.152)

Moreover, even if it did just so happen that the good things were all and only those that we desired to desire under conditions of full imaginative acquaintance, that would once again be, at best, an *a posteriori* truth, not an *a priori* truth. The fact that vividly imagining X causes [reaction] is thus not constitutive of X's being a value at all. What matters is, at best, whether vividly imagining X *justifies* the [reaction]. At this point we therefore begin moving towards Charybdis.

On the other horn of the dilemma, Charybdis, we make an evaluative judgement in specifying what the relevant [reaction] is, or who the relevant [persons] are, or what the relevant [circumstances] are. Blackburn's examples are these (1993, pp. 272–3).

> X is good iff X is such as to elicit desires from good people when they come across it.
>
> X is good iff X is such as to elicit desires from people under the ideal circumstances, i.e. those under which people desire good things.

His objection on this horn is, accordingly, not that the biconditional is false or at best only *a posteriori* true, but rather that it makes no analytic advance.

> It takes not observation but ethical judgement to determine whether something is such as to elicit desires from good people, since you have to judge who are the good people. Of course, in principle an advance within ethics could come about this way, since it might be somehow easier to judge who are the good people than it appears to be to judge X's. But this will not be an advance in our understanding of ethical judgement *per se*. It would be a strictly local advance in first order moral theory. (Blackburn 1993, pp. 272–3)

On Charybdis we therefore make no headway in our attempt to understand the nature of an evaluative judgement. If we were initially puzzled whether the judgement that X is good expresses a desire or belief, then being told that it is equivalent to the judgement that X is such as to elicit desires from people under the circumstances under which people desire good things is hardly going to help. We will simply be undecided whether that expresses a desire or belief.

If Blackburn is right then it seems that response-dependent analyses of value cannot help us block the argument from internalism to non-cognitivism. If the analysis is reductive, then though it succeeds in telling us which belief an evaluative judgement is supposed to express, it is evidently false that evaluative judgements express the beliefs thus identified. And if it is non-reductive then we make no analytic advance. The alleged analysis simply doesn't tell us that evaluative judgements *do* express beliefs. The argument for non-cognitivism thus remains intact.

My task in the present paper is to show that Blackburn's dilemma is no dilemma at all. I will argue that because Blackburn overlooks the role of platitudes in conceptual analysis he does not see that we can use these platitudes to spell out the cognitive content of an evaluative judgement in non-reductive response-dependent terms. I begin at the beginning, by explaining what, precisely, the role of platitudes in an analysis is.

2. Platitudes and conceptual analysis: the case of colour

When we acquire mastery of any term in a language what we acquire is a certain sort of skill in the use of that term: we acquire a set of dispositions to make inferences and judgements along certain lines (Smith 1994, Ch.2). Let's call the description a theorist might give of these inferences and judgements a set of 'platitudes'. What might these platitudes be?

Consider, to begin, the case of colour, and in particular the concept of being red. What are the red-platitudes? The red-platitudes describe the inferences and judgements we make in virtue of being masters of the term 'red'. They therefore include platitudes about the relations between redness and the other colours. 'Red is more similar to orange than to yellow', 'Red is more similar to purple than to blue', 'Red is maximally dissimilar to green', 'Red is more similar to pink than to white', 'Red is more similar to plum than to black', and so on. They include platitudes about the relations between colour experiences and colour judgements. 'Someone who judges an object to be red in the presence of that object has an experience as of the object's being red, provided something unusual isn't going on', 'The colours of objects typically cause us to see those objects as the colours that they are', 'Most everything we see looks coloured', 'There's no seeing a colour without seeing an extended coloured patch', 'Blind people don't know what colours are', and the like. They include corrective platitudes linking real as opposed to illusory colours to features of perceivers and their environments. 'If you want to know what colour something is, have a look at it', 'Things don't usually look the colour they really are in the dark so if you want to see what colour something really is, take it into the daylight', 'If your eyes aren't working properly you might not be able to tell what colour things really are', 'Unperceived objects are still coloured', and the like. And, finally, they include platitudes about the ways in which we learn colour terms by linking them up with features of the world. 'If you want to teach someone what the word for red means, show her some red objects and then say the word for red', 'Teach what the word for red means at the same time as you teach what the other colour words mean', and so on.

To say that these are platitudes is not to say that their precise formulation is uncontroversial. On the contrary, it is presumably very controversial what the judgements and inferences we make as masters of the term 'red' are.[2] Moreover, the fact that we make the inferences and judgements that we do, as masters of the term 'red', is consistent with the possibility that we are wrong to do so. We would, for example, change our habits if we were shown that the judgements and inferences that we make as masters of the term 'red'—those captured by the platitudes themselves—were incompatible or inconsistent with each other. Importantly, however, it would take something like being convinced of such inconsistency to make us change our inferential and judgemental habits. And the reason why is easy enough to state.

At the limit, giving up on the inferences and judgements we make as masters of colour terms, in virtue of being masters, is to give up on using *colour* terms altogether. The platitudes that describe these inferences and judgements therefore have a prima facie *a priori* status, and gain *a priori* status simpliciter by surviving as part of the maximal consistent set of platitudes constitutive of mastery of colour terms. That this is so should not be surprising if, as I have already suggested, these platitudes together describe the pattern of inferences and judgements licensed by our colour concepts themselves. For, other things being equal, these inferences and judgements are themselves *a priori* knowable. Someone who has mastery of the term 'red', and who understands the red-platitudes, needs only to think the matter through carefully in order to assent to them.

If an account along these lines of what it is to have mastery of colour terms is on the right track, then a certain natural picture emerges of how we might go about giving an analysis of the concept of being red. Since such an analysis should tell us everything there is to know *a priori* about what it is for something to be red, it follows that it should give us explicit knowledge of all and only the red-platitudes: that is, the maximal consistent set of platitudes that describes the inferences and judgements we make as masters of the term 'red'. And this in turn suggests that an analysis of the concept of being red is itself simply constituted by, or derived from, a long conjunction of these platitudes. In this way an analysis helps to make the implicit explicit.

---

2. It follows that the formulations of the red-platitudes in the text may therefore be incorrect, a possibility that I will abstract away from in what follows.

3. Colour-platitudes and cognitivism

We have seen the materials from which we are to construct an analysis of the concept of being red, and we have seen what the goal of such an analysis is. Before we even attempt to construct such an analysis, however, we must first ask whether colour judgements in general are to be analysed cognitively or non-cognitively. For this will have a crucial effect upon the nature of our analysis.

It is a striking fact that nearly everyone agrees that colour judgements express beliefs about the colour properties possessed by objects. No one seems to think that they are mere expressions of our experiential reactions. But why? What justifies this cognitivist stance? The answer is: the colour-platitudes themselves (Smith 1993). For while the colour-platitudes force us to recognise an intimate connection between colour experiences and colour judgements, they also force us to recognise all sorts of ways in which our colour experiences can mislead us as to the real colours of objects. In this way they force us to make an is/seems distinction. Colour judgements thus purport to tell us about a stable property possessed by objects, a property objects can retain quite independently of various inconstancies in our experiences of them. Having a colour experience is thus neither necessary nor sufficient for making a colour judgement.

In this respect colour-platitudes contrast with the platitudes that describe the proper ways in which we are to use overtly expressive terms. Consider, for example, an expressive term such as 'ech', as in 'That tastes bitter. Ech!'. In learning to use this term we learn nothing that requires us to suppose that the unpleasant experiences which give rise to our saying 'Ech!' may in some way be mistaken. The ech-platitudes themselves thus in no way force us to make an is/seems distinction. Having an unpleasant experience is indeed both necessary and sufficient for the judgement 'Ech!' to be appropriate. This is why ech judgements, unlike colour judgements, are best construed non-cognitively, as mere expressions of our distaste for our experiences.

4. Colour-platitudes and the response-dependent analysis of colour

Now that we have seen that and why colour judgements in general are to be analysed cognitively, we are in a position to ask more specific questions about the cognitive content of these judgements. In particular, we are in a position to ask whether we should analyse the cognitive content of colour judgements in response-dependent terms.

It seems to me that we most certainly should analyse colour judgements in response-dependent terms, and that once again it is the colour-platitudes themselves that justify this response-dependent stance. In order to see why, we need merely to look again at the red-platitudes, and, in particular, at the platitudes that connect our colour experiences with our colour judgements on the one hand, and the various corrective platitudes on the other. For these platitudes are remarkable precisely because they force us to make the is/seems distinction in a characteristic response-dependent way: that is, by telling us when it would and would not be appropriate to use the colour experiences of perceivers of a certain sort, in certain sorts of environmental conditions, as criterial of the real, as opposed to the merely apparent, colours of the objects perceived. They tell us that an object is red, as opposed to merely appearing to be so, just in case it has a property that causes it to look red to normal perceivers under standard conditions.

Of course, the terms 'normal perceivers' and 'standard conditions' do not themselves occur in a statement of the red-platitudes. But their role in the analysis is clear enough. They serve simply to help summarise the particular response-dependent way in which the red-platitudes enable us to make the is/seems distinction.

5. Can we give a reductive analysis of colour?

We have now seen that and why we are to give a response-dependent analysis of the cognitive content of colour judgements. We are therefore in a position to ask whether the response-dependent analysis on offer is reductive or non-reductive.

According to the response-dependent analysis an object's being red is a matter of its having a property that causes it to look *red* to normal perceivers under standard conditions. Someone who does not already understand the concept of being red is therefore in no position even to understand the analysis. And this means in turn that the analysis is most certainly non-reductive. For we have not been given a way of understanding what it is to be red in terms that do not themselves presuppose an understanding of what it is to be red (Smith 1986a).

Importantly, however, this does not in any way undermine the claim that the response-dependent analysis constitutes an *analysis*. For, to repeat, the task of an analysis of the cognitive content of judgements to the effect that an object is red is simply to give us more or less explicit knowledge of what we otherwise knew at best implicitly in virtue of being masters of the term 'red': that is, knowledge of the red-platitudes, the judgements and inferences we are disposed to make in virtue of being masters of the term 'red'. A non-reductive response-dependent analysis accomplishes this task. For it makes explicit the fact that an object's being red is a matter of its looking red to normal perceivers under standard conditions. It makes explicit the fact that the red-platitudes force us make the is/seems distinction in this particular response-dependent way.

The fact that the response-dependent analysis of the cognitive content of judgements to the effect that an object is red is not reductive does not show that no reductive analysis is possible, of course. But it seems to me that we can in fact provide an argument for this stronger conclusion. For the only technique I know of for deriving reductive analyses from platitudes is the technique described by David Lewis (1970, 1972, 1989). However, as we will see, judgements to the effect that an object is red elude analysis in Lewis's reductive terms. Let me explain why this is so.

In trying to provide a reductive analysis of the cognitive content of judgements to the effect that an object is red the first step is to rewrite all of the colour-platitudes so that every mention of red, blue, green and the rest is in property-name style.[3] 'If you want to teach someone what the word for red means, show her some red objects and then say the word for red' becomes 'If you want to teach someone what the word for the property of being red means, show her some objects with the property of being red and then say the word for the property of being red', and so on. And each mention of the word 'colour' becomes mention of a big disjunction of all of the property-names of the colours. 'If you want to see what colour something really is, take it into the daylight' becomes 'If you want to see whether something really has the property of being red or the property of being green or the property of being blue or...., take it into the daylight'.

The second step is to conjoin all the platitudes, and to represent their long conjunction as a relational predicate 'T' true of all the various colour

---

3. My presentation of Lewis's style of analysis follows Jackson (1992).

properties. Where the properties of being red, green, blue and so on, are represented by the letters 'r', 'g', 'b' and the like, the conjunction will be represented by:

T[r g b ...]

Once we have this long conjunction, the third step is to strip out each mention of each of the property-names of the colours and replace it with a free variable:

T[x y z...]

Once we have done this we can say that, if there are colours, the following must be true:

∃x ∃y ∃z... T[x y z...] & (x*) (y*) (z*)... T[x* y* z*...] iff (x=x*, y=y*, z=z*...)

In other words, if there any colours, then there are properties which are in fact related to each other and to the world in just the way that the big conjunction of platitudes says the colours are related to each other and the world.

If the variable 'x' replaced the property of being red when we stripped out all mention of the particular colours, then we can define the property of being red as follows:

the property of being red *is* the x such that ∃y ∃z... T[x y z...] & (x*) (y*) (z*)... T[x* y* z*...] iff (x=x*, y=y*, z=z*...)

What we have here thus purports to be a definition of the property of being red in terms of the network of relations this property bears to the other colours, and to all of the things that are mentioned in the platitudes about the colours: features of perceivers, features of the environment, and the like. Importantly, however, the analysis itself mentions no colour terms at all. No colour term is needed to say what 'T' means. It therefore purports to be a reductive definition of the property of being red, a definition in *non-colour* terms.

I said earlier that colour judgements elude a reductive analysis. But haven't I just explained, in schematic terms at least, how to provide such an analysis? The judgement that an object is red is simply the judgement that the object has the x such that ∃y ∃z ... T[x y z...] & (x*) (y*) (z*)... T[x* y* z*...] iff (x=x*, y=y*, z=z*....). The answer is that the schematic terms in which this analysis is given mask a serious flaw in the purported definition, a flaw whose nature emerges once we make explicit what 'T' really means.

'T' is simply a long conjunction of the colour-platitudes: the red-platitudes, the orange-platitudes, the yellow-platitudes, and so on. But now reflect for a moment on these platitudes. Remember, in doing so, that they include platitudes about the relations between the colours, platitudes that reflect our ordinary understanding of the colours as standing in certain similarity relations to each other, relations that can be captured on a continuous colour wheel. And remember also that they include platitudes connecting colour experiences with colour judgements, and also various corrective platitudes, platitudes that we have already seen can be usefully summarised in the manner of a response-dependent analysis.

Bearing all this in mind, the red-platitudes can then be seen to entail the following claims: the property of being red causes objects to look red to normal perceivers under standard conditions, and the property of being red is more similar to the property of being orange than it is to the property of being yellow, and so on. The orange-platitudes entail the following claims: the property of being orange causes objects to look orange to normal perceivers under standard conditions, and the property of being orange is more similar to the property of being yellow than it is to the property of being green, and so on. The yellow-platitudes entail the following claims: the property of being yellow causes objects to look yellow to normal perceivers under standard conditions, and the property of being yellow is more similar to the property of being green than it is to the property of being blue, and so on. And so we could go on.

Let's now make a substantial assumption. Assume that there are no platitudes about the colours that entail any claims beyond these about the properties of being red, or orange, or yellow, or the rest. I will have something to say about the plausibility of this substantial assumption presently. With this assumption in place, however, look at what happens to our reductive network style analyses when we make the meaning of 'T' more explicit. Simplifying somewhat, we find that:

> the property of being red *is* the x such that $\exists y \exists z...$ objects have x iff they look x to normal perceivers under standard conditions, and x is more similar to y than it is to z.. &..(uniqueness)

the property of being orange *is* the y such that ∃z ∃u… objects have y iff they look y to normal perceivers under standard conditions, and y is more similar to z than it is to u.. &..(uniqueness)

the property of being yellow *is* the z such that ∃v ∃w … objects have z iff they look z to normal perceivers under standard conditions, and z is more similar to v than it is to w.. &..(uniqueness)

and so on. But now look at the network of relations specified by the definitions on each right hand side. It is the *very same* network of relations in each case. Our so-called 'definitions' therefore fail to distinguish the colours from each other. The properties of being red, orange, yellow and the rest all turn out to have the same definition, and so to mean the same thing. Thoroughly reductive network style analyses of the various colours therefore lose *a priori* information about the *differences* between them. Let's call this the 'permutation problem'.[4]

Can we solve the permutation problem? In order to do so, there would have to be some additional platitudes we can use to enrich our understanding of 'T', platitudes which are such that, by adding them into the mix, we could distinguish the colours from each other. I have been assuming that there are no platitudes beyond those already mentioned. But is the assumption correct? It might be thought that the assumption is incorrect. After all, wouldn't claims like 'Red is the colour of blood', 'Orange is the colour of ripe mandarins', 'Yellow is the colour of a new born chicken', and the like, stop the permutations if only we made the meaning of 'T' depend, *inter alia*, on them? And aren't we entitled to make the meaning of 'T' depend on them, given that they are all platitudes, in at least one sense of the term 'platitude'?

The answer is that, though they would indeed stop the permutations, they are not platitudes in the relevant sense of the term 'platitude'. Claims like 'Red is the colour of blood', 'Yellow is the colour of a new born chicken', and the like, are certainly widely believed to be true, and in that sense they are indeed platitudes. But, unfortunately, being widely believed to be true is neither necessary nor sufficient for being platitudes in the relevant sense. Platitudes, in the relevant sense, have a *prima facie a priori* status because they constitute a description of the judgements and inferences we make in virtue of being masters of colour concepts. But claims like 'Red is the colour

---

4. I owe this useful term to Philip Pettit.

of blood', 'Yellow is the colour of a new born chicken', and the rest, are at best merely widely believed *a posteriori* truths about the colours. We therefore cannot use them to enrich our definitions of the colours.[5]

As I see it, so long as we try to provide a thoroughly reductive network style analysis of colour, nothing short of adding *a posteriori* information of the sort described will allow us to solve the permutation problem. We have indeed added all the *prima facie a priori* truths into the mix. The only conclusion to draw, it seems to me, is that we should therefore give up attempting to provide a thoroughly reductive network style analysis of colour and make the meaning of 'T' depend instead, in some way, on information that is characterised in *colour* terms. And the way in which we should do so is plain.

What distinguishes the property of being red from the property of being orange? The answer is obvious: the property of being red is the one that typically causes objects with the property to look *red*, whereas the property of being orange is the one that typically causes objects with the property to look *orange*. But this is just what a non-reductive response-dependent analysis of red and orange tells us, and, as we have seen, these analyses are indeed *analyses*. It seems to me that we should therefore abandon the project of analysing the cognitive content of colour judgements in a thoroughly reductive network style, and conclude, instead, that a non-reductive response-dependent analysis is the very best that we can hope for.

6. Lessons learned by reflecting on the case of colour

We have considered the case of colour in some detail. Let's recap, and generalise the lessons we have learned.

First, we have seen that in order to decide whether to be cognitivists or non-cognitivists about a certain class of judgements, those involving a certain concept C, we should look at the platitudes that describe the inferences

---

5. Suppose the best theory of colour tells us that the colour wheel is not perfectly symmetrical—that, say, reds and blues have a feature that the other colours don't have. Might we use that feature of the reds and blues to solve the permutation problem? As is perhaps evident, the answer depends on whether it is plausible to suppose that it is *a priori* that reds and blues have the feature in question. My own view is that though it may be discovered that the reds and blues have a feature that the other colours don't have, it would be at best an *a posteriori* truth that this is so.

and judgements we make as masters of C. If they enable us to make an is/seems distinction then it is plausible to suppose that the C-judgements have cognitive content, whereas if they do not then the C-judgements should be analysed non-cognitively.

Second, we have seen that in order to decide whether we should give a response-dependent style analysis of a concept C we should look at the platitudes that describe the inferences and judgements we make as masters of C in order to see whether they enable us to make the is/seems distinction in a characteristic response-dependent way. If the C-platitudes suggest that there are certain responses to objects, and certain conditions, which are such that the presence of that response, in those conditions, to the objects in question is criterial of the instantiation of C in those objects, then we should give a response-dependent analysis of C.

Third, we have seen that at least some concepts are to be given, at best, a non-reductive response-dependent style analysis. The fact that a certain concept is to be given, at best, a non-reductive response-dependent analysis does not call into question the status of the analysis as an *analysis*, however, because such an analysis may still do everything that an analysis is required to do. It may make explicit what we otherwise knew at best only implicitly in virtue of being masters of C: that is, it may make explicit the fact that the C-platitudes force us to make the is/seems distinction in a particular response-dependent way.

7. Platitudes and conceptual analysis: the case of value

Let's now consider the case of value. As with any concept, mastery of evaluative concepts is constituted by a disposition to make inferences and judgements along lines that can be described by a rich set of platitudes. In analysing evaluative concepts, then, our task will be to capture all and only these evaluative-platitudes. What are some of these platitudes?

Obviously enough there are platitudes about the internal or necessary connection between evaluative judgements and the will. 'If someone judges her ϕ-ing to be desirable, then, other things being equal, she will be disposed to ϕ', 'Weakness of will, compulsion, depression and the like may explain why someone isn't moved in accordance with her evaluative beliefs', 'Reasons for judging acts to be desirable and undesirable are reasons for acting and refraining from acting accordingly', 'We sometimes do what we do because we judge we have a reason to do so', 'The reasons why acts are desirable are sometimes the reasons why people perform those acts' and so on. There are platitudes about the objectivity of evaluative judgements. 'When A says that ɸ-ing is desirable, and B says that it is not the case that ɸ-ing is desirable, then at most one of A and B is correct', 'Whether or not ɸ-ing is desirable can be discovered by engaging in rational argument', 'Provided A and B are open-minded and thinking clearly, an argument between A and B about the desirability or undesirability of ɸ-ing should result in A and B coming to some agreement on the matter', and so on. And, finally, there are platitudes concerning the procedures by which we can discover how to make the substance of evaluative judgements more precise. Rawls famously gave system to such platitudes when he described what he calls the method of 'reflective equilibrium' (Rawls 1951, 1971). For not only is it a platitude that desirability is a property that we can discover to be instantiated by engaging in rational argument—something we just saw in connection with the platitudes that relate to objectivity—it is also a platitude that such arguments have a characteristic coherentist form. 'Those evaluative principles that provide the most unified and coherent justification for A's evaluative judgements are the ones to which A is committed', 'Those evaluative judgements that do not cohere with the evaluative principles to which A is committed are the ones that he has reason to reject', and the like.

This is by no means an exhaustive list of the platitudes describing the inferences and judgements we make as masters of evaluative concepts. They will, however, suffice for present purposes.

8. Evaluative-platitudes and cognitivism

How do the evaluative-platitudes bear on the debate between cognitivists and non-cognitivists? As I see it, much as in the case of colour, the evaluative-platitudes bear on that debate by giving support to a cognitivist rather than a non-cognitivist analysis of evaluative judgements.

This may seem surprising. After all, as I have said, the evaluative-platitudes do force us to recognise an important connection between evaluative judgement and motivation, and this is the internal or necessary connection between evaluative judgement and the will I described at the outset, the connection that provides the crucial premise in the argument for non-cognitivism. But the evaluative-platitudes also force us to recognise that there are all sorts of ways in which we may be motivated to pursue things that we do not even believe to be desirable, and to believe desirable things we are not in the least motivated to pursue. Being motivated to ϕ is thus neither necessary nor sufficient for judging it desirable to ϕ. And the evaluative-platitudes also force us to recognise that there all sorts of ways in which, even when our motivations and our evaluative judgements do match up with each other, our evaluative judgements, and so our motivations, may yet be directed at something that is not desirable. Thus there is the possibility of weakness of will, compulsion, depression and the like on the one hand, and there is the possibility of correcting our evaluative judgements via the method of reflective equilibrium on the other.

In this way the evaluative-platitudes therefore force us to make an is/seems distinction in the case of value, an is/seems distinction much like the is/seems distinction in the case of colour. They do so by forcing us to recognise that both our motivations and our evaluative judgements may bear little relation to the real value of things. The function of an evaluative judgement thus seems to be not merely to give expression to a motivation, as the non-cognitivists tell us. Its function seems rather to be to report the value of that things have whether or not we are presently motivated to pursue them, and the value they have whether or not we are presently inclined to judge that they have it. Evaluative judgements should therefore be analysed cognitively, rather than non-cognitively.

9. Evaluative-platitudes and response-dependence

Now that we have seen that and why evaluative judgements in general are to be analysed cognitively, we are in a position to ask more specific questions about the cognitive content of these judgements. In particular, we are in a position to ask whether we should analyse the cognitive content of evaluative judgements in response-dependent terms.

It seems to me that we most certainly should analyse evaluative judgements in response-dependent terms, and that once again it is the evaluative-platitudes themselves that justify this response-dependent stance. In order to see that this is so, we need merely to look again at the evaluative-platitudes, and, in particular, at the various platitudes connecting evaluative judgements with our motivations and our reasons for action on the one hand, and the various platitudes associated with the method of reflective equilibrium on the other. For these platitudes are once again remarkable precisely because they force us to make the is/seems distinction in a characteristic response-dependent way: that is, in this case, by telling us when it would and would not be appropriate to use the desires of an agent of a certain sort as criterial of the real value of the actions desired. In short, the evaluative platitudes seem to tell us that φ-ing in certain circumstances C is desirable just in case, if we had a maximally unified and coherent desire set—that is, if we were fully rational—we would desire that we φ in C.

Of course, the phrase 'the desires we would have if we fully rational' does not itself occur in a statement of the evaluative-platitudes. But, much as with the 'normal perceivers' and 'standard conditions' clauses in the anlaysis of colour terms, the role of this phrase in the analysis is clear enough. It serves simply to summarise the import of the evaluative-platitudes for us in a useful way: that is, it summarises the particular response-dependent way in which the evaluative-platitudes—as opposed to the colour-platitudes, say—enable us to make the is/seems distinction.

10. Can we give a reductive analysis of value?

We have now seen that we can analyse the concept of value in response-dependent terms. We are therefore in a position to ask whether the analysis on offer is reductive or non-reductive.

According to the response-dependent analysis, φ-ing in certain circumstances C is desirable just in case our fully rational selves would desire that we φ in C. The analysis itself therefore appears to be non-reductive, for someone who does not already understand what it is for something to be desirable would be in no position to understand what it is for something to be the object of a desire of her fully rational self: that is, a self who has a maximally unified and coherent desire set. For an understanding of the latter requires an understanding of the method of reflective equilibrium, and that in turn requires an understanding of what it is for something to be desirable. In order to see that this is so, look again at the explanation we gave of that method.

The mere fact that the response-dependent analysis of value is not reductive does not entail that a reductive analysis of value is impossible, of course. But it seems to me that we might even be able to construct an argument for this stronger conclusion. The argument would be that, given the holistic and symmetrical nature of our evaluative concepts—the fact that our concepts of the desirable and the undesirable, the better than and the worse than, the coherent and the incoherent, must all be interdefined while preserving the appropriate oppositions—it follows that a reductive network style analysis of value, an analysis in the spirit of Lewis, would be vulnerable to a permutation problem, a permutation problem of much the same kind as that we found in the case of colour.

I will not attempt to construct such an argument here, however. For my present aim is not to argue that the only possible analysis of value is an analysis in non-reductive response-dependent terms. My aim is rather simply to insist, as against Blackburn, that the idea that this is so is at least coherent, if not plausible.[6] As a matter of fact I do believe the stronger conclusion (Smith 1994: 54–6, 161–4). But it is not important for me to establish the stronger conclusion in the context of the present paper. The important point is rather this.

Even if value is to be given, at best, a non-reductive response-dependent style analysis, remember that this does not in any way undermine our claim to have provided an *analysis* of the cognitive content of evaluative claims. To repeat, the task of an analysis of the cognitive content of an evaluative judgement is simply to make explicit what we otherwise knew at best only implicitly in virtue of being masters of evaluative concepts: that is, its task is to give us more or less explicit knowledge of the evaluative-platitudes, the judgements and inferences we are disposed to make in virtue of being masters of the evaluative concepts.

A non-reductive response-dependent analysis succeeds in this task. It succeeds because it makes explicit the fact that the desirability of ϕ-ing in C is a matter of ϕ-ing in C being what our fully rational selves would desire. It makes explicit the fact that the evaluative-platitudes force us to make the is/seems distinction in this particular response-dependent way.

11. The argument for non-cognitivism again

Does the non-reductive response-dependent analysis of value we have been considering so far enable us to bring out the crucial flaw in the argument for non-cognitivism described at the beginning of this paper? It does indeed (Smith 1994, 1995a).

The argument for non-cognitivism is, in essence, that there could be no internal or necessary connection between evaluative judgements and the will if evaluative judgements were expressions of beliefs, whereas there could be such an internal or necessary connection if evaluative judgements were

---

6. I argue that value is best analysed non-reductively in Smith (1995b).

expressions of motivations. In order to bring out the crucial flaw in this argument, it will be sufficient for us to show that if the beliefs in question have the non-reductive response-dependent content we have been considering so far, then there could indeed be such a connection. The task, then, is to show that someone who believes that she would desire that she ϕs in circumstances C if she were fully rational—that is, if she had a maximally unified and coherent desire set—will, at least absent weakness of will and the like, desire that she ϕs in C. How might we argue that this is so?

Note, to begin, that an agent who *both* believes that she would desire that she ϕs in C if she had a maximally unified and coherent desire set *and* desires that she ϕs in C, has a more coherent psychology than another who has the belief that she would desire that she ϕs in C if she had a maximally unified and coherent desire set, but who doesn't desire that she ϕs in C. Coherence is thus on the side of those who have evaluative beliefs, with their non-reductive response-dependent cognitive content, and corresponding desires, rather than the side of those who have evaluative beliefs but lack corresponding desires.

But if now we add in the additional, and plausible, assumption that an agent who is not suffering from weakness of will and the like is one whose psychology exhibits the sort of coherence just specified (Pettit and Smith 1993; Kennett and Smith 1994), then it follows immediately that those who believe that they would desire that they ϕ in circumstances C if they had a maximally unified and coherent desire set will, at least absent weakness of will and the like, desire that they ϕ in C. For the coherence in their overall psychological state *guarantees* a match between their evaluative beliefs and their motivations.

In this way the non-reductive response-dependent analysis of value enables us to do just what it was supposed to do. It provides us with a way of thinking of evaluative beliefs as beliefs about our desires, and so allows us to see why there is an internal or necessary connection between evaluative judgements and motivations. Moreover, the explanation it provides is consistent with the claim that belief and desire are distinct existences. Indeed, it entails that evaluative beliefs and motivations are distinct existences because it leaves open the possibility that someone whose psychology fails to exhibit the requisite coherence might believe it desirable to ϕ in C *without* desiring that she ϕs in C.

12. Blackburn's dilemma again

We are now in a position to reconsider Blackburn's dilemma for response-dependence. Does it still look like a dilemma? Granting Scylla, consider again Charybdis.

On Charybdis the response-dependent theorist claims to be giving us a non-reductive response-dependent analysis of the cognitive content of an evaluative judgement. Blackburn's complaint is, in essence, that we have no reason to believe that this is what we are really being given. Rather, as he sees things, because the analysis is non-reductive—that is, because an understanding of the analysis presupposes an understanding of the content being analysed—so the form of words used in the analysis may therefore be best analysed non-cognitively. This is why he concludes that we have made no analytic advance.

But this simply cannot be the right response. It would prove too much. After all, as we have seen, no-one seriously denies that colour judgements have cognitive content. Everyone thinks that colour judgements express beliefs. Yet we have also seen that the very best we can do by way of an analysis of the cognitive content of a colour judgement is an analysis in non-reductive response-dependent terms. Suppose someone offers us such an analysis. Would it be appropriate for Blackburn to complain that we have no reason to believe that the analysis is really an analysis of *cognitive* content? Certainly not. For Blackburn must think, along with everyone else, that colour judgements do indeed have cognitive content. He must therefore face the task, along with everyone else, of squaring this fact with the fact that a non-reductive response-dependent analysis of the cognitive content of colour judgements is the best that we can come up with. In short, then, Blackburn's argument on Charybdis fails because, if it succeeded, a parallel argument would show that colour judgements do not express beliefs. Since colour judgements do express beliefs, this constitutes a *reductio* of the argument on Charybdis.

More generally, however, it seems to me Blackburn's whole line of argument betrays his failure to recognise the crucial importance of spelling out platitudes when our task is to analyse a concept. If he had done so he might well have seen that, in the case of both colour and value, the platitudes themselves force us to make an is/seems distinction, and so force us to be cognitivists about both colour and value. And, if he had done so he might well have seen that, in the case of both colour and value, the platitudes themselves force us to make the is/seems distinction in a characteristic response-dependent way, and so force us to give a response dependent style analysis of the cognitive content of both colour judgements and evaluative judgements. Finally, if Blackburn had recognised the crucial importance of spelling out platitudes when our task is conceptual analysis, he might well have seen that a failure to provide a reductive analysis of value is no criticism of the analysis *as an analysis*.

This last is the point that needs to be underscored. For, as we have seen, the task of an analysis of the cognitive content of an evaluative judgement is simply to make explicit what we otherwise knew at best only implicitly in virtue of being masters of evaluative concepts: that is, its task is to give us more or less explicit knowledge of the evaluative-platitudes, the judgements and inferences we are disposed to make in virtue of being masters of evaluative concepts. A non-reductive response-dependent analysis of the kind we have been considering succeeds in this task by making explicit the fact that the desirability of ϕ-ing in C is a matter of ϕ-ing in C being what our fully rational selves would desire. It makes explicit the fact that the evaluative-platitudes force us to make the is/seems distinction in this particular response-dependent way.

This point is worth emphasising, and not just because this particular analysis allows us to defeat the argument for non-cognitivism. It is worth emphasising because it allows us to agree with Blackburn that his own example of a non-reductive response dependent analysis of value is indeed as hopeless as he says it is. His own example, you will recall, is this:

> X is good iff X is such as to elicit desires from people under the ideal circumstances, i.e. those under which people desire good things.

This is indeed hopeless because, as his own expansion of 'ideal circumstances' makes plain, the term 'ideal circumstances' *is not* being used as a summary of the various ways in which the evaluative-platitudes enable us to make the is/seems distinction, but is rather being used simply as shorthand for 'circumstances in which people desire good things'. Just as Blackburn says, the analysis in his example makes no analytic advance.

But this is where it is important to see just how different things might have looked to Blackburn if he had first first spelled out the evaluative-platitudes in some detail. For he might then well have seen that a term like 'ideal circumstances' can be used in another way, namely, as a summary of the particular response-dependent way in which the evaluative-platitudes enable us to make the is/seems distinction: that is, *inter alia*, as a summary of the various platitudes concerning the procedures by which we can discover how to make the substance of our evaluative judgements more precise. Perhaps then he would have seen that non-reductive analyses can indeed make an analytic advance. Such an advance is made, after all, when we analyse the desirability of φ-ing in C in terms of φ-ing in C being what our fully rational selves would desire.[7]

Research School of Social Sciences
Australian National University
Canberra ACT 0200
msmith@coombs.anu.edu.au

---

7. My argument against Blackburn has had the form of an *ad hominem*. Even he must agree that colour judgements express beliefs, and even he must agree that a non-reductive response dependent analysis of colour is the only analysis available. It follows that he is therefore in no position to object, in principle, to the idea that evaluative judgements express beliefs, and yet that a non-reductive response-dependent analysis of value is the only analysis that is to be had. Yet his objection on Charybdis amounts to just that. But what if Blackburn decides to bite the bullet? What if he turns my argument around and concludes instead that, if a non-reductive response-dependent analysis of colour is the best that we can come up with, then colour judgements too must be analysed non-cognitively? What should we say then? My temptation—and I must emphasise that it is merely a temptation at this stage—is to argue that in that case Blackburn would have think that *all* judgements are to be analysed non-cognitively: that is, he would be forced to think, *incoherently*, that there are no *beliefs* at all. The argument I am tempted to give for this conclusion is that, in light of the rule-following considerations, *all* judgements must be analysed, *inter alia*, in non-reductive response-dependent terms. To have mastery of any concept C is to be disposed to find salient similarities among the Cs, at least under favourable conditions, where, as far as I can see, there is no prospect of giving a non-C characterisation of any of these conditions (compare Pettit 1990). Unfortunately, however, there is no space here to explore this particular argument for the possibility of non-reductive response-dependent analyses of cognitive content. Here we must rest content with the *ad hominem*.

References

Blackburn, S. 1984 *Spreading the Word*, Oxford: Oxford University Press.

Blackburn, S. 1993 "Circles, Finks, Smells and Biconditionals" in James E. Tomberlin, ed, *Philosophical Perspectives, Language and Logic*, Volume 7, 259-79.

Gibbard, A. 1990 *Wise Choices, Apt Feelings*, Oxford: Clarendon Press.

Hare, R.M. 1952 *The Language of Morals*, Oxford: Oxford University Press.

Jackson, F. 1992 "Critical Notice of Susan Hurley's *Natural Reasons: Personality and Polity*", *Australasian Journal of Philosophy*, 70, 475-88.

Johnston, M. 1989, "Dispositional Theories of Value", *Proceedings of the Aristotelian Society* Supplementary Volume, 63, 139-74.

Kennett, J. and M.Smith 1994, "Philosophy and Commonsense: The Case of Weakness of Will" in Michael Michaelis and J. O'Leary-Hawthorne, eds, *Philosophy in Mind: The Place of Philosophy in the Study of Mind*, Dordrecht: Kluwer Academic Publishers, 141-57.

Korsgaard, C. 1986 "Scepticism about Practical Reason", *Journal of Philosophy*, 83, 5-25.

Lewis, D. 1970 "How to Define Theoretical Terms", *Journal of Philosophy*, 67, 427-46.

Lewis, D. 1972 "Psychophysical and Theoretical Identifications", *Australasian Journal of Philosophy*, 50, 249-58.

Lewis, D. 1988 "Desire as Belief", *Mind*, 97, 323-32.

Lewis, D. 1989 "Dispositional Theories of Value", *Proceedings of the Aristotelian Society* Supplementary Volume, 63, 113-37.

McDowell, J. 1978 "Are Moral Requirements Hypothetical Imperatives?", *Proceedings of the Aristotelian Society* Supplementary Volume, 52, 13-29

McDowell, J. 1985 "Values and Secondary Qualities" in Ted Honderich, ed., *Morality and Objectivity*, London: Routledge and Kegan Paul, 110-29.

Pettit, P. 1990 "The Reality of Rule-Following" in *Mind*, 99, 1-21.

Pettit, P. and M. Smith 1993 "Practical Unreason" in *Mind*, 102, 53-79

Rawls, J. 1951 "Outline of a Decision Procedure for Ethics", *The Philosophical Review*, 60, 177-97.

Rawls, J. 1971 *A Theory of Justice*, Oxford: Oxford University Press.

Smith, M. 1986a "Peacocke on Red and Red", *Synthese*, 60, 559-76.

Smith, M. 1986b "Should We Believe in Emotivism?" in Graham Macdonald and Crispin Wright, eds, *Fact, Science and Morality: Essays on A.J.Ayer's Language, Truth and Logic*, Oxford: Basil Blackwell, 289-310.

Smith, M. 1987 "The Humean Theory of Motivation", *Mind*, 96, 36-61

Smith, M. 1989 "Dispositional Theories of Value", *Proceedings of the Aristotelian Society*. Supplementary Volume, 89–111.

Smith, M. 1993 "Objectivity and Moral Realism: On the Significance of the Phenomenology of Moral Experience" in John Haldane and Crispin Wright, eds, *Reality, Representation and Projection*, Oxford: Oxford University Press, 235-55.

Smith, M. 1994 *The Moral Problem*, Oxford: Blackwell.

Smith, M. 1995a "Internal Reasons" in *Philosophy and Phenomenological Research*, 55, 109-31.

Smith, M. 1995b "Internalism's Wheel" in *Ratio*, 277-302.

Wright, C. 1988 "Moral Values, Projection and Secondary Qualities", *Proceedings of the Aristotelian Society* Supplementary Volume, 62, 1-26

HUW PRICE
Two Paths to Pragmatism II

1. Introduction

Particular topics of conversation seem to be inaccessible to speakers who lack an insider's view of the subject matter concerned. The familiar examples involve sensory deficiencies: discourse about music may be inaccessible to the tone deaf, wine talk to the anosmic, the finer points of interior decorating to the colour blind, and so on. The traditional secondary qualities thus provide the obvious cases of concepts which seem to exhibit this form of subjectivity—this dependence on specific and quite contingent human capacities.

It is easy to think of further cases, resting on more specific perceptual and quasi-perceptual disabilities. (Could someone with no ball sense understand what it is like to be a batsman, for example?) But is this the end of the matter? How far does this phenomenon extend in language? How precisely should it be characterised? And what is its significance, if any, for the metaphysical status of the concepts concerned? Questions of this kind have been the focus of considerable attention in recent years. The original impetus for much of this work seems to have been the suggestion that there might be a useful analogy between moral concepts and the secondary qualities. This

---

This is a revised version of, not a sequel to, a paper which first appeared in P. Menzies (ed.), *Response-Dependent Concepts (Working Papers in Philosophy, No. 1)*, Canberra: Philosophy Program, Research School of Social Sciences, ANU, pp. 46–82. The original paper was written for a weekend conference on response dependence at ANU in June, 1991. I am grateful to David Macarthur for extensive comments on an early version, to Peter Menzies and Michaelis Michael for helpful discussions before the conference, and to Mark Johnston and Philip Pettit, especially, for comments and discussion at the time of the conference.

rather specific issue has then given rise to a more general interest in the nature and significance of the kind of subjectivity exhibited by the secondary qualities (and/or moral concepts). Writers such as Mark Johnston and Crispin Wright have sought to develop general formal frameworks within which to represent the dependence of concepts of a certain kind on particular human capacities.[1]

As Johnston well appreciates, one excellent motive for seeking a general characterisation of the kind of subjectivity in play in the case of the secondary qualities is to equip oneself for an assault on one of the most fascinating issues in philosophy: How much of the conceptual framework we apply to the world is simply taken over from the world itself, and how much of it 'comes from us'? In a philosophical climate often dismissive of the sort of pragmatism that takes this question seriously, is it pleasing to see the attention it receives in Johnston's hands.

All the same, it seems to me that Johnston has done pragmatism a disservice. His advocacy of response dependence as the general species of subjectivity apparently exhibited by the secondary qualities has helped to obscure an attractive alternative path into the same territory. The effects of this are evident in Johnston's own position. In 'Objectivity Refigured' Johnston argues tellingly that there is space for a species of pragmatism distinct from verificationism and Putnam's internal realism. He then assures us that the route to a pragmatism of this kind 'goes by way of developing and applying the notion of response-dependence.' (OR, p. 103) So it comes as something of an anti-climax when he concludes that the notion of response depen-

---

1. See their respective contributions to J. Haldane and C. Wright, eds, *Reality, Representation, and Projection,* Oxford: Oxford University Press, 1993: Wright's 'Realism: The Contemporary Debate—W(h)ither Now?', pp. 63–84, and Johnston's 'Objectivity Refigured: Pragmatism Without Verificationism' (hereafter OR), pp. 85–130. See also Johnston's contribution to the symposium 'Dispositional Theories of Value' (hereafter DTV), *Proceedings of the Aristotelian Society,* Supplementary Volume LXII, 1989, and Wright's *Truth and Objectivity,* Cambridge, Mass.: Harvard University Press, 1992. In keeping with the focus of the conference for which this paper was first prepared, I shall concentrate on Johnston's work. However, given that Wright's account invokes biconditional content conditions similar to those employed by Johnston, and that my main concern is to argue for a quite different means of explicating the significance of the relevant linguistic expressions, I think that much of what I say would equally stand opposed to Wright's approach.

dence is of limited application, even in the hands of philosophers who are prepared to revise ordinary usage to put it on respectable metaphysical foundations. Though Johnston attempts to salvage some general consequences from a response-dependent treatment of theoretical 'rightness', pragmatists hoping for historic victories on the field of metaphysics will feel a sense of anticlimax.

I want to show that the problem lies in the choice of response dependence as the path to the general issue of the extent of subjectivity in our representation of the world. There is an alternative route, and one which promises bigger dividends. Indeed, it suggests that the subjectivity in question is global, infecting all parts of language (though different parts to different extents). In endorsing a form of global pragmatism I concur with Philip Pettit.[2] However, Pettit follows Johnston in regarding response dependence (or a closely related notion) as the proper path to such a pragmatism, and apparently in failing to appreciate that there is an alternative. (He disagrees with Johnston mainly in arguing that the resulting pragmatism is globally applicable.) But the global enterprise turns out to be particularly sensitive to the choice of route: the alternative path has advantages even in local cases, but becomes mandatory if the pragmatist's project is to be generalised in this way. So while I join Pettit in the quest for global pragmatism,[3] I want to argue that in setting a course in terms of response dependence, he is guiding our common ship by the wrong star.

So the main task of this paper is philosophical cartography. I want to put the alternative path to pragmatism on the philosophical map, and draw attention to some of its advantages. The aim is to chart the least hazardous course for those of us who cannot resist the lure of a world whose conceptual joints all owe something to ourselves; and to present the complete picture for the benefit of less adventurous souls, so that at least they may see towards what monsters we set sail.

2. Two ways of explicating meaning

The two paths to pragmatism are distinguished by the fact that

---

2. Philip Pettit, 'Realism and Response-Dependence' (hereafter RRD), *Mind* 100, 1991, 587–626.
3. Indeed, we both sail under the rule-following banner. See RRD, p. 588 and my *Facts and the Function of Truth* (hereafter FFT), Oxford: Basil Blackwell, 1988, pp. 192–5.

they rely on different theoretical strategies for explicating the significance of a concept or linguistic expression. The first strategy—that employed by response theorists—is exemplified by the following simple version of Johnston's 'basic equation':

(1)   X is C iff X is disposed to produce response R_C in normal subjects under suitable conditions

I shall call this a *content condition*. Not much hangs on the terminology. Johnston, Pettit and others warn us not to interpret such biconditionals as reductive *analyses* of the concepts referred to on the LHS. However, the term 'content condition' will serve to mark a contrast with a second sort of explication of the significance of an expression, which is what I shall call a *usage condition*. The general form of such a condition is something like this:

(2)   The utterance S is prima facie appropriate when used by a speaker who has a psychological state ϕ_S.

The particular usage condition which contrasts to (1) will then be:

(3)   The utterance 'X is C' is prima facie appropriate when used by a speaker who experiences response R_C in the presence of X.

A usage condition thus tells us something about the *subjective assertibility conditions* of an expression—about what condition must normally obtain *in the speaker* for the utterance of an expression to be appropriate. As such, it is of course only the very first step in a theoretical description of linguistic practice. It leaves out the Gricean hierarchy of intentional attitudes, to mention just one aspect of the larger picture. All the same, it may be an important first step, as a few familiar examples will illustrate.

Emotivism
The utterance 'X is good' is prima facie appropriate when used by a speaker who approves of (or desires) X.

Adam's Hypothesis
The utterance 'If P then Q' is prima facie appropriate when used by a speaker who has a high conditional credence in Q given P.

Assertion and Belief
The assertion 'A' is prima facie appropriate when used by a speaker who has the belief that A.

Again, these principles are only the most basic elements of a pragmatic account of the usage conditions of the utterances concerned. So it would be beside the point to object at this point that it is not always appropriate to say 'X is good' when one approves of X. It is not always appropriate to say 'P' when one believes that P, but there is still something important and informative in the principle that one should normally assert that P only if one does believe that P.

I shall be arguing that the insights of pragmatism are better served by usage conditions than by content conditions. However, I emphasise that I am not suggesting that content-specifying conditions have no role to play in the philosophical project of explicating meaning. In my view a pragmatist is likely to find as much use as anybody else in a content-specifying truth theory of the Tarski-Davidson sort, and should have no more qualms about

(4)   'X is good' is true iff X is good

than about

(5)   'X is electrical charged' is true iff X is electrical charged.

My argument simply concerns the appropriate vehicle for the distinctive points a pragmatist wants to make about the dependence of particular areas of discourse on human capacities or points of view. I want to urge that these points are better made in terms of usage conditions than in terms of the kind of biconditional content conditions that writers on response dependence have offered us.

I noted above that my description of these biconditionals as 'content-specifying' might be thought contentious, given that Johnston and others take pains to point out that these principles are not to be read as straightforward reductive analyses. I don't want to become entangled in a discussion of the possible varieties of conceptual analysis. I simply want to show that even if we put these labels to one side there is a clear distinction between response theorists and a usage pragmatist, in that usage conditions do not yield several of the key conclusions that Johnston and Pettit draw from their versions of response dependence. This will be enough to show that content conditions and usage conditions represent two incompatible paths to pragmatism. It will also give us some reasons for preferring the latter path.

One more terminological point: once it is appreciated that content conditions and usage conditions provide two distinct strategies for explicating the dependence of particular discourses on human abilities, responses and capacities, then a decision is needed as to whether we should take the term 'response dependence' to be applicable to both, or only to the content-based approach. As my use of the term 'response theorist' already indicates, I take the latter course. Given the central role of biconditional content conditions in the work of those who have introduced the term 'response dependence', I think it would be misleading to apply it to an approach which rejects these biconditionals. I therefore refer to writers who rely on these content conditions as *response theorists*.

It should be emphasised that many of the general remarks response theorists make in characterising their pragmatic stance are quite compatible with a usage-based approach. In the first paragraph of 'Realism and Response-Dependence', for example, Pettit asks us to

> Consider the concepts of smoothness, blandness and redness. They are tailor-made for creatures like us who are capable, as many intelligences may not be, of certain responses: capable of finding things smooth to the touch, bland to the taste, red to the eye. The concepts, as we may say, are response-dependent.

We may agree with Pettit that concepts such as these depend on particular human responses or capacities, and yet deny that this entails that they should be (let alone *need be*) seen as response-dependent, in the technical sense of the term that Johnston has introduced. The main point of this paper is to show that there is an alternative to response dependence, providing a better way to explicate the relevant species of dependence on particular responses. It is perhaps a pity that the useful descriptive term 'response dependent' has come to be associated with a less than general account of what the general phenomenon amounts to, but there it is. The crucial point to keep in mind is that the general pragmatic program is not at issue here. The dispute concerns the correct strategy for putting the program into effect.

Finally, it should be noted that Johnston himself distinguishes two sorts of conclusion the pragmatist might aim for. The first is a descriptive doctrine about a discourse as it stands in ordinary use. The second is the revisionary proposal to replace an existing discourse with a discourse couched in acceptable pragmatic terms. My main interest is in the descriptive doctrine—in the question as to how to explicate actual linguistic practice. I want to show that the usage-based approach does better at this descriptive level than the response theorist's alternative. But we shall see that because it does better here, the usage approach avoids some difficulties which the response theorist might take to motivate the revisionary doctrine. As always, the linguistic revisionist bears an onus to justify the proposed change. For a response theorist the claimed justification might be that the (non–response-dependent) concepts presently employed in some area of discourse do not properly reflect their evident dependence on contingent human capacities; the proposed revision is intended to make this dependence explicit. However, the usage-based approach shows that this is a solution to a non-existent problem. Usage conditions provide an alternative way to represent the dependence of particular discourses on human responses and capacities, and response theorists have simply looked in the wrong place. The discourses in question may adequately reflect their subjective origins as they stand, and hence be in no need of revision.

More later on the advantages of the usage approach. The first task is to show that the usage and content approaches are genuinely distinct. The best way to do this is to show that the usage approach does not have certain consequences that response theorists rightly draw from their content-based accounts.

3. Usage conditions: their theoretical austerity

If the Johnston's biconditional is to be called the basic equation then perhaps the alternative usage condition should be referred to as the *more* basic equation. For the usage condition embodies a very austere, general, and theoretically fundamental perspective on linguistic practice. Because it is so general and so austere, its philosophical consequences are correspondingly thin. It is committed to little, compatible with much. It is compatible with the most thoroughgoing realism, for example—realists about a particular subject matter will not deny that assertions about that subject matter are governed by a usage condition of the kind sketched above under *Assertion and Belief*.

Similarly, the usage perspective does not of itself commit us to the view that speakers' responses or psychological states provide privileged access to the truth of the utterances concerned. This is clear in the case of *Assertion and Belief*, where the mistake of thinking otherwise is the Protagorean mistake of thinking that because we assert that P when we believe that P, to assert that P is to *say* that one believes that P (and is therefore true if one believes that P).

More interestingly, it seems that the usage perspective is not committed to privileged access to truth even in the cases which will provide the direct alternative to the response theorist's biconditional, such as (3). For example, consider an explicitly fallibilist version of Moorean moral intuitionism. Here, the primary usage condition for 'X is good' will be said to be whatever manifests the intuition that X is of moral worth. But this might be regarded as a fallible and defeasible condition, perhaps in such a way that normal speakers might be systematically mistaken about the moral status of certain kinds of entities. (Normal speakers might exhibit an irrational bias in favour of the so-called deserving poor, for example.) Normal consensus would thus be regarded as neither necessary nor sufficient to guarantee truth. Another example might be provided by realism in mathematics, coupled with a usage condition in terms of the belief that one has a proof. In this case normal community consensus might be sufficient but not necessary for truth. So even in these cases, *the usage perspective is not necessarily response-privileging*. It is compatible with a more 'cosmocentric' brand of realism, to use Pettit's term.

On the other hand, a usage-based approach is also compatible with a much less realist overlay than the response theorists offer us. In particular, it is compatible with the view that the area of discourse in question does not have truth conditions, or is non-factual in character. Examples are provided by the two principles headed *Emotivism* and *Adam's Hypothesis* above. Emotivism is usually associated with the view that moral judgements are non-factual and lack truth conditions; while Adam's Hypothesis is held by some to be the centrepiece of a non–truth-conditional view of indicative conditionals.

The fact that the usage-based theory is compatible with non-factualism perhaps marks the most striking and interesting contrast with content-based accounts. A response-dependent account is automatically truth-conditional. This is of course implicit in the biconditional form of the basic equation—there is nothing to stop us adding '…is true' to the LHS, after all. Response theorists thus get their factualism for free, and therefore find it difficult to give serious consideration to alternative views. Johnston suggests that the fault lies with the opposition:

> An appropriate response-dependent account [of value] may thus threaten to make quasi-realism redundant. The quasi-realist programme is to *somehow* defend our right to employ the truth-conditional idiom in expressing evaluations.

However, the

> response-dependent account of value ... implies that there is no need to *earn* the right to the truth-conditional form of expression. ... [W]e have a natural conceptual right to this truth-conditional form. (DTV, pp. 173–4)

Pettit simply passes over the point, noting that 'there is no pressure from the traditional response-dependent thesis to go towards an instrumentalist ... theory.' (RRD, p. 607) Surely this is an indication that something has been missed. It is clear that philosophical attention to the dependence of particular concepts and discourses on human capacities has often found expression in non-factualist theories of one sort or another. Emotivism provides one familiar example, but there are many others. Simon Blackburn's quasi-realist program provides a whole range of cases, for example—cases which, as Blackburn points out, may trace their ancestry to prominent themes in Hume.[4] These examples demonstrate that the pragmatist's concern to exhibit the dependence of language on human capacities and responses is not incompatible with non-factualism. So if the response theorist's reading of the pragmatist program cannot find room for non-factualism, so much the worse for that reading—or at least for the view that it is the sole available reading of what the pragmatist is up to.

At any rate, the usage approach provides a viewpoint from which the quasi-realist's concerns re-emerge. It characterises a pattern of usage using the very materials to which dispositional theories of value appeal, namely the existence on the part of speakers of dispositions to value certain things and states of affairs. But it does so in terms which don't prejudge the issue as to whether (and if so why) a pattern of usage meeting this characterisation need take a truth-conditional form. On the face of it, speakers might display the relevant dispositions in language in a very minimal way, if at all. Humans might boo and cheer. Many animals successfully express their likes and dislikes in all sorts of pre-linguistic ways. So a lively disposition to value some things and disvalue other things need not sustain a *truth-conditional* linguistic practice, and it is entirely appropriate to enquire why, and with what justification, we ourselves do express certain evaluative dispositions in assertoric form. This is the quasi-realist's concern. It is a concern clearly addressable from the usage perspective, and hence the fact that a response-

---

4. See Blackburn's *Essays in Quasi-Realism,* Oxford: Oxford University Press, 1993.

dependent account cannot make sense of it serves to emphasise the difference between the usage perspective and the content perspective. Both are pragmatic; both characterise evaluative discourse in terms of human responses. But content conditions and usage conditions engage with these responses in very different ways.

In trying to show that usage conditions provide the better path to pragmatism, I shall offer four main arguments. The first (§ 6) turns on the consequences of the view that the species of pragmatism with which we are concerned is global in its application to language. I endorse this view, but argue that it leads to incoherence unless couched in terms of a usage pragmatism. Because it turns on globality, this first argument is not directly effective against a response theorist such as Johnston himself, who takes response dependence to be a local doctrine (and indeed potentially a revisionary doctrine). Against this position, my second argument (§ 7) is in a sense a reversal of Johnston's above redundancy claim concerning quasi-realism. I argue that wherever there are the resources for a response-dependent reading (or re-reading) of a discourse, there are also the resources the quasi-realist needs for an adequate *explanation* of truth-conditional practice. So the response theorist's re-reading works only where it is unnecessary. But the relation is not symmetric: the usage-based approach often works where response dependence would not. In particular, it is entirely compatible with the minimalist metaphysical position that Johnston sees as the main rival to a response-dependent pragmatism with respect to many philosophically interesting topics.

In defence of a revisionary response-dependent reading it might be claimed that at least in certain cases, it alone enables us to *justify* judgements that play important roles in our lives. My third argument (§§ 8–9) counters this claim, and in the process shows that the usage-based approach does a better job of explaining the characteristic role of judgements of various kinds. All parties agree that an account of evaluative judgements should explain why they motivate us (and *should* do so); an account of probabilistic judgement should explain its connection with decision under uncertainty, and so on. I want to show that the response theorists do rather poorly on this crucial task—a failure masked to some extent by a characteristic equivocation concerning the notion of rationality.

Finally (§§ 10–13) I argue that the usage approach gives a more accurate explanation of some of the subtleties of ordinary language. In particular, it makes much better sense than its content-based rival of the peculiar mix of objectivity and subjectivity we encounter in discourses subject to no-fault disagreements.[5] This should recommend the approach to those less sanguine than Johnston seems to be about the prospect of wholesale revision of linguistic practice.

The next two sections establish some of the groundwork for these arguments, particularly by drawing attention to useful analogies between response dependence and more familiar philosophical strategies.

4. *Assertion and Belief*: some Protagorean lessons

The principle *Assertion and Belief* embodies the uncontroversial idea that an account of the historical and psychological foundations of language will give a central explanatory role to the notion of belief; perhaps not to the full-blown propositional attitude, but at least to some weaker notion of behavioural commitment. For in an obvious sense, belief underlies and sustains the linguistic activity of *assertion*. Creatures who didn't have beliefs couldn't make assertions. Whatever else we say about assertion, we'll want to mark the fact that speakers typically assert that P only if they believe that P. Yet none of this entails that in saying that P a speaker asserts *that* he or she believes that P. True, it means that we can ordinarily infer that a speaker believes that P from the fact that she says that P. But there are several simple objections to identifying the content of an assertion with the belief which it normally expresses.

In particular, such an identification leads to analytic regresses, arguably vicious, of more than one kind. Suppose, for example, that our interest is in a general account of assertion. The view in question tells us to interpret the assertion that P as the assertion that the speaker concerned believes that P. Here the target notion of assertion occurs again, central and yet unanalysed.

Alternatively, let's focus on the content of the assertion that P. The view in question now leads us to the principle that this content is in some sense equivalent to that of the assertion that the speaker believes that P. The content of the latter assertion is then in the same sense equivalent to that of the assertion that the speaker believes that the speaker believes that P, and so on. The way is clear to a denumerable infinity of content sentences, whose

---

5. All discourses have to potential to exhibit such disagreements, in my view; hence the global character of a usage-based pragmatism. See FFT, ch. 8.

related contents are all equivalent in the specified sense. So far what we have is not necessarily vicious. After all, it is a familiar idea that a denumerable infinity of logically equivalent sentences may all have the same content. But it teeters on the brink of viciousness: if the slightest analytic pressure is put on the RHS of the relevant biconditionals, the whole structure collapses. For example, if we say on the psychological plane that to believe that P is to believe that 'P' is true—that is, to believe that one believes that P—then immediately we are lost. Or if we say on the semantic plane that what *makes true* my assertion that P is the truth of the proposition that I believe that P, then again the regress carries us away. If not already incoherent, then, the position in question is at least highly unstable.[6]

One further point: if a reference to belief were a universal ingredient of the content of assertoric judgement in this way, then an obvious theoretical strategy would be to try to factor it out, and to concentrate on what varies from assertion to assertion, namely the content of this embedded belief—which would just take us back to where we started. This might well be the best practical strategy, as well. If *all* assertion were initially of the form 'I believe that P', then the most advantageous strategy might be to let the qualification drop away; to invent a discourse of quasi-assertions, which pretended to talk about the world in an unqualified way. All the materials would be already at hand. The principle governing truth ascription would thus be that we should not worry about what *really* made one of these quasi-assertions true—they are, after all, only a game of our own devising—but simply that we should be prepared to *say* that one was true or ('quasi-true') when we had the relevant belief. Thus one should be prepared to quasi-assert that P, or ascribe quasi-truth to the quasi-assertion 'P', when and only when one believes that P.

Thus the Protagorean's own materials allow us to construct a non-Protagorean practice. To close the trap, we need simply point to the possibility that the latter practice may be our actual practice. Later, this will be my strategy against content-based response theories.

---

6. In OR, p. 106, Johnston suggests that circularity will be a problem for the Protagorean 'only if it made the biconditionals and their associated identities empty'—i.e., if the Protagorean was aiming for a reductive definition, and the biconditional was too weak too supply it. But the infinite regress threatens because the biconditional is too strong, not because it is too weak.

5. Self-descriptivism

Thus in the familiar case of *Assertion and Belief*, it is easy to distinguish the role that belief properly plays in a usage-based account of the linguistic activity of making assertions, from a role that it might mistakenly be thought to play in a content-based theory of the content or truth conditions of assertoric utterances. In less commonplace places, however, it seems to have been less easy for philosophers to keep the distinction firmly in mind. Consider, for example, the familiar kind of non-cognitivist (or non-factualist) view that utterances of some disputed class do not express *beliefs*, but rather some other kind of propositional attitude. This is what a simple kind of emotivism says about moral judgements, or what a simple subjectivism says about probabilistic judgements. In these cases the relevant propositional attitudes are *approval* and *credence*, respectively: the emotivist says that 'It is good that P' expresses a speaker's approval that P, not her belief that it is good that P; while the subjectivist says that 'It is probable that P' expresses a speaker's high degree of credence that P, not his belief that it is probable that P.

These familiar expressivist positions are usage-based, not content-based: they give us usage conditions, not content conditions, for moral and probabilistic utterances. But they have often been confused with the following *self-descriptive* interpretations of moral and probabilistic claims: the view that in saying 'It is good that P' a speaker *says that* she approves of the fact that P; and the view that in saying 'It is probable that P' a speaker *says that* he has a high degree of credence that P. However, I hope it is clear, at least on reflection, that self-descriptivism is actually quite different from expressivism. The difference is just like that between the (correct) view that we typically say that P *when* we believe that P and the (incorrect) view that in saying P we say *that* we believe that P. In each case the difference rests on that between two distinct possible roles for the psychological state concerned: a usage-based role in an *explanation* of a linguistic practice, and a content-based role in an *analysis* or *explication* of the content of the utterances comprising that practice. Expressivism is usage-based, self-descriptivism is content-based.

However, while the self-descriptive interpretation is easily seen to be close to incoherency in the standard case of belief and assertion, it is not so obviously mistaken as an alternative to emotivism and probabilistic subjectivism. Indeed, it may seem to have some attractions, foremost of which might be thought to be that it doesn't leave us with any mystery as to what moral or probabilistic judgments actually mean, or as to why they look like regular assertions. They are regular assertions on this view, the only oddity being that their subject matter is not what it seems to be: they are about their utterer's state of mind, rather than about moral or probabilistic aspects of the world. (These views are not non-cognitivist, and are only non-factualist about their *apparent* factual referents.) A self-descriptivist might thus express puzzlement at the emotivist's concern with the issue as to why moral judgements take indicative form, and appear truth-conditional. 'Once we explicate moral judgement in the way I suggest', the self-descriptivist might say, 'We see that we have a natural conceptual right to the truth-conditional form of expression.'

The response theorist's content conditions are not as implausible as those of these naive self-descriptivists, of course. All the same, I think that there is a valid comparison between the two kinds of position. In my view, the fallacy of interpreting expressivism as self-descriptivism involves simply a more graphic form of the same blindness that characterises the response dependence program—that is, a blindness to the very possibility of a usage-based account built on the same psychological foundations. If nothing else, then, it will be helpful to have the self-descriptivist fallacy available as cautionary lesson, as I try to bring back into focus the possibility and advantages of a usage-based approach.

6. The consequences of global pragmatism

As I noted in §1, Philip Pettit argues that all concepts are response-dependent. His case turns on Wittgensteinian considerations about rule following: in virtue of the inability of any finite class of exemplars to constrain an intended concept to future cases in a unique way, the applicability of a concept F to a new potential instance X is always, in the last resort, dependent on the disposition of the members of a speech community to regard X as F. (The point is perhaps more evident if cast in terms of terms rather than concepts.) If endorsed, as I think it should be, Pettit's point has important ramifications for our present concerns. It invites a global generalisation of the dispositional method of analysis. If

(6)   X is good iff X is disposed to evoke (i.e. is such that it evokes) the 'valuing' response in us.

then why not also

(7) X is F iff X is disposed to evoke (i.e. is such that it evokes) the 'Seeing as relevantly similar to paradigm F's' response in us.

This suggestion cannot be rejected on the grounds that there is something illegitimate about the nature of the response referred to on the RHS. The point of Pettit's argument, and ultimately of the rule-following considerations themselves, is that language depends on responses or dispositions of this kind. Our use of the word 'chair' ultimately depends on the fact that we have a certain ability to generalise to new cases on the basis of exposure to a small number of exemplars.[7]

What are the consequences of taking (7) seriously, however? In considering this question, let us pretend for the moment that the response theorist's biconditionals are to be taken as outright content specifications: if not as reductive analyses, then at least as indications of conceptual equivalence, or common content on both sides of the biconditional. Apparently, then, the consequence of (7) is that we cannot talk about the world as such, but only about its effect on us. All content becomes relational and anthropocentric in this way.

Recall that this is just what happens according to the Protagorean view that to assert that P is to assert that one believes that P. In §4 I mentioned several objections to this view, turning mainly on the idea that it threatens a vicious regress. Similar problems would appear to afflict any attempt to take (7) as the general form of an analysis of concept ascription. The biconditional describes, if not an equivalence between contents, then at least an equivalence relation (viz., sameness of truth conditions). If the doctrine is to be universal, then the fact that the RHS is at the same time more complex and yet of the same basic logical form as the LHS—the form 'X is G'—will guarantee us a denumerable infinity of content sentences, all specifying contents that stand to one another in the same equivalence relation. From here viciousness threatens in the same way as before: if the slightest weight is put on the RHS, the whole structure is liable to collapse.

---

7. Reductive definition of a term is a possibility, of course, but this simply delays the inevitable, as Kripke points out in *Wittgenstein on Rules and Private Language*, Oxford: Basil Blackwell, 1982.

Can a response theorist avoid this difficulty, by insisting that the relevant biconditionals have *no* analytic significance? It seems doubtful. As in the Protagorean case, even the suggestion that the RHS specifies what makes the LHS truth-apt will be enough to tip the balance, and it does seem that the response theorists are committed to this. As we have seen, Johnston relies on the biconditional to illustrate the response theorists 'natural conceptual right' to truth conditions, for example, while Pettit apparently takes it as the basis of his suggestion that response dependence provides no pressure towards non-factualism.[8] But if the LHS has its truth value (or truth aptness) *in virtue* of that of the RHS, and the RHS has to acquire its own truth value (or truth aptness) in the same way, then the regress is certainly vicious. (By way of analogy, let's say that an object is well-grounded if it is standing on top of an object which is itself well-grounded. Now suppose that it's turtles all the way down. Can we show that the top turtle is well-grounded? No, for the same issue arises all over again at every level in the hierarchy of turtles.)

I think this is a decisive objection to a content-based global response theory. It is not a problem for local response theorists, of course, and nor is it a problem for a theory which accepts that language is globally dependent on dispositions 'to go on in the same way', but explains the role of these dispositions in usage conditions rather than in content conditions. We can indeed be global pragmatists, then, but only if we abandon response dependence in favour of usage conditions.

7. The redundancy argument

In §4 I mentioned another objection to the Protagorean view. It was that the Protagorean's own materials suffice to construct an alternative 'language game', with respect to which the appropriate reference to belief takes the form of a usage condition rather than a content condition. In effect, then, the Protagorean's own resources provide a plausible alternative model of what might be going on in actual discourse. Unlike the regress point itself, this idea can be developed again local versions of content-based response theories.

---

8. Pettit also indicates (RRD, p. 608) that the LHS of such a biconditional might be empirically falsified, in virtue of the lack of the various responses and conditions mentioned on the RHS.

Let's consider the raw materials required for a response-dependent account of, say, redness. What must be true of the members of a speech community in order for the dispositional account of colour to yield truths of the form 'Roses are red, violets are blue'? Simply that by and large, the members of the community share stable dispositions to experience similar responses in response to similar objects on similar occasions. The response theorist then tells us that when a member of the community says 'Roses are red', what they say is true if and only if roses have the disposition to produce a particular psychological condition—the 'redness' response—in normal members of the community under suitable conditions.

Suppose that a particular community have the appropriate responses, currently use the term 'red' in accordance with this model, and are theoretically sophisticated enough to realise that this is what they are doing. It is open to them, in principle, to make the following linguistic policy decision. From now on, when they teach their children how to use the term 'red' they will pretend that there is a response-independent property of redness in the world, and conform their practice to this pretence. I don't mean that they will explicitly say to their children that redness is response-independent; just that they will introduce 'X is red' as the sort of claim that is capable of being true or false, independently of human dispositions to see things as red. Now it is a moot point just what is required to inculcate such an understanding. If our naive notion of colour is already response-independent, as Johnston suggests it may be, then presumably these linguistic policy makers need only decide to follow the teaching practices actually followed by unsophisticated English-speaking folk. But if this is not enough, they could add explicit lessons in the fallibility of human access to colour, taking care to pretend epistemological modesty with respect to colour. The crucial point is that even this is not incompatible with a reliance on the usual means of indicating to novices the extension of these properties, namely the use of paradigm cases. (All it requires is the additional lesson that even the paradigms are defeasible.)

The policy makers thus set out to instil in the practice of novice speakers two main habits or principles. The first principle is the primary usage condition governing assertions of the form 'X is red'—the relevant instance of (3), in effect. The second is the habit of taking redness to be something that falls under the objective mode of speech. Against the general background of assertoric practice, the way to combine these lessons will be to teach novices to describe their redness experiences in terms of the notions of perception and belief—ordinary, world-directed perception and belief, of course, not any introspective variety. In treating the distinctive redness response as defeasible perceptual grounds for a corresponding belief, we open the way to such comments as 'You believe that it is red, but is it *really* red?' This in turn may call into play the standard methods of rational reassessment. In virtue of their acquaintance with the objective mode *in general*, speakers will be lead into the practice of subjecting their colour judgements to reflective scrutiny by themselves and others. The objective mode brings with it the methods and motives for rational enquiry. But notice the way rationality gets into the picture here. It is not a part of a content specification for the utterances in question, but a gift that comes for free with any choice to adopt the objective mode of speech, to use the indicative form, to speak of truth and belief. One of the attractions of usage-based rather than content-based pragmatism seems to me to be that it puts rationality in its proper place—extrinsic rather than intrinsic to the discourse. (More on this in the next section.)

Of course, we are not free to adopt the objective mode wherever we like; or rather, it won't get very far in some cases. It works in the colour case because our colour responses are sufficiently alike, across the community, for rational reassessment to get some grip. But notice that the requirements are extremely flexible. The practice is quite capable of tolerating a considerable degree of difference. For one thing, it may be quick to exploit pockets of similarity, small communities of like-minded responders. But it does this not by relativising its claims to the standards of the community, but by exploiting the fact that the similarity within the community makes possible some degree of rational agreement on unrelativised claims.

Again, I'll come back to this. In §11 I'll argue that this flexibility with respect to the scope of the speech community provides another advantage of the usage-based approach. For the moment I simply want to emphasise the more basic point that where we have the resources in terms of which the content-based response theorists construct their accounts—i.e. a sufficiently uniform pattern of responses across a community—these same resources provide sufficient foundation for a non–response-dependent discourse, characterised theoretically (and in effect to its novice speakers themselves) in terms of a usage condition. Thus it is the response theorist's account which now seems in danger of redundancy.

The response theorist might object that this so-called alternative will actually be equivalent to the content-based response-dependent account of the discourse in question. One way to see that this is not so is to observe that unlike the response-dependent account, the usage-based alternative is not committed to the a priori impossibility of global error. In principle the impossibility of such error might be accessible from one or both of two perspectives: to practitioners in the discourse in question, to theoreticians reflecting on the nature of the discourse, or to both. However, from the practitioners' point of view there is nothing in the usage-based account that rules out the possibility of global error. The discourse was explicitly designed not to exclude this (while the general possibility was illustrated in §3 by the case of the fallible moral intuitionists). This leaves the theoreticians' point of view, and from here talk of error is simply a category mistake: because a usage-based theory is semantically austere, it tells us not when the utterances concerned are *true*, but how they are properly *used*.[9]

This point about theoretical perspective also provides the answer to a response theorist who asks what the truth conditions of the imagined discourse would be—hoping perhaps to show that there is no space for an alternative pragmatism at this point, between response-dependent truth conditions, on the one hand, and realist truth conditions, on the other. The answer is that *as theorists* we simply need not be in the business of providing truth conditions in the first place. As *speakers*, we may say with the crowd that 'X is red' is true if and only if X is red. As *theorists*, we are simply interested in how discourse of this kind is *used*. (True, one important aspect of usage concerns the speakers' use of the terms 'true' and 'false', and this needs to be explained. However, there is no a priori argument in this for the kind

---

9. It is becoming a familiar point that semantic minimalism and metaphysical minimalism tend to go hand in hand. Here, semantic austerity accompanies metaphysical austerity. As I noted in §3, the usage-based theory tells us very little about the metaphysical commitments of the community in question. But it is compatible with, and perhaps encourages, the minimalist metaphysical position that Johnston (OR, §4) regards as the most serious challenge to a revisionary response-dependent reading of several philosophically interesting topics. What Johnston fails to see is that in rejecting response dependence the metaphysical minimalist need not reject pragmatism. The usage path to pragmatism remains open.

of realism which would embarrass a usage pragmatist, at least as long as quasi-realism remains a viable alternative.)

The alternative is thus a genuine one. But could there be some reason for preferring the response-dependent practice; some reason for revising practice, if it is not already response dependent? A possible suggestion is that only a response-dependent account enables us to *justify* the practice in question.[10] This would tie in with the observation just made, namely that only the content-based approach yields talk of truth at the theoretical level. Only this approach provides a framework in which, with luck, it may turn out to be demonstrable that at least some of the claims we take to be true actually are true.

This is a tempting idea, but I think it is mistaken. In my view, response dependence tends to buy justification at the cost of devaluing the practice for which we wanted justification in the first place. This is brought out most starkly in cases in which the commitments typical of the original discourse have certain characteristic consequences for action, so that to justify the commitments concerned would be to justify the actions to which they give rise. The most important examples involve concepts of value and probability. I want to show that the response-dependent substitutes for these notions do not have the proper connections with action, and hence that justifying the substitute judgements does not serve to justify the associated behaviour. As we shall see, the point has been obscured by some ambiguities in the use that response theorists make of the notion of rationality. When these ambi-

---

10. The quest for justification or legitimation of linguistic practices is a prominent theme in Johnston's OR. In the opening paragraph he tells us that what 'deserved the name of a progressive pragmatism' would be a critical philosophy which asked 'whether the real explanations of our practices allow us to justify them.' One possible answer to this question would of course be a negative one, in particular the view that it is hardly more appropriate to try to justify our linguistic practices than it is to try to legitimate (say) our digestive practices. In both cases we can describe the practices concerned, and perhaps say what function they serve in our lives, but little more than that. I suspect that Johnston would be unhappy with a pragmatism that yielded no more than this. At any rate, in the next section I shall try to show that someone who does want more won't find it in response dependence. True, they won't find it in a usage-based pragmatism, either. My point is that a content-based theory does not offer any advantage in this respect.

guities are resolved, response dependent accounts of probability and value turn out to do rather worse than their usage-based rivals.

8. Justifying choices

Moral cognitivists need to explain how moral beliefs can be genuine beliefs, on the one hand, and yet of an essentially motivating character, on the other. There seems to be an analytic connection between believing that X is good and desiring that X. Why should this be so? I call this the *Approval Problem*.[11]

There is an analogous problem on the other side of decision theory. Cognitivists about probability need to explain how beliefs about probability can be genuine beliefs, on the one hand, and yet have some non-contingent connection with particular degrees of belief (and hence with betting behaviour), on the other. Someone who believes that it is probable that P tends to be confident that P, and to act accordingly. Again, why should this be so? I call this the *Confidence Problem*.[12]

One of the great attractions of expressivist views of probability and morality is that they provide a very simple solution to these problems. If moral claims express evaluative attitudes, for example, then the Approval Problem vanishes: moral commitments simply *are* desires, in effect, and we don't need any further explanation of why they tend to be accompanied by desires. These are problems for cognitivists about value and probability, then—problems for people who think that there is a significant psychological distinction to be drawn between a belief about probability and the corresponding degree of confidence, or between a belief about value and the corresponding affective disposition. If there are important psychological distinctions of this kind, it needs to be explained why the mental states so distinguished tend to occur together.

In both cases the problem can be given either a descriptive or a normative flavour. Why *do* people who believe X is good tend to desire that X? And why *should* they do so? In either flavour, however, these problems need to be distinguished from a more general problem of justifying our desires and cre-

---

11. I use this terminology in FFT, ch. 4. Michael Smith (DTV, p. 89) calls the same issue 'the Moral Problem'.
12. See my 'Does "Probably" Modify Sense?', *Australasian Journal of Philosophy* 61, 1983, 396-408, and FFT, ch. 4.

dences (and hence the behaviour which flows from them). The easiest way to see the more general problem is to suppose that we had solved the Approval and Confidence problems, in their normative versions. Suppose, in other words, we could show that our desires and credences were justified in the light of our beliefs about value and probability. It would still make sense, apparently, to wonder whether we had the right beliefs about value and probability, and hence the right desires and credences in this broader sense.

In effect, this broader problem is that of justifying the behavioural dispositions with which, as decision makers, we meet the world. I'll call this the *Behavioural Justification Problem* (or 'Behavioural Problem', for short). In order to solve it, cognitivists about value and probability need not only normative solutions to both the Approval and Confidence problems, but also a means of justifying our evaluative and probabilistic beliefs themselves.

What is involved in justifying our evaluative and probabilistic beliefs? It depends, obviously, on the content of these beliefs. One of the attractions of response dependence seems to be that it provides contents which make the task look manageable. After all, if moral and probabilistic claims are very general claims about human dispositions, then the knowledge required to justify them is a kind of self-knowledge. The subject matter of morality and probability becomes more accessible—as well as more palatable, metaphysically speaking, to those of a naturalistic frame of mind.

If the Approval and Confidence problems could be solved under their normative readings, then, the Behavioural Problem would reduce to that of justifying moral and probabilistic beliefs. And if that problem starts to look approachable from the response theorist's point of view—because these beliefs are about our own psychological dispositions, in some sense—an attractive vista opens up. A solution to the Behavioural Problem might seem to be in sight. I want to show that this prospect is quite illusory, however. In effect, response theorists can have one half of the solution or other, but not both together. Which half they get depend on what precisely goes into their biconditional content conditions, and the illusion rests on equivocation.

Let's think first about the Confidence Problem. I noted that the two-step solution to the Behavioural Problem requires a *normative* solution of the Confidence Problem—in other words, a demonstration that an agent who believes that it is probable that P is *justified* (and not merely *disposed*) to be confident that P. However, if the response theorist says that 'It is probable that P' means that (or is true if and only if) normal people are disposed to be confident that P, then a normative solution to the Confidence Problem will not be forthcoming. After all, put yourself in the position of the agent concerned. You believe that normal people in your circumstances are disposed to be confident that P. But what have the habits of other people (normal or not!) got to do with whether *you* should be confident that P?

The usual approach at this point to put some normativity in by hand, so to speak, in the form of the notion of rationality. Roughly, the response theorist's suggestion is that 'It is probable that P' means (or is true if and only if) a *rational* person would be confident that P. I want to show that this strategy is a dead end, or rather a whole neighbourhood of dead ends, distinguished by a range of possible readings of the notion of rationality. I'll begin with the probabilistic case, and then apply the same lessons to the evaluative case.

The idea of analysing probability in terms of rational partial belief has long seemed attractive. I call it the rationalist approach to probability. Roughly, it amounts to saying that P is probable if and only if a rational person would be confident that P, if properly acquainted with the relevant evidence.[13] How does a rationalist handle the Confidence Problem? In its normative version, the problem now comes to this: Why should a person who believes that it is *rational* to be confident that P, *actually* be confident that P?

There are a number of possible approaches, turning on different readings of the relevant notion of rationality. It would be almost impossible to be exhaustive at this point, of course, but the following alternatives will serve to illustrate the nature of the problem:

---

13. Among recent writers, Hugh Mellor has a theory of chance of this kind, for example (though in his case it is part of a hybrid theory including propensities, thought of as dispositions to produce arrangements of chances). See Mellor's *The Matter of Chance*, Cambridge: Cambridge University Press, 1971. Mellor takes his theory to be in the spirit of F. P. Ramsey's view, developed in 'Truth and Probability', in *Foundations*, D. H. Mellor ed., London: Routledge & Kegan Paul, 1978. Despite the apparent differences between Ramsey and Keynes on this topic, Keynes too might be thought of as an early exponent of the rationalist treatment of probability, given that his 'logical' probability relations are characterised in terms of degrees of *rational* belief; see Keynes's *A Treatise on Probability*, London: Macmillan, 1921.

I   *Rationality cashed in terms of our own cognitive dispositions.* Either (a) the concept of the rational is the concept of what we are disposed to accept, or (b) the term 'rational' is used to express a disposition to accept a claim to which it is applied.

II *Rationality cashed in terms of practical utility.* Rational partial belief is useful partial belief.

III *Objective rationality.* Rationality is an objective cognitive value, and our practice in the present case reflects our awareness of its presence and nature.

Option I(a) amounts to a response-dependent account of the relevant notion of rationality. Roughly, it says that a cognitive move is rational if and only if it is a move we are disposed to make. To say that it is rational to be confident that P is thus to describe a disposition on our own part to be confident that P. (There are at least two readings of 'our' here: it might be the speaker personally, it might be the community.) Option II(b) has a more expressive flavour: to say that it is rational to φ is to *express* (not *describe*) a disposition to φ. (In this case the bearer of the disposition is presumably just the speaker.) On either version of Option I, however, the idea that the response theorist's appeal to rationality leads to normative justifications for our behavioural dispositions turns out to be illusory: if rationality itself is cashed in descriptive or expressive terms, so too is whatever notion of justification rides on its back.

Option II may look more promising. It is world-directed, taking rational belief to be belief that works. But what is useful about a particular degree of credence? At best, only that it is (increasingly) *probable* to lead to success in the (increasingly) long run. Taken in this sense, then, the analysis of probability in terms of rationality is circular, at least in the sense that a rationalist account of probability is powerless to help with the Confidence Problem. The problem simply re-emerges at the new level.

Option III is more interesting. It countenances an objective cognitive value, and interprets probability in terms of the value, in this objective sense, of certain degrees of partial belief. Why is it the case that people who believe that it is probable that P do, or should, also have a high degree of confidence that P? Because to say that P is probable is to say that it is valuable to have such a credence, in this objective sense of value. So if people believe that P is probable then they believe that they *should* have a high credence that P, by their own evaluative lights.

So far so good, but this answer won't satisfy someone who has noticed the Approval Problem. For we now have what might be called the Rationality Problem: What is the connection between rationality and motivation? The question again has a descriptive and a normative aspect: Why does someone who believes that it is rational to F *actually* F (or at least typically have an inclination to F)? And why *should* they? Why does rationality matter, and why should it?

Just as in the case of the Approval Problem, the Rationality Problem might incline us to a response-dependent or expressive account of rationality. In the present context, however, these were the views we considered under option I. So if Option III is to remain distinct we must reject this course—and yet the problem now seems intractable. Still, if one is prepared to live with this problem in the evaluative case then there is no need to bite another bullet for the probabilistic case. Rationalism shows us how to use the same evaluative bullet for both cases.

In sum, then, does a rationalist account of probability succeed in providing a normative solution to the confidence problem? It depends on what we mean by rationality. There seems to be three possibilities, comprising two dead ends and one diversion:

(i) On a response-dependent or expressivist reading of the rationality claim, the connection between the probabilistic belief and credence is merely descriptive. At best, the disposition expressed or described by a probability judgement simply *gives rise to* the corresponding credence. It doesn't *justify* the adoption of that credence.

(ii) On a utilitarian reading of the rationality claim the rationalist account of probability is circular.

(iii) On a normative reading of the rationality claim the Confidence Problem is replaced by a version of the Approval Problem.

Rationalist response theorists thus do rather poorly on the normative aspect of the Confidence Problem. At best they succeed in shifting the issue to the evaluative case.

Perhaps not surprisingly, however, it turns out that much the same difficulties arise in evaluative case (and here, of course, there is nowhere else to hide). To illustrate the nature of the problem, suppose we follow the response theorist in equating the good, or the valuable, with what substantial rationality leads us to value. In its normative aspect, the Approval Problem is now the question as to why we should actually value what we believe to be valuable in this sense. Why should we value what substantial rationality leads us to value? Once again, the structure of the answer turns on our understanding of the rationality claim. There seems to be three main possibilities, which roughly parallel those in the probabilistic case.

I* *Response-dependent or expressive rationality.* These approaches cash rationality itself in terms of our own psychological dispositions. As in the probabilistic case, they provide descriptive but not normative solutions to the Approval Problem.

II* *Rationality as a cognitive value.* This approach interprets rationality in terms of evaluative categories already in play. For example, it takes what it is rational to value to be what it is valuable to value. As in the probability case, the effect of this is to make rationality unhelpful in providing an account of value. The analysis leads in a circle.

III* *Rationality as a sui generis cognitive value.* If rationality is an independent value then the Rationality Problem is distinct subspecies of the Approval Problem. Indeed, for rationalist response theorists it becomes the core species, to which other versions of the Approval Problem reduce.

Let's think about the normative aspect of the Rationality Problem in the light of III*. Given this *sui generis* notion of rationality, why should someone who believes that it is rational to ϕ, actually ϕ? One possible move is say that the solution is analytic, because 'should' itself needs to be cashed in terms of this notion of rationality. If rationality itself is the core normative notion, there is no non-trivial normative issue to be raised at this point.

However, recall our reason for being interested in the normative versions of the Confidence, Approval and Rationality problems in the first place: if successfully negotiated, they seemed likely to provide response theorists with the second half of a two-stage solution to the Behavioural Problem. The first stage of the solution required justification of our evaluative and probabilistic beliefs themselves. Here response theorists seemed well placed to make progress, in virtue of the fact that they take such beliefs to refer to our own psychological dispositions. However, if the notion of rationality invoked in the response theorist's content conditions is normative and irreducible, this easy progress is quite illusory. Justification now depends on access to the dispositions of *rational* agents, not merely those of *actual* agents. And the enquiry itself seems in danger of a problematic regress, if the notion of justification involved is to be cashed in terms of the same notion of rationality.

The underlying moral of this discussion is a simple one, which applies in both the probabilistic and evaluative cases. If the response theorist's content conditions invoke irreducibly normative notions, they leave unresolved all the old difficulties about normativity in a natural world. One issue left unresolved is the epistemological one: How could creatures like us have access to normative facts of the relevant kind? How could we be *justified* in holding particular beliefs about such facts?[14] On the other hand, if the response theorist's content conditions are not irreducibly normative, then the Confidence Problem and the Approval Problem loom large: Why should our behaviour as agents be guided by what we believe about the psychological dispositions of our fellows? Only someone who equivocates about the normativity of the relevant notion of rationality could imagine that a response-dependent account of probability or value escapes both horns of this traditional dilemma.

9. Action as a fixed point

The previous section was motivated by the suggestion that a response theorist might answer the redundancy argument by claiming that a content-based account is better placed than its various rivals to justify our beliefs. In a sense this claim is true, of course. Because the effect of the response theorist's biconditionals is to read all our commitments in the relevant domains as partially self-descriptive, the commitments as interpreted are often easier to justify than they would be under other readings. However, opponents on both sides of the response theorist—more traditional realists on one side, and irrealists of various kinds on the other—are likely to feel that there is a trick involved. In effect, the response theory solves the problem by changing the subject.

---

14. There is a double problem here, of course, because what is being called for is *justification* for our beliefs about matters of *justification*.

The nice thing about the evaluative and probabilistic cases is that here the trick, if we may call it that, is blocked by the fact that the psychological states which play the role of the response in these cases—desire and credence—have direct connections with behaviour. This means that they provide psychological fixed points, toward which the quest for justification is ultimately directed. When the response theorist tries to reconstrue evaluative or probabilistic belief, the necessary connections with credence and desire bring the issue of justification back to the same point. These connections are the core of the Confidence and Approval problems, respectively—problems which arise for any view which recognises a gap between believing that X is valuable and desiring X, or between believing that P is probable and being confident that P. As I noted earlier, one of the great attractions of expressivist views is that they minimise these gaps.

In the case of the traditional secondary qualities, however, there are no psychological fixed points of this kind. There is no distinctive behavioural manifestation of 'seeing red', for example, such that an account of the content of the belief that X is red has to explain why people who have this belief typically do (or should) display this behaviour. 'Seeing red' simply doesn't play that sort of a role in our mental lives. This might explain why the response-dependence strategy has long seemed so attractive in these cases. When it came to seem that there was no place for the folk properties of colour in a scientific account of the objective contents of the world, the strategy of revising in favour of the Lockean dispositional account did not have to confront anything analogous to the Confidence and Approval problems. So the attractions of the Lockean account—for example, the fact that by sacrificing their observer-independent status, colours retain a respectable place in the scientific world—are not offset by difficulties elsewhere.

With colour properties so construed, of course, the scientific view *can* justify our colour ascriptions. As always, response dependence interprets our commitments in a way which makes them more accessible. Whatever the merits of this move in the colour case, I have argued that it doesn't work in the probabilistic and evaluative cases. Here, the justification we want is justification for our credences and desires, and the dispositional revision doesn't give it to us.

As long as the secondary qualities constitute an isolated case, there is an evident attraction in keeping them within the scientific fold by reading them dispositionally. This advantage would be undermined by the acceptance that whatever the nature of the subjectivity in play here, it is a global feature of language. For in this case it infects our scientific discourse as well, and hence cannot be quarantined where it occurs in other discourses by means of the revisionary dispositional reading. True, we may see an advantage in reducing multiple sources of infection to one, taking the view that the scientific discourse is the most hygienic we have. But if it is acknowledged that we live (and have no choice but to live) with the infection in this case, an obvious thought is that we might just as well do so in other cases as well. This would be to defend our right to the old unsterilised naive discourse about colour, relying on our internal systems of cognitive quarantine to avoid serious conflict with our scientific beliefs. This would in a sense be quasi-realism about colour, but a quasi-realism defended by the claim that in virtue of the global nature of the relevant kind of subjectivity, the same quasi-realist attitude is appropriate everywhere. There is no embarrassing divide between 'real' realism and quasi-realism, on this view—a divide which several of the quasi-realist's critics[15] have identified as a weak spot.

10. Making sense of usage

I have argued that globality is incompatible with a thoroughly content-based approach to explicating the sort of subjectivity with which we are here concerned; that wherever a content-based account may be given, the materials also exist for a usage-based account; and that in the moral and probabilistic cases there is no advantage for the content-based account—quite the contrary, if anything—concerning the justification of the relevant action-guiding psychological states. To finish, I want to exhibit a further advantage of the usage-based approach. Like the redundancy point, this turns on the fact that the usage-based theory is more austere and less demanding than its rival. Here the effect is not simply that the usage-based theory works wherever the content-based theory claims to work, but a stronger point: in accounting for folk linguistic practice the usage approach often works smoothly where the content-based approach does not. As we shall see, this advantage is most evident in the case of discourses whose patterns of usage exhibit a subtle combination of objective and subjective aspects.

---

15. Including me; see FFT, ch. 4, 'Metaphysical Pluralism', *Journal of Philosophy*, 89, 1992, 387–409.

11. Truth conditions: the objective-subjective dilemma

Let's return to the self-descriptivist misreading of emotivism. It has often been noted that self-descriptivism is unable to make sense of ordinary intuitions about moral objectivity, and in particular about the possibility of moral error and moral ignorance. For example, there is nothing particularly counterintuitive about

(8) I believe that X is good but I may be wrong

or about

(9) There are many good things of whose existence I am quite unaware.

Apparently, however, the self-descriptivist is required to parse these propositions as something like

(10) I believe that I approve of X, but it may be the case that I do not approve of X

and

(11) There are many things of which I approve without being aware that they exist,

respectively. But (11) is clearly counterintuitive, and (10) mislocates the source of moral error, taking it to involve a mistake about oneself. (In folk moral practice it simply isn't true that self-knowledge excludes moral error.) In this respect, then, the self-descriptivist's paraphrases do not do justice to a degree of moral objectivity which is claimed by ordinary usage.

The problem becomes even more acute in cases of moral disagreement. Folk intuition regards the utterances 'X is good' and 'X is bad' as prima facie incompatible, even if said by different speakers. In response to the assertion 'Discipline is good', for example, the utterance 'Discipline is bad' would normally be taken to amount to a clear (if rather stilted) expression of dissent. Yet the self-descriptivist should see no more conflict between these propositions, expressed by different speakers, than between 'I approve of discipline' and 'You disapprove of discipline'.

These are familiar objections to self-descriptivism, of course. They turn on the fact that the self-descriptivist's truth conditions for moral claims are too subjective to account for the apparent objectivity of ordinary moral discourse, and a promising response is therefore to 'objectify' in one or both of two respects: (a) by taking moral claims to refer not to the evaluative dispositions of the individual speaker, but to those *normal* in the speech community as a whole; or (b) by appealing not to *actual* responses, but to possibly counterfactual responses under *ideal* conditions. Taken together, these moves give the self-descriptivist something like this:

(12) X is good iff a normal person would approve of X, if acquainted with X under ideal conditions.

In other words, the effect of these moves is to bridge the gap between naive self-descriptivism and response-dependence. As response theorists recognise, of course, this opens the way for moral error and ignorance. To the extent that an individual speaker is abnormal, or less than ideally situated, his or her evaluations may be out of step with the objective standard. It also makes possible moral disagreement: two speakers may simply disagree about how the normal speaker would react to some state of affairs under ideal conditions.

So much for capturing the objectivity of moral usage. But moral usage is also notoriously subjective, in the sense that it appears to leave room for speaker-relativity, for no-fault disagreements: cases of moral difference in which usage appears to allow that neither speaker need be at fault. Can the modified self-descriptivist theory make sense of these? On the face of it not, for surely it is a perfectly objective matter whether a given X is such as to evoke a given response in normal people under specified conditions.

Response theorists have an answer to this challenge, whose adequacy I'll consider in a moment. First note that the problem cannot be avoided by denying moral relativity, or it some other way appealing to the special features of the moral case. For the problem turns on the possibility of no-fault disagreements, and these are not simply a feature of the moral case. Indeed they are potentially global, in virtue of the same rule-following considerations that lead Pettit to conclude that response dependence is global: because the application of any general term is finitely based, it is always conceivable that a speech community will divide on the issue of a future application. If it turns out that such a division underlies an apparent disagreement, that disagreement will be held to involve no fault.[16] In gen-

---

16. See FFT, ch. 8.

eral, wherever language depends on a response which might vary from speaker to speaker, we have a potential source of no-fault disagreements.[17] So our present concern is not peculiar to the moral case.

In so far as it acknowledges the possibility of no-fault disagreement, the solution the response theory proposes is to invoke an indexical specification of the relevant 'response community'—for example, to suggest:

(13) X is good iff *I* would approve of X, if I were acquainted with X under ideal conditions.

Roughly speaking, the strategy is thus to dispense with (or at least water down) the notion of normality, but to retain a reference to ideal conditions (thereby, hopefully, retaining the ability to deal with the objectivity problem).

The revised account can certainly make some sense of moral error: I might simply be mistaken as to how I would respond under ideal conditions. But can it make sense of moral disagreements? We noted earlier that a naive self-descriptivist should see no more prima facie conflict between 'X is good' and 'X is bad', said by different speakers, than between 'I approve of X' and 'He disapproves of X'. Clearly, the same applies to this indexical version of the content-based theory. Normality was thus doing important work, and the problem re-emerges if it is omitted.

Response theorists thus face the following dilemma. If they leave out the notion of normality, the resulting account is insufficiently objective to make sense of ordinary prima facie disagreements about the matters in question. If they put in normality, on the other hand, the account cannot make sense of the very real possibility of no-fault disagreements, arising in cases in which there is statistically significant divergence in patterns of response.

In practice, response theorists may choose a different horn of this dilemma in different cases. They may favour subjectivity where no-fault disagreements are most obvious, such as in the moral case, and objectivity ('normal response') elsewhere. This is mere damage control, however. Both choices are unsatisfactory, and in any case any such division is bound to be arbitrary. No-fault disagreement is a global phenomenon in language, and its incidence varies only by degree from one discourse to another.

---

17. Are there other potential sources? Yes, in various kinds of context-dependencies. See FFT, ch. 8.

Let's focus on a case in which response theorists do invoke normal conditions, and consider the sensitivity this engenders to the issue as to whether there are statistical norms in the community in question in the given respect. Pettit recognises (RRD, p. 608) that it is a consequence of the content-based theory that if there is no normal response, the relevant property ascription should be regarded as false. A related conclusion is that as long as the bounds of the community are indeterminate, so too is the content of the property ascription concerned. But consider the consequences of this in perfectly ordinary cases. Canberra is a small city, with a lot of open space. By Sydney standards, it is a quiet place. But if I were to deny that Canberra is a bustling place, would I speaking to the rather refined bustle-sensitivities of Canberra residents themselves, to those of my own Sydney community, or to some other 'normal' class? A disadvantage of the content-based approach is that until the issue is resolved, the significance of what I have said is simply not determinate.

A great advantage of the usage-based approach is that it avoid these ambiguities *at the level of the meaning specification*. Roughly, Canberra residents and Sydney residents learn to use the term 'bustle' in accordance with the same usage condition: the assertion 'This place is bustling' is prima facie appropriate when one experiences the 'Oh, it's so busy!' response. This provides the sense in which the two communities speak the same language in using the term. But it leaves room for divergence later, if it turns out that Canberra residents and Sydney residents are differently sensitive to experiencing this response. The response theorist has to try to account for this divergence in terms of a difference in meaning which—perhaps unknown to the participants—has been present in their linguistic practice all along. (The term 'bustle' simply latched onto different concepts in Canberra and Sydney.) By specifying meaning in terms of usage, in contrast, my kind of pragmatist is able to explain the fact that in one important sense, the term does mean the same to the members of the two speech communities—and to explain the divergence in its application by differences between the speakers which lie in the background, as preconditions for the practice in question.

There are two main arguments for leaving these differences in the background, rather than incorporating them into the content of the assertions concerned. First, it makes much better sense of ordinary usage. Naive Canberra and Sydney folk need have no sense that their notion of bustle is not universal, and to insist on such gross indeterminacies in content unreasonably detaches meaning from speakers' understanding. (There is a theoretical redundancy point lurking here. Even if initially we thought there were such content indeterminacies, an obvious and appealing theoretical move would be to factor them out, thus concentrating on what would have better claim to be thought of as speaker-accessible meanings.) Second, and ultimately even more telling, not all the preconditions of language can be made explicit, in the sense of figuring in the content of the linguistic expressions for which they are preconditions. This is a familiar point, related to what the Tortoise said to Achilles. Something must stay in the background, crucial and yet unsaid. Whatever it is, it might vary from speaker to speaker, or from community to community. In this way, we'll get precisely what we have in the case of 'bustle': a divergence in application which rests not on any difference in content, and not on any mistake by either party, but simply on a difference in the background.

Many discourses handle these no-fault disagreements surprisingly smoothly. We are able to 'switch off' the objective mode sufficiently to accommodate such irreconcilable differences, without seriously undermining its useful application in ordinary cases. We thus combine objectivity with a certain tolerance of subjectivity (or relativity). (In *Facts and the Function of Truth* I tried to explain this in terms of an account of what in general the objective mode is *for*.) A usage-based account can readily make sense of this feature of language, but a content-based theory is bound to be torn between the objective and subjective aspects of practice.

In particular, a usage-based account puts normality in its proper place. There is a direct comparison here with a coherence theory of truth. Opponents of such a theory can agree, of course, that in the long run what we *take to be true* is what we converge on believing—roughly, what normal people come to believe in the ideal limit of rational discussion. But this is simply a consequence of the more basic usage condition for truth, viz., that it is prima facie appropriate to assert that 'P' is true only if one believes that P. Against a background of communal reassessment of belief, this basic condition guarantees, more or less, that what normal people *take to be true* in the long run will be what the community converges on. Since this fact about usage can be explained by any theory of truth which accepts the minimal usage condition, it provides no argument for the coherence account's attempt to explain it analytically, by analysing truth in terms of normal rational convergence. On the other hand, the coherence theory does violence to usage at other points. (With respect to the phenomenology of truth, for example: as correspondence theorists like to point out, what we seem to care about in rational enquiry is not whether we'll all come to agree that P, but whether P is in fact the case.)

As for the coherence theory, so for the content-based approach in general: the right place for the notions of normality, rationality, and the like is in an account of the consequences, after the fact, of the adoption of a usage rule which makes no mention of these things.

12. Pragmatics to the rescue?

We have been considering the objection that content-based theories do a poor job of accounting for certain features of ordinary usage. In various respects, for example, the ordinary use of the notions of truth and falsity is not what it should be, if the response theorist's biconditionals captured the content of the utterances concerned.

In reply, response theorists may well try to invoke various 'pragmatic' factors about language use, to explain the apparent mismatch. Depending on the version of the response theory on offer, the task may to explain apparent objectivity or apparent subjectivity. If (13) is the preferred reading of moral judgements, for example, then problem will be to explain the possibility of moral disagreement: to explain why 'X is good' and 'X is bad' are normally taken to be incompatible, even when uttered by different speakers.[18] A number of suggestions might be made at this point. For example, it might be suggested that the benefits of social cohesion provide a reason for attempting to 'align' the evaluative attitudes of the different members of a speech community, and that this is encouraged by treating such cases as if they embody a genuine disagreement.

There are other possibilities—linguistic pragmatics is fertile territory—but I think they are uniformly misguided. However, the fault lies not with the pragmatic considerations themselves, but with the ailing program they are called on to patch up. For the irony is that the content-based theory has now taken on the quasi-realist's project, but with the added handicap of

---

18. Alternatively, if the preferred content-based response theory errs towards the objective side, the task will be to account for the apparent subjectivity of no-fault disagreements. One possibility, to which Johnston seems attracted at least as a last resort, is to simply deny that the parties concerned are speaking the same language. See DTV, p. 170.

having to explain not only why usage bestows 'apparent' truth conditions, but also why it does not accord with real truth conditions. Initially it might have seemed that the content-based theory provided an attractive way to bypass the quasi-realist's rather tedious concern with this business of explaining usage: invoke one's natural conceptual rights, and get on with something more interesting. Tripped up on the awkward tendency of usage to combine objectivity in some respects with subjectivity in others, however, the content-based theory now finds itself bogged in the same messy territory. And it is burdened, as the quasi-realist is not, with a doctrine about the 'real' truth-conditions of the utterances in question.[19]

True, a disdain for the painstaking work of pragmatism may not have been the only factor that led the content-based theory to reject the quasi-realist path in the first place. Another motive might have been the feeling that it is the quasi-realist who does violence to ordinary usage by suggesting that folk truth is not univocal—by distinguishing between genuine truth (where realism is appropriate attitude to discourse) and constructed truth (where quasi-realism is as close as we get). I want to emphasise that in this respect the usage-based theory I recommend sides with the content-based theory. It takes the view that there is no sharp divide in language where real truth conditions cease and ersatz ones take over. Rather, throughout language the explanatory task is the same: to account for the fact that dispositions to respond to the world in certain ways come to be expressed in the objective assertoric mode.

Finally, it might be felt that there is a powerful argument for the content-based theory in the intuition that truth conditions play a crucial role in a theory of meaning (or theory of linguistic competence). Certainly this intuition seems to have been influential in underpinning resistance to non–

---

19. One consequence of this burden will be that the content-based response theorist will be bound to admit that there are some circumstances in a speaker's own judgements of truth and assertibility may part company: either she grants that P is true but declines to assert that P (or disagrees with the assertion that P); or she asserts that P, but declines to claim that P is true. Moreover, note that the content-based response theorist should really now explain why usage accords with underlying truth conditions when it does do so, as well as why it sometimes parts company. In effect, this means that the content-based response theorist needs a complete pragmatic account of the usage conditions of the utterances in question, not merely a patch for a few exceptional cases.

truth-conditional treatments of various topics, such as conditionals. The point might well be linked to the previous one: it will be at least inelegant if a theory of meaning has to offer one sort of account of the meaning those indicative sentences that do have genuine truth conditions, and another sort of account of those that do not.

This suggestion calls for three responses. First, there is another conception of knowledge of meaning, apart from that of knowledge of truth conditions—namely knowledge of (subjective) usage conditions. The usage-based theory is tailor-made for a role in such a theory. Roughly, knowledge of the meaning of a descriptive term will amount to knowledge as to which response that term expresses. Second, we have just seen that the content-based theory cannot fully account for the ordinary use, and hence the meaning, of the relevant utterances in terms of the truth conditions it provides for them. An appeal to pragmatic features is also necessary. This concession deflates any general appeal to the idea that meaning is simply a matter of truth conditions.[20] And third, the role of truth in a general theory of meaning is in any case widely acknowledged to be fulfilled by a very thin disquotational notion. Such a truth predicate can easily be added to a language by stipulation, if need be, and is unlikely to be of relevance to the issues at stake between the content-based theory, on the one side, and the usage-based theory and quasi-realism, on the other.[21]

---

20. Perhaps there is tendency to underestimate the necessary role of a pragmatic element in a theory of meaning, even where truth conditions are well behaved. It is easy to overlook the need for a truth-conditional theory of content to be supplemented by a theory of assertion—a pragmatic theory which relates the truth conditions of an asserted sentence to the *point* of asserting it. In my view this project is of doubtful coherency, since it assumes in effect that the notion of truth is prior to that of assertion (and hence *correct* assertion). But even if it is coherent, the existence of this project inevitably undermines the apparent theoretical advantages of the truth-conditional approach. For one thing, it will presumably be an ingredient of the required pragmatic account that (canonically) it is appropriate to assert that P when one believes that P. This takes us back to the usage-based theory's subjective assertibility conditions, with the difference that we now lack a suitably general account of belief (or judgement). The usage-based theory has this built in: beliefs (or judgements) are just what we come to call our responses of the relevant kinds, when these responses come to be expressed in the objective truth-conditional mode.
21. For more on this point see FFT, ch. 9.

13. Conclusion

In sum, the usage path to pragmatism has the following four main advantages. It avoids a vicious regress that threatens a global version of the content-based approach. In any local case, it makes more economical use than the content-based approach of the same raw materials—the same facts about shared human responses. It gives a much better account of some of the subtleties of ordinary usage, particularly of the peculiar mix of objectivity and subjectivity we find in discourses prone to no-fault disagreements. And it avoids the Approval Problem and the Confidence Problem, while doing no worse than its rivals at *justifying* our credences and evaluative attitudes.

Let me finish by mentioning what may seem the most unattractive feature of a usage-based pragmatism. Such an approach requires us to distance ourselves from our own linguistic practices, to such an extent that we are able to ask not *what* we are saying—what its content is—but *why* we are saying it; why we use those words and concepts in the first place. Many philosophers seem to be troubled by this detached perspective, feeling that it threatens our right or ability to continue to engage in these practices in a meaningful way. The attempt to regard one's practices 'from the outside' thus engenders something akin to agoraphobia—a fear that one is losing touch with one's values and community. I don't know what to do about this problem, beyond pointing out that the external viewpoint concerned is only a small aspect of the perspective on ourselves that human biology already offers us. It *is* sometimes unsettling to take this detached view of practices so central to our lives. At least since Darwin, however, there has been no honest escape from this kind of problem. We cannot avoid the source of the discomfort, except by self-deception. The best treatment seems to be to try to alleviate the symptoms. Lasting relief requires the ability to be untroubled by a certain cognitive distance between one's theoretical standpoint and one's everyday linguistic activity.[22]

---

22. Australians might thus be expected to make good usage pragmatists. The ability to be untroubled by distance is a national characteristic, and Australians are used to contemplating matters of interest from great remove. This view from the middle of nowhere is not without its advantages. The advantages are those of critical distance, of seeing the big picture. Often it is important to step backwards, to move off Broadway in order to contemplate its activities objectively.

In my view, however, the prognosis is favourable. In other areas of life we seem to be able to accommodate the two perspectives quite painlessly. Our appetites are not less urgent, their satisfactions less enjoyable, in the light of what we know about their biological basis. Pain itself is not less unpleasant because we know what it's for. Unless there is something special about our linguistic behaviour, then, these cases suggest that the complaint is a little theatrical. Ordinary humans find it relatively easy to combine the internal and external perspectives in one satisfying cognitive life.

School of Philosophy
MainQuad, A14
University of Sydney
NSW Australia 2006
huw@mail.usyd.edu.au

Ignoring the pessimistic thought that it is quite possible to have too much of a good thing, it is thus an engaging speculation that an aptitude for a detached, sceptical and explanatory stance might yet prove a more enduring characteristic of Australian philosophy than the famous local brand of naive realism.

The usual naturalistic explanation of Australian naive realism attributes it to the bright Australian light. As David Armstrong puts it, reality forces itself upon one in these conditions. There are rival hypotheses, of course, including the mischievous suggestion that Australian philosophers only became naive realists when they stopped protecting their heads by wearing hats. But a more plausible hypothesis is that naive realism is itself a response to isolation—a straw-clutching attempt to steady oneself against the vertigo induced by distance.

These chauvinistic comments are prompted by a footnote in early versions of Mark Johnston's 'Objectivity Refigured' (sadly, it is missing from the published version) in which Johnston notes the possible emergence of a distinctively Australian pragmatism. As I have indicated, this worthy project seems to rest on sound geographically foundations. All the same, it may be that those Australian pragmatists whose hearts are too close to Broadway have yet to achieve the cognitive distance required to cast such a pragmatism in its most desirable form.

JIM EDWARDS
Response-Dependence, Kripke and Minimal Truth

1. Introduction

Saul Kripke's infamous Sceptical Solution to the problem of rule-following takes as its central notion the *assertibility conditions* of an utterance (Kripke 1982). More accurately this is not Kripke's own solution but that of Wittgenstein according to Kripke, but let's for brevity pretend that the proponent of the Sceptical Solution is Kripke himself. Taking assertibility conditions to be the central notion of an account of language use is reminiscent of Michael Dummett's suggestion to make assertibility conditions the central notion of a theory of meaning. But there are crucial differences. Kripke denies that utterances whose assertibility conditions are satisfied are apt for truth or falsity. He denies that utterances have truth conditions as well as assertibility conditions. Dummett's suggestion, in contrast, although it does place some restriction upon truth conditions, allows that assertible utterances are apt for truth and falsity. A second feature of Kripke's Sceptical Solution is that he takes the assertibility conditions of an utterance to be response dependent—i.e., to be determined at bottom by a consensus in the judgements of the language-using community. Again this is in contrast to Dummett.

Kripke takes as his example arithmetic utterances of the form "$x + y = z$". Let us contrast Kripke's radical picture of how we use the sign "+" with the intuitive picture. Intuitively, we assume a picture in which a competent user has learned the meaning of "+" and that meaning bestows truth conditions upon her utterances employing "+". In the intuitive picture, she endeavours to make such utterances as accord with those truth conditions and correspond to the mathematical facts[1] relevant to those truth conditions, so that her utterances are therefore true utterances, and it is the general success of language users in this enterprise which accounts for their common agreement concerning utterances which employ "+", to the extent that they do agree. Kripke, in contrast, holds that there is no fact about a competent language user that constitutes her meaning addition by the sign "+".[2] Thus, in Kripke's view, there is no meaning fact about Jill which bestows truth conditions and therefore truth values upon her utterances employing "+", and no similar meaning fact about Jack, and hence no such facts to explain their agreement in judgements employing "+", if they do agree. Rather, in Kripke's picture, the practice of using "+" is governed merely by assertibility conditions, whereby a correct use of "+" is an utterance which the language community at large do, or would, endorse. Kripke's alternative picture is that there are no individual graspings of a meaning, and no consequent truth conditions which that meaning bestows upon arithmetic utterances. Hence no endeavours to accord with those truth conditions *explain* our common agreement in usage. Any explanation of that common agreement is at a non-rational, purely causal level.

Thus Kripke claims, in contrast to the intuitive picture, that there is no fact about a language user, call her "Jill", which is her meaning something by the sign "+". So her utterances employing "+" have no meaning which bestows truth conditions upon those utterances. However, Kripke recognizes that there may be another source of truth conditions. The assertibility conditions which he does recognize these utterances to have may themselves generate truth conditions for those utterances. Kripke remarks:

> Wittgenstein's theory should not be confused with a theory that, for any *m* and *n*, the value of the function we mean by 'plus', *is* (by definition) the value that (nearly) all the linguistic community would give as the answer. Such a theory would be a theory of the *truth* conditions of such assertions as "By 'plus' we mean such-and-such a function." or "By 'plus' we mean a function, which, when

---

1. My talk of assigning meaning and accessing mathematical facts is intended to be neutral and innocent of any particular metaphysics and epistemology of mathematics.
2. Kripke considers and dismisses the claim that Jill's meaning addition by "+" is an occurrent, introspectible mental state, the claim that it is a *sui generis* mental state, and the claim that it is a disposition to answer questions of the form "n + m = ?" with whatever numeral it is which stands for the sum.

applied to 68 and 57 as arguments, yields 125 as value." (An infinite, exhaustive totality of specific conditions of the second form would determine which function was meant, and hence would determine a condition of the first form.) The theory would assert that 125 is the value of the function meant for given arguments, if and only if '125' is the response nearly everyone would give, given these arguments. Thus the theory would be a social, or community-wide version of the dispositional theory, and would be open to at least some of the same criticisms as the original form. I take Wittgenstein to deny that he holds such a view ... (Kripke 1982 p. 111).

In this paper I shall be concerned to develop arguments designed to show that, supposing utterances with "+" have communal assertibility conditions, those assertibility conditions do not generate truth conditions for such utterances. Some of these arguments will be taken directly from Kripke, but others are only loosely based upon his discussion. Kripke focuses his discussion upon arithmetic assertions, but the sceptical conclusion he reaches is intended to apply to all assertions. It is not intuitively plausible that arithmetic utterances do have response dependent assertibility conditions, although this is not a claim I shall question in this paper. However, talk of colours is perhaps the most worked out example in which it is plausible to claim that assertibility conditions are (at least partly[3]) determined by human responses. The question arises whether the response dependent assertibility conditions of colour talk bestow truth conditions upon colour talk. One way of tackling this question is to take the arguments developed to show that the (assumed) response dependent assertibility conditions for utterances with "+" do not generate truth conditions, and to ask whether those arguments transpose from arithmetic to colour talk.

---

3. The extensions of colour concepts are at most only partly determined by human responses. Objects in the dark are also in the range of colour concepts. How is it canonically determined whether an object in the dark is or is not red? One answer is that we presuppose that the colours things look to normal observers in standard conditions supervene upon some perhaps disjunctive set of physical properties of the objects in question. If so, and if the object in the dark has whatever physical property it is that things which look red to normal observers in standard conditins supervene upon, then the object in the dark is red, and otherwise it is not red. Hence the responses of observers only partly determine the extension of the concept of being red, supervenience relations also play a part.

In the next section I shall develop three such arguments for utterances with "+", and show that they do *not* transpose to utterances with "red". However, in the following two sections I shall develop a further argument to show that the (assumed) response dependent assertibility conditions for utterances with "+" do not generate truth conditions for those utterances, and in the final section I shall show that this argument, unlike the others, *does* transpose to utterances with "red". This paper will thus present a challenge to response dependent accounts of the assertibility conditions of colour words. The threat arising from Kripke's work is that such accounts will deprive colour talk of truth conditions.

2. Three arguments which do not transpose from arithmetic utterances to utterances about colour

In this section we shall consider three arguments for the conclusion that the (assumed) response dependent assertibility conditions for utterances with "+" do not generate truth conditions for those utterances, and proceed to show that these arguments do not transpose to utterances with "red".

Our first argument attempts a reductio of the supposition that the assertibility conditions of utterances with "+" do generate associated truth conditions. What *would be* the relation between the assertibility conditions of arithmetic utterances and their associated truth conditions, *if* those assertibility conditions did indeed generate truth conditions? The passage from Kripke quoted above implies that the truth conditions of utterances containing the sign "+" are given by the following meaning rule:

($M^{"+"}$)   For any ordered triple of numbers <k,l,m>, <k,l,m> satisfies "x + y = z" if and only if (nearly) all the linguistic community would judge of <k,l,m> that they satisfy "x + y = z".

It is not plausible that this is the rule which the language users would be likely to be self-consciously following if their assertions employing "+" were challenged. If that were the rule the language users were self-consciously following, then when they wanted to answer the question "n + m = ?" they would explicitly ask themselves the *linguistic* question

What number i completes the triple <n,m,i> which satisfies "x + y = z"?

rather than asking the corresponding *arithmetic* question (assuming their meaning for "+")

What number i is equal to m + n?

More plausibly, when language users are considering whether to make an arithmetic utterance, they ask themselves an arithmetic question. So I think we should read Kripke as implying that, if *we were to suppose that assertibility conditions do generate truth conditions,* the linguistic rule ($M^{"+"}$) determines the truth conditions of their arithmetic utterances, because their responses to the arithmetic questions, when true, conform to that rule. The corresponding arithmetic rule which they might self-consciously take themselves to be following is:

(R^+)   For any numbers n and m, n + m is equal to the number that (nearly) all the linguistic community would judge to be n + m.

But to understand this arithmetic rule we must give the sign "+" in it the meaning determined by the linguistic rule ($M^{"+"}$). Only then is (R^+) an a priori truth, as it needs to be if it expresses a rule they might appeal to if challenged to justify their answer to some arithmetic question.

We are not supposing that people do follow (R^+), where we are to read "+" in (R^+) by ($M^{"+"}$). Rather, we are supposing that *if their assertions using "+" did have truth conditions,* they would be following such a rule, with "+" so understood. However, the reductio continues, in fact we treat (R^+) as an a posteriori contingent claim. We think the linguistic community might be prone to error and wrongly judge of some k,l,m that k + l = m. However unlikely in practice, a community wide arithmetic error is possible. (R^+), on the other hand, makes community wide arithmetic error impossible, since the community's verdict defines the 'sum'. Hence our understanding of "+", whatever that may amount to, does *not* conform to ($M^{"+"}$). Hence our utterances with "+" have only assertion conditions and not truth conditions.[4]

---

4. It is not essential to this argument that the rule they would be following defines the sum of n and m to be the number that nearly all the linguistic community would judge to be the sum of n and m. Instead, their rule could be

   (R^{*+})   For any numbers n and m, n + m is the number that nearly all the linguistic community would reach if they counted a set of n objects and then continued by counting a non-overlapping set on m objects, without starting again from one.

Whatever the merit in the case of "+" of this argument developed from Kripke, does the argument transpose from the case of "+" to the case of the colour-word "red"? We need to decide what is the response, and what the community who by giving this response determine the assertibility conditions of colour talk. Here I'll just gesture quickly at what we need to borrow from Crispin Wright's account of the response dependent nature of colours.[5] The question of whether a certain object x is or is not red is determined, if it is seen in optimal conditions by normal observers, by whether it looks red to them or not. If something *looks* red to someone competent in the application of the concept of redness, then they will judge that

> if the conditions are optimal and I am a normal observer, then it *is* red.

Let this judgement be the response which at least partially determines the assertibility of sentences employing the word "red".

What is it for conditions to be optimal and the observer normal? We cannot define optimal conditions and normal observers as

> whatever conditions and kind of observer x are sufficient to guarantee that y is red if and only if x judges that [y is red if I am normal and conditions are optimal].

For such a definition of optimal conditions and normal observers presupposes that whether or not y falls under the concept of redness has been otherwise determined. Rather, to use a phrase of Crispin Wright, whose ideas I have been following, the specification of optimal conditions and normal observers needs to be "substantial":

And the related meaning-rule would be

(M^{*+}) For any ordered triple of numbers <k,l,m>, <k.l.m> satisfies "x + y = z" if and only if (nearly) all the linguistic community, if they were to count a set of k objects and then continue by counting a non-overlapping set of l objects, without starting again from one, would reach m on completion.

So long as n + m is defined by a communal response—whether a communal judgement as to the sum, or a communal judgement as to the outcome of a practical operation—we must understand "+" according to a meaning rule (M^{+}) or (M^{*+}). Otherwise we get the modality wrong: a supposedly a priori rule (R^{+}) or (R^{*+}) will be, by our lights, a contingent statement.

5. Mainly in Wright (1992) Appendix to Chapter 3, and Wright (1988).

they must be specified in sufficient detail to incorporate a constructive account of the epistemology of the judgements in question, so that not merely does a subject's satisfaction of them ensure that the conditions under which she is operating have "whatever-it-takes" to bring it about that the judgement is true, but a concrete conception is conveyed of what it actually does take. (Wright 1992 p. 112.)

Let us suppose that such a substantial account of what it is for conditions to be optimal and observers normal has been provided.

Now we can transpose the argument to the case of the colour-word "red". *For the sake of an intended reductio, we take assertibility conditions of colour talk to have associated truth conditions.* The truth conditions of utterances containing the word "red" are (at least partly) given by the following meaning rule:

($M^{\text{"red"}}$) (x)(y)((x is an object in optimal viewing conditions & x is viewed by normal observer y & y is a member of the linguistic community) → (x satisfies "red" ↔ y would judge of x that [if the conditions are optimal and self is a normal observer, then x satisfies "red"])).

Again, we need not take Kripke to imply implausibly that the language users would be self-consciously employing this linguistic rule. Rather, the claim should be that in considering whether to issue an utterance containing "red" and concerning a given object x, a language user considers such colour questions as

Is x red?

But with "red" understood in terms of the linguistic meaning rule ($M^{\text{"red"}}$). Our provisional supposition is that the meaning rule determines the truth conditions of their utterances employing the word "red"—in that those utterances when true accord with the meaning rule and the condition of the object. If we now ask for a corresponding rule *using* "red" which they might self-consciously follow, we get

(R^{red}) (x)(y)((x is an object in optimal viewing conditions & x is viewed by normal observer y) → (x is red ↔ y would judge of x that [if the conditions are optimal and self is a normal observer, then x is red])).

But, unfortunately our intended reductio, by the lights of the response dependent theory of colour concepts outlined above, (R^{red}) is indeed a priori and necessary. (R^{red}) is an instance of what Wright calls a "provisoed biconditional" (Wright 1992, p. 119), which he uses to *define* a response dependent account, and which he claims, inter alia, is a priori and necessary (ibid. pp. 114–7).

We now have an important contrast between the case of the sign "+" and the case of "red". In the case of "+", if we suppose Kripke's assertibility conditions generate associated truth conditions, then a general statement (R^+) about numbers which we intuitively think contingent and a posteriori would have to be reclassified as necessary and a priori, by reading it in accord with the meaning rule ($M^{"+"}$). This gives us, by reductio, an argument to say that *our* assertibility conditions for *our* arithmetic utterances do *not* go along with truth conditions. Thus we have philosophical room to claim that our statements employing "+" have assertibility conditions but not truth conditions, given that Kripke is right about their assertibility conditions. On the other hand, in the case of the word "red", if we suppose Kripke's assertibility conditions for our utterances employing "red" generate truth conditions, no parallel counterintuitive result follows—supposing that we have already accepted a response dependent theory of colour concepts—since (R^{red}) is required to be necessary and a priori if the assertibility conditions have associated truth conditions, and (R^{red}) is indeed necessary and a priori according to an intuitively plausible response dependent theory of colour concepts. So we have as yet not found an argument to claim that our uses of colour words lack truth conditions.

However, there are other arguments to be considered which Kripke produces in the case of "+"—arguments for denying that assertion conditions generate truth conditions. We need to see whether any of these transfer from the case of the sign "+" and the meaning rule ($M^{"+"}$) to the case of the word "red" and the meaning rule ($M^{"red"}$). Kripke remarks of theories of the meaning of "+" based on rules like ($M^{"+"}$):

> Such a theory [of the meaning of "+"]… would be a social, or community-wide, version of the dispositional theory, and would be open at least some of the same criticisms as the original form. (Kripke 1982 p. 111)

The "original form" to which Kripke is referring was a proposal to identify the fact of *Jill* meaning something by "+" with her *individual disposition* to respond to questions of the form: "n + m = ?". ($M^{"+"}$) can be read as identifying the meaning of "+" with a *communal disposition* to converge on answers to questions of the form "n + m = ?". Kripke evidently thinks that at least some of the criticisms he made of the proposal to identify the meaning of "+" for Jill with her individual disposition carry over to the present proposal to identify the meaning of "+" with a community-wide disposition. Two questions arise: What criticisms is Kripke referring to? And: Do they transfer from the case of the sign "+" and the meaning rule ($M^{\text{"+"}}$) to the case of the word" red" and the meaning rule ($M^{\text{"red"}}$)?

Kripke made two criticisms and, we shall find, neither criticism obviously applies in the case of ($M^{\text{"red"}}$). The original form of the dispositional theory to which Kripke was referring was a proposal to identify Jill's meaning addition by "+" with the her being disposed to respond with the sum to questions of the form: "x + y = ?", where x and y are any numerals. Kripke's first criticism of this proposal was that Jill has in fact no such disposition. Actual dispositions to answer such questions cannot account for the infinitude of the addition function, cannot fix the value of "x + y" for numerals too long for Jill to take in, and hence too long for her to give any answer to. Jill cannot even raise a question of the form "x + y = ?" for numerals too long for her to take in. This objection need not detain us, since it does not transpose to the project of identifying the meaning of "red" by ($M^{\text{"red"}}$). When we consider how we refer to the individual objects in the range of the predicate "red"—the individual candidates for being red, or not being red, that is—there is nothing comparable to the system of ever-expanding numerals by which we canonically refer to each of the individual candidates in turn. Our ability to refer to particular candidates does not give out after some finite initial segment of canonical names.

However, there is a comparable problem. We cannot assume that the community is disposed to assign or withhold the word "red" of each relevant object.[6] Some objects in the range of the predicate "red" are too small, too far away, or too big for even the community to assess them for redness by sight, so the community is disposed neither to assert nor to deny the predicate "red" of such objects. Hence, it seems, we cannot take the communities disposition to apply or withhold "red" by sight to determine the extension of "red" for such objects. Yet intuitively some such objects may be red.

---

6. I am grateful to an anonymous referee of this paper for pointing this out.

To solve this problem, the response dependent account of colour we are considering only claims that the disposition of normal observers operating in optimal conditions *partially* determines the extension of the predicate "red". The account also claims that the colours of objects which are seen by normal observers in optimal conditions supervene upon some perhaps disjunctive set of unobservable physical properties of those objects. The account claims that objects in the dark, or too small, or too big, or too far away to be viewed by normal observers in optimal conditions are red just in case they have whatever physical properties they have which fall within the supervenience base of redness, where that base is in fact determined by normal observers viewing other objects in optimal conditions.

The problem was that, if we take the disposition of normal members of the community to determine the extension of the predicate "red", then seemingly the extension is undetermined for objects in the dark, or too small, or too large, or too far away. The solution to the problem starts from the observation that the dispositions of normal observers *directly* determine the extension of "red" only for objects viewed in optimal conditions by normal observers. Thus ($M^{\text{"red"}}$) will deliver a verdict only in such cases, because only such cases fulfil the antecedent of the conditional.

($M^{\text{"red"}}$) (x)(y)((x is an object in optimal viewing conditions & x is viewed by normal observer y & y is a member of the linguistic community) → (x satisfies "red" ↔ y would judge of x that [if the conditions are optimal and self is a normal observer, then x satisfies "red"])).

The response dependent account claims that the following is a material presupposition of our language game with "red":

($MP^{\text{"red"}}$) (x)(y)((x is an object in optimal viewing conditions & x is viewed by normal observer y & y is a member of the linguistic community) → (∃P)(x has P ↔ y would judge of x that [if the conditions are optimal and self is a normal observer, then x satisfies "red"])).

Provided that Nature honours this material presupposition, the full extension of the predicate "red" is then determined by the following meaning rule:

($*M^{\text{"red"}}$) (x)(∃P)((x satisfies "red" ↔ x has P) & (y)((x is an object in optimal viewing conditions & x is viewed by normal observer y & y is a member of the linguistic community) → (x has P ↔ y would judge of x that [if the conditions are optimal and self is a normal observer, then x satisfies "red"]))).

Thus the dispositions of normal observers *indirectly* determine the extension of the predicate "red" even for objects in the dark, or too small, or too big, or too far away.[7]

Kripke's second criticism of the original proposal—to identify Jill's meaning addition by "+" with the her being disposed to respond with the sum to questions of the form: "x + y = ?", where x and y are any numerals—was that Jill's dispositions to linguistic behavior are simply facts about her, so that identifying her meaning with her dispositions to behave cannot capture the essentially normative dimension of meaning. Jill's disposition to respond to questions of the form "x + y = ?" only determines how she *would* respond to such a question, not how she *ought* to if she intends to mean addition by "+".

---

7. The meaning rule ($M^{\text{"red"}}$) is a priori. But the full meaning rule ($*M^{\text{"red"}}$) is not, because it incorporates a substantial presupposition—viz., that there is such an unobservable subvenient property P. We are used to meaning rules incorporating substantial presuppositions, and hence not being a priori. For example, it is plausible that the meaning rule for "water" takes the set of observable properties which 'fix the reference' of the word "water", and then uses them together with a substantial empirical presupposition as follows: x satisfies "water" ↔ x is of whatever natural kind is in fact dominantly causally responsible for those properties in the majority of samples which have those observable properties. This meaning rule incorporates the a posteriori presupposition that the majority of the samples so described are indeed of a single natural kind.

I have taken the property P to be an unobservable physical property (more likely an open disjunction of such properties) upon which redness itself supervenes. Another response dependent account takes the unobservable physical property P to be the property of redness. The visual experiences of normal observers in optimal conditions *fix the reference* of the predicate "red", but do not present the actual property of redness to the viewer, which is in fact the physical property P (Pettit 1991). Another view would also identify P as the property of redness, but would hold that visual perception presents that very property to the viewer (Campbell 1993). However, it is doubtful whether this last view is a response dependent account, since it is doubtful whether, on this view, the provisoed biconditional (R^{red}) is a priori.

However, this objection does not transpose to the project of equipping *communal* assertibility conditions with truth conditions, either for "+" or for "red". For the meaning rule ($M^{"+"}$) does, on Kripke's own account, generate normative constraints upon individual users of "+". Although Kripke enjoins us to look and see

> under what circumstances attributions of meaning are made and what roles these play in our lives

what we see when we look is that the practice of assertion is constrained by *norms*. We note

> what circumstances actually *license* such assertions and what role this *license* actually plays (Ibid. p. 86/7, my emphases.)

Despite Kripke's emphasis on the actual features of the practice, the feature in question is a *license* to assert, a normative notion. An individual member of the language community is licensed to make an assertion employing "+", or employing the word "red", when that assertion is, or would be, endorsed by the community, or a relevant portion of the community. So, if the meaning and truth conditions of utterances employing "+" or "red" are determined by community-wide dispositions, then there is room for a distinction between the uses Jill *does* make of "+" or "red", and the uses she *ought* to make of "+" or "red". An individual's usage is subject to the normative constraint that it ought to coincide with what the community would judge.[8]

In the case of the word "red", therefore, there is so far no objection to allying assertibility conditions with truth conditions, and thereby turning the so-called sceptical solution to the problem of rule-following into a straight solution. However, in the next two sections I shall develop a further argument to show that the (assumed) assertibility conditions for utterances with "+" do not generate truth conditions, and in the final section I shall show that this last argument does transpose to talk employing "red".

---

8. It remains an open question whether these normative constraints on utterances are of the right kind to sustain the claim that the utterances have meaning and truth values. Indeed, the sceptical argument, to be developed in what follows, claims that they are not.

3. The Minimal Requirements for Truth

Kripke's assertibility conditions are intended not to go along with truth conditions. But as yet we have not found a reason in Kripke to deny that colour talk is governed by a response-dependent meaning rule which sustains truth conditions. To progress, I propose to borrow from Crispin Wright's discussion of the relation which *should* obtain between assertibility conditions and truth conditions, *if* a discourse is to have both.[9] I propose to develop a necessary condition which assertibility conditions must meet if the discourse in question is to have both assertibility conditions and truth conditions. Armed with that necessary condition, we shall then return to the discussion of scepticism about truth conditions.

Consider a language community, perhaps our own, which employs a vocabulary of colour words. Suppose that, like us, they also employ a predicate "is true". What does it take for that predicate to mean truth? Wright argues that there are a number of necessary conditions to be satisfied whose joint satisfaction is sufficient. We will consider three.

Firstly, instances of the following schema, called the equivalence schema, need to be trivially a priori in the language of the community:

It is true that P iff P.

This ensures that truth conditions coincide in positive normative force with assertibility conditions. For any circumstances which warrant the assertion that P will—moving from right to left across the platitude—warrant the assertion that P is true. And any circumstances which warrant the assertion that P is true will—moving from left to right across the platitude—warrant the assertion that P. Thus any circumstances which warrant the assertion that it is true that P, warrant the assertion that P, and vice versa. But equally trivially and a priori, any circumstances which warrant the assertion that P will also warrant the assertion that it is assertible that P. And vice versa, any circumstances which warrant the assertion that it is assertible that P will warrant the assertion that P. Hence, by transitivity of the biconditionals, any circumstances which warrant the assertion that it is assertible that P also warrant the assertion that it is true that P, and vice versa. Thus the predicates "is assertible" and "is true" in the language of the community coincide in positive normative force—to have reason to apply one to P is to have reason to apply the other.

---

9. In Wright (1992), Chapters 1 and 2.

Secondly, instances of the following schema also need to be trivially a priori in the language of the community

It is not true that P iff it is true that not-P

which in turn implies that instances of the following schema are trivially a priori

If it is not true that P, then it is true that not-P.

This last ensures that assertion conditions and truth conditions, although coincident in normative force, may nonetheless differ in extension. Our practice with colour words admits what Wright calls 'neutral states of information'. If Jill sees the shadow of a rose in the dark, her state of information does not warrant the assertion that the rose is red, and does not warrant the assertion that the rose is not red. But it does not follow that it is not true that the rose is red, since that would imply, by the above a priori platitude and the equivalence schema, that the rose is not red, and the latter we have agreed is also not assertible by Jill. So the predicate "is true" and the predicate "is warrantedly assertible" used relative to Jill's given state of information, may differ in extension. Thus the truth conditions of "The rose is red" and its assertibility conditions may differ, since it may be true for all she knows, but it is not assertible by her.[10]

The first two a priori platitudes forge a link but also force a difference between assertibility conditions and truth conditions.[11] The final a priori platitude places a condition upon assertibility conditions—if they are to support a notion of related truth conditions. The third a priori platitude is:

True statements correspond to the facts.

---

10. The rose example considers a state of information which could easily be enlarged to determine whether the rose is red or not - Jill could simply open the curtains. But neutral states of information can also be relatively robust. If Jill is an expert on chameleons and she sees the shadow of a chameleon darting around in the dark, her state of information does not warrant her asserting that the chameleon is red, and does not warrant her asserting that the chameleon is not red. She knows that come daylight it will take on the colour of whatever background is then current, but she doesn't think it is changing colour now to match the colour of whatever leaf or flower it is currently on in the dark - what would be the evolutionary point of that?
11. For a contrary view see Neil Tennant (1995), and for a reply see Edwards (1997).

We already know that a warrant to assert that P is, by the first platitude, a warrant to assert that it is true that P. And hence, by the above platitude, a warrant to assert that an assertion that P corresponds to the facts. But if an assertion that P corresponds to the facts, then further investigations as to whether it is a fact that P, insofar as those investigations are successful, will encounter the same fact. So we can claim:

(1) A warrant to assert that P is a warrant to assert that any further investigations as to whether P whose results accord with the fact of the matter concerning P, will also warrant the assertion that P.

I have said that the results *accord* with the fact and not that they *correspond* to the fact of the matter concerning P. To see why, suppose that the results take the form of certain meter readings, but that P is a proposition about the course of some microevents. Obviously neither the meter readings nor the propositions that the meters so read *correspond* to the fact that P, if it is a fact that P, in the way that the proposition that P corresponds to the fact that P. It is this last relation which the correspondence platitude refers to, so I need another relation, which I am calling 'accord', between the results of the investigation and the fact under investigation. However, I decree by fiat that the relation of accord is a suitably strong relation: if the results *accord* with the fact that P, then they *warrant* the assertion that P.[12]

We now have a constraint upon assertibility conditions, if the assertions in question are also to have truth conditions. The conditions which warrant an assertion that P place a constraint upon the outcome of further investigations as to whether or not P. Satisfying the assertibility conditions warrants the claim that the outcome of further investigations which accord with the

---

12. (1) is acceptable to a realist. Suppose that we have a warrant to assert that P. A realist may suppose that Nature will not afford us a second glimpse of reality, no further opportunity to confirm whether or not P. But a realist can agree that *if* Nature *does* afford us another glimpse which accords with the facts, then our original warrant to assert that P warrants the prediction that the second glimpse will also warrant P.

(1) is also consistent with the claim that a current warrant to assert that P is defeasible and may be overturned on further investigation by a new warrant which accords with the fact that not-P. For the original warrant warranted the claim that investigations-whose-results-accord-with-the-fact-would-warrant-P, and if the first warrant is defeasible, then that only implies that the second warrant is likewise defeasible—whatever defeats the first defeats the second.

fact of the matter in question will also warrant the assertion that P. Thus, conditions which warrant the assertion that P warrant a prediction about the outcome of further investigations which accord with the fact as to whether or not P, viz., that the outcome will also warrant the assertion that P. All this, of course, assuming that the assertion that P has truth conditions.

4. Kripke's Sceptical Solution and Arithmetic Utterances Again

Kripke claims that utterances have assertibility conditions but not truth conditions. We have seen that a necessary condition of a discourse having truth conditions as well as assertibility conditions is that the circumstances which satisfy the assertibility conditions should warrant a prediction about certain other states of information and the assertions which they would warrant. Kripke considers someone who has hitherto been orthodox in her arithmetic judgements, but who surprisingly proceeds to assert the utterance "68 + 57 = 5". The surprise is that she takes the circumstances which have warranted her various previous arithmetic judgements to commit her to asserting this particular utterance, whereas the rest of us would take the circumstances which warranted those former arithmetic utterances to commit us to denying this particular utterance. The upshot of Kripke's discussion, I think, is that nothing about the circumstances which warranted the earlier arithmetic utterances commit either her or us to endorsing or denying a new arithmetic utterance. In general, Kripke claims, the circumstances which warrant one set of arithmetic judgements have no implications for the assertibility of other arithmetic judgements. Our task in this section is to find an argument to support this claim.

There are in general two ways in which the stock of arithmetic judgements can be added to. It can be added to by passing judgement on new sums, as in Kripke's own discussion, or the corpus of judgements can be added to by the reappraisal of old sums. In both types of case, I think, Kripke's claim would be that there was nothing about us the judges, nor about our applications of the assertibility conditions to license the former judgements, which binds in any way our applications of the assertibility conditions to license the later judgements. The canonical assertibility conditions for any judgement are, according to Kripke's sceptical solution, whatever is or would be the consensus of accumulated judgements on the question to date. That is the highest authority to which a judgement is answerable. Kripke's claim is that there is nothing in that consensus which commits future judgements one way or another—so a community who proceeded to endorse "68 + 57 = 5" instead of "68 + 57 = 125" would be perfectly in order. Similarly, a community who first agree "68 + 57 = 125" but, when they come to reconsider the matter, their enlarged corpus of judgements converges on "68 + 57 = 5" instead would also be perfectly in order. The consensus they had achieved earlier in no way committed the consensus achieved in the enlarged corpus of judgements one way or the other.

Suppose our present consensus favours "68 + 57 = 125", it might seem that on standard inductive grounds we do have a warrant to assert that any future enlarged consensus will continue to favour "68 + 57 = 125". Of course, it still might turn out in fact that an enlarged consensus favours "68 + 57 = 5" instead. But such is the risk of any prediction based upon an inductive warrant. Just so we may have current evidence in favour of a scientific theory T, and since that theory predicts that the outcome of some experiment will be P, we currently have an inductive warrant to predict that the outcome will be P. Despite our warrant the outcome might actually turn out to be not-P, and the theory T to be false. But that does not detract from the fact that before the outcome of the experiment was known we did have a warrant to assert T and to predict that the outcome would be P. The outcome not-P only shows that inductive warrants are defeasible. Similarly, it might seem, our present consensus gives us an inductive but defeasible warrant to predict that any future enlargement of the corpus of judgements will continue to favour "68 + 57 = 125", contrary to Kripke's claim.

Inductive inference is a large and disputatious philosophical field in itself. All I propose to do here is dogmatically sketch a position regarding the validity of inductive inferences which is (i) philosophically defensible and (ii) will serve Kripke's purpose.[13]

---

13. I am developing Kripke's position in a way that essentially relies upon a view of inductive inference. In doing this I am going beyond Kripke's text. At various places Kripke notes a formal analogy between his own discussion and Nelson Goodman's New Riddle of Induction, between his own 'bent' concept of quus and Goodman's similarly 'bent' concept of grue. But when doing so Kripke draws a distinction between his scepticism about meaning and Goodman's scepticism about induction. I think the topic of induction is more germane to Kripke's scepticism about meaning and truth conditions than he recognises in his text.

Suppose all the ravens we have observed so far have turned out to be black. Does that cumulative observation to date warrant the prediction that all ravens are black? No doubt the observation provides *some* evidence for the prediction, but the question is whether the evidence *warrants* the prediction that all ravens are black? I claim that whether or not it does depends upon our relevant background theory. If for example, we held that the coloration of a bird's feathers is strongly genetically determined, so that it is invariant under changes of diet or climate in the range of the bird, and 'centrally' genetically determined—i.e. colour is one of the traits which distinguishes one bird species from another—then we would take the prediction to be warranted by the observations so far. On the other hand, if our theoretical assumptions were that the colour of bird's feathers is sensitive to diet and climate, or like the colour of human hair only peripherally genetically determined, then we would need more information about the sample—Did the observations include ravens enjoying other climes and diets? Were the observations scattered over the various habitats of the species?—before we took the observation to warrant the prediction. Furthermore, assuming the colour of a bird's feathers is only peripherally genetically determined, even if these conditions are known to be met, the resulting prediction would be relatively 'local' in its scope. We would not assume that the ravens of very long ago or any ravens in the far future were or will be black—since their diet and climatic range may have been or may become very different from those of present ravens.[14]

Obviously there is much more to be said, but the general point I wish to make is that although the observation of a uniformity is always *some* evidence for its inductive projection to the population as a whole, the *strength* of that evidence, whether or not it amounts to a warrant to judge that the uniformity holds of the whole population, and whether the inductive conclusion applies to a population as a whole, or to some relatively local subset of the population and what the parameters defining that subset should be, is

---

14. The discovery of black swans in Australia showed that the colour of swans was only peripherally and not centrally genetically determined. The gene pool of antipodean swans had become isolated from the rest of the stock, so that the black variation was geographically confined. We remain confident of the local induction that swans in the northern hemisphere are white.

highly sensitive to changes of background theoretical knowledge. Further, I claim the following is an a priori truism about induction:

(TI)   Without the assumption of any background theory at all, an observed uniformity does *not* give a warrant to project that uniformity upon the population as a whole.

Interpreting the term "theory" widely as covering any background knowledge, (TI) merely reflects that without a background theory we have no notion of what the relevant parameters are for deciding whether the observed sample is a fair sample, and no notion of whether we should draw a conclusion about a local population or about all the population. Without answers to these questions we are not warranted in drawing an inductive conclusion.

(TI) is all that Kripke needs. So far our community has as a matter of fact endorsed "68 + 57 = 125". We want to know whether this gives us a warrant to predict that any future enlargement of the pool of judges will preserve this consensus, and not converge on, say, "68 + 57 = 5" instead? Kripke's view is that we have no explanation of our current consensus. If there is an explanation of our current consensus it is an unknown causal explanation, and if there is an explanation of a later surprising consensus that too will be an unknown causal explanation. Since it is the consensus which licenses our present assertion, nothing about our current license to assert "68 + 57 = 125" implies anything about later assertibility, licensed by an enlarged corpus of judgements. The most we can say as a matter of simple observation is that, in the case of our own arithmetic community, such consensuses have *hitherto* proved *locally* stable upon enlargement of the licensing corpus of judgements. So there is *evidence* that, if we enlarge the corpus of judgements by reconsidering the same arithmetic question tomorrow, the enlarged corpus of judgements will continue to converge by endorsing "68 + 57 = 125". But, by (TI), that evidence does not amount to a *warrant* to project our consensus to *all* enlargements of the pool of judges, since we have no background theory to explain why our consensus was reached.

Let us contrast the traditional folk explanation of our current consensus, an explanation which Kripke is concerned to reject. Traditionally we suppose that there is a rational explanation of our consensus—roughly, that enough of us grasp and assign the same meaning to "+" and access the same mathematical facts. Furthermore, that meaning and those facts will require of any other judges that they too endorse "68 + 57 = 125" and reject "68 + 57 = 5", on pain of their judgements being out of accord with that meaning or those facts. A warrant to judge that "68 + 57 = 125" is itself a warrant to judge that any enlarged corpus of judges who also assign the same meaning and access the same facts will endorse the judgement.

In our discussion above of the minimal requirements for truth, we arrived at a necessary condition for an utterance to be apt for truth or falsity, viz. that the following be a priori:

(1) A warrant to assert that P is a warrant to assert that any further investigations as to whether P whose results accord with the fact of the matter concerning P, will also warrant the assertion that P.

Applied to the case in hand, and taking a warrant to assert that P to be a warrant to assert "P", this necessary condition becomes: The following is a priori:

(2) A warrant to assert "68 + 57 = 125" is a warrant to assert that any further investigations as to whether "68 + 57 = 125" is assertible whose results accord with the fact of the matter concerning 68 + 57 = 125, will also warrant the assertion of "68 + 57 = 125".

Mathematical truths, if there are such, do not change with time, or so we intuitively think. Further investigations even though later are therefore reinvestigations of the same fact of the matter, if there be a fact of the matter. The Sceptical Solution gives consensus of judgement as *the* canonical assertibility condition for a mathematical utterance. I interpret this as equivalent to the claim that a mathematical assertion backed by such a consensus is *guaranteed* to accord with the mathematical fact of the matter, assuming there is a mathematical fact of the matter. For if there is a mathematical fact of the matter for the assertion to correspond or fail to correspond to, how could certain conditions canonically warrant the assertion if they did not suitably 'connect' with this fact? So results of investigations which accord with the fact of the matter will be results which match the consensus current at the time. We can modify (2) to:

(3) A warrant to assert "68 + 57 = 125" is a warrant to assert that any further investigations as to whether "68 + 57 = 125" is assertible whose results satisfy the canonical conditions for asserting or denying "68 +

57 = 125", will also warrant the assertion of "68 + 57 = 125".

If arithmetic utterances have truth conditions, assuming their canonical assertibility conditions are as given in the Sceptical Solution, then (3) is a priori.

However, we have seen that, according to the Sceptical Solution, an earlier consensus which warrants the assertion "68 + 57 = 125" is not itself a warrant to assert that a later enlarged consensus will also warrant "68 + 57 = 125". At best the earlier consensus provides evidence short of a warrant for the claim that the judgement will continue to be the consensus of the indefinitely enlarging corpus of judgements. We must recall that, according to the Sceptical Solution, there is no rational explanation of the earlier consensus. From the point of view of reasons for judgement the consensus is just a brute fact, having an unknown causal explanation. So there is nothing about that earlier consensus which itself warrants a prediction as to any future consensus. But consensus is the condition which warrants the assertion or denial of "68 + 57 = 125", so the earlier warrant to assert "68 + 57 = 125" is not a warrant to assert that further investigations as to whether "68 + 57 = 125" whose results satisfy the canonical conditions for asserting or denying "68 + 57 = 125", will also warrant the assertion that "68 + 57 = 125". Thus (3) fails, and arithmetic utterances, given the assertibility conditions provided by the Sceptical Solution, do not meet the minimal requirements to be apt for truth or falsity. They do not have truth conditions.

We now have an argument running from the premise:

Arithmetic utterances have response-dependent assertibility conditions,

to the conclusion:

Arithmetic utterances do not have truth conditions.

The argument is that arithmetic utterances fail a necessary condition for having truth conditions—viz., (1) above, in the specific form of (3). As remarked in the introduction above, it is not intuitively plausible that arithmetic utterances do have response-dependent assertibility conditions, so the argument might be valid and yet the conclusion false. However, plausibly, colour talk does have response dependent assertibility conditions, so if the argument transposes from arithmetic talk to colour talk, the conclusion that colour talk lacks truth conditions will be plausible.

5. Kripke's Sceptical Solution and Colour Talk

Does the argument of the last section transpose to colour talk? That is to say: Does colour talk satisfy (1)?

(1) A warrant to assert that P is a warrant to assert that any further investigations as to whether P whose results accord with the fact of the matter concerning P, will also warrant the assertion that P.

When we turn from the generality of (1) to assertions employing colour words, we can be more specific. Having accepted a response dependent theory of colour concepts, we have an a priori guarantee that the results of investigations as to colour carried out by normal observers in optimal conditions will accord with the colour facts.[15] Hence, if "P" ascribes a colour to an object:

(4) A warrant to assert "P" is a warrant to assert that further investigations by normal observers in optimal conditions as to whether "P" is assertible would produce results which warrant the assertion of "P".

We need to be clear that any reinvestigations as to whether, say "This rose is red" is assertible are investigations of the same original fact of the matter. Obviously, if investigations by normal observers in optimal conditions warrant the assertion of "This rose is red", that is not a warrant to assert that a further investigation of its colour tomorrow will also warrant "This rose is red", for it may change colour between now and tomorrow. Colour facts are not timeless. So (4) requires that any further investigations are of the same fact as the original investigation—any demonstratives or other indexical elements in "P", like tense, must take the same values in the new investigation as they did in the original investigation.[16]

---

15. This result does not generalise to all predicates for which there are optimal conditions of investigation and normal observers. Some optimal test procedures may be probabilistic, in which case a warrant to assert that P is a warrant to assert that further optimal tests by normal observers are *unlikely* to produce results which fail to warrant the assertion that P. Even optimal test procedures may give misleading results to even normal observers when the test procedures are probabilistic—see Edwards (1996).
16. It is plausible that aesthetic and moral judgements are response dependent, and are also timeless.

Because objects may change colour through time, there are practical difficulties in enlarging the corpus of judgements as to whether the rose is red. We need to suppose that the enlarged corpus of judgements concerns the colour of the rose at the same time. Let us suppose that one team of normal observers has observed the rose in optimal conditions and declared it to be red at time t. Thus they have canonical conditions warranting the assertion of "The rose is red". Suppose that the rose was also observed in optimal conditions by a second team of normal observers, but without either team knowing of the other's existence at the time. The second team recorded their communal verdict as to the colour of the rose at time t separately and placed it in a sealed envelope. The a priori assertion of (4) is a necessary condition for colour talk having truth conditions as well as assertibility conditions. So the issue of whether colour talk has truth conditions turns on whether the warrant to assert that the rose is red provided by the first team of observers is itself a warrant to claim that on opening the envelope they will find that the second team's verdict too was that the rose is red?

Kripke should claim that it is not. The first consensus in judgements provides evidence for, but fails to provide a warrant for predicting the outcome of any enlarged consensus. The reason for the failure is as in the arithmetic case. If there is an explanation of the first team's consensus it is an unknown causal explanation. So, by (TI), no predictions are warranted about the outcome of enlarging the corpus of judges. We do not know, lacking a background theory, what constraints there may be, if any, on projecting a current consensus. But to satisfy (4) we would need a *warrant* to judge that the consensus is stable under *all* enlargements of the corpus of judges as to whether or not the rose is red. This we do not have, and hence (4) is not satisfied and colour talk lacks truth conditions.

Recall that we cannot appeal to the traditional rational explanation of the first team's consensus—that they had achieved their consensus for the reason that enough of them grasped and assigned the same meaning to "red" and had access to the relevant facts about the rose. We cannot use these alleged facts about how the first team achieved their consensus to justify a prediction that the second team will endorse that consensus. We cannot argue that, assuming the second team assign the same meaning to the word "red" as the first, then that meaning and the state of the rose together require of the second team that they too endorse "The rose is red", on pain of their judgements being out of accord with what that meaning requires in the case of this rose. This is the picture Kripke wants to reject.

We can focus the discussion of whether colour talk has truth conditions as well as assertibility conditions upon the status of ($M^{\text{"red"}}$)—which, in a response dependent account of colour, partially detemines the extension of the predicate "red".

($M^{\text{"red"}}$) (x)(y)((x is an object in optimal viewing conditions & x is viewed by normal observer y & y is a member of the linguistic community) → (x satisfies "red" ↔ y would judge of x that [if the conditions are optimal and self is a normal observer, then x satisfies "red"])).

It is definitive of a response dependent account that ($M^{\text{"red"}}$) is a priori. When we look at our practice of colour talk, we find an a priori assumption built into the practice: viz., that any consensus of normal observers viewing in optimal conditions is stable under enlargement of the corpus of such viewers. Thus we take the following to be assertible a priori:

(5)   (x)(y)(z) ((x is a normal observer & x views z in optimal conditions & y is a normal observer & y views z in optimal conditions & x and y are members of the linguistic community) → (x would judge of z that [if the conditions are optimal and self is a normal observer, then z satisfies "red"] ↔ y would judge of z that [if the conditions are optimal and self is a normal observer, then z satisfies "red"])).

(5) is a consequence of ($M^{\text{"red"}}$). (5) will imply, a priori if ($M^{\text{"red"}}$) is itself a priori, that the enlarged consensus provided by the second team will agree with the consensus of the first team. So if ($M^{\text{"red"}}$) is a priori, (4) will be satisfied, and colour talk will have truth conditions.

Kripke presents a response theorist with a dilemma concerning the status of ($M^{\text{"red"}}$). Either the users of "red" themselves have a background theory with which to explain why normal observers in optimal conditions agree in their judgements with "red" or they do not.[17] On the one hand, suppose

---

17. We should remember that a response dependent account gives 'substantial' accounts of what it is to be a normal observer, and of what it is to be optimal conditions. The specification of normal observers and optimal conditions does not imply that if both teams are of normal observers observing in optimal conditions, then their judgements will agree.

they do have such a theory, call it (T). The challenge to a response theory is to show that the players can hold this theory and still hold ($M^{\text{"red"}}$) *a priori*. Even if the responses of normal observers in optimal conditions do in fact concur, it is plausible that (T) will make conceivable to them conditions under which consensus would fail—indeed, it is difficult to see how (T) could explain the de facto consensus if it did not do this. But now ($M^{\text{"red"}}$) is no longer a priori, it is conditional upon the a posteriori theory (T). The central tenet of a response dependent account is that some judgemental response, or consensus of judgemental responses, is epistemically privileged—privileged in that this response or these responses partially determine the extension of the predicate "red". There is no ulterior *reason* that the judges can produce which *justify* their judgements employing "red". On a response dependent account there is no logical room to question a consensus achieved by normal observers in optimal conditions. But (T) provides the logical room to question that consensus, ($M^{\text{"red"}}$) is no longer a priori.

On the other hand, suppose the users of "red" do not themselves have any background theory with which to explain why normal observers in optimal conditions agree in their judgements with "red". Any explanation of stability of their judgements to date is unknown and causal. The most they should say is that, as a simple observation in the case of their own community, such consensuses have hitherto been stable upon enlargement of the licensing corpus of judgements. So if the first team converge on endorsing "The rose is red", then they have *evidence* that, when they enlarge the corpus of judgements by opening the envelope, the enlarged corpus of judgements will continue converge by endorsing "The rose is red". But this evidence does not amount to a *warrant* to predict stability of judgement. Without a warrant to project the consensus, they are not entitled to assert (5), nor therefore ($M^{\text{"red"}}$) a priori. Either way, then, a response dependent account collapses. A response dependent account of assertibility conditions cannot, it seems, sustain truth conditions. This is the challenge as I see it arising from Kripke's Sceptical Solution.[18]

---

18. I would like to thank Helen Beebee, Bob Hale, Scott Meikle, Pat Shaw, John Skorupski, Crispin Wright and Nick Zangwill for helpful comments upon an earlier draft of this paper.

Department of Philosophy,
University of Glasgow,
Glasgow G12 8QQ,
U.K.
J.Edwards@Philosophy.arts.gla.ac.uk

References

Campbell, J. 1993 "A Simple View of Colour", in Haldane J. and Wright C., eds., *Reality, Representation and Projection* Oxford: Oxford University Press, 257-268.

Edwards, J., 1996 "Anti-Realist Truth and Concepts of Superassertibility", *Synthese*, 109, pp. 103–120.

Edwards, J. 1997 "Is Tennant Selling Truth Short", *Analysis*, 57, pp. 152–158.

Kripke, S., 1982 *Wittgenstein on Rules and Private Language*, Oxford: Basil Blackwell.

Pettit, P., 1991 "Realism and Response-Dependence", *Mind* 100, 587-626.

Tennant, N., 1995 "On Negation, Truth and Warranted Assertibility", *Analysis*, 55, 98-104.

Wright, C., 1988 "Moral Values, Projection and Secondary Qualities", in *Proceedings of the Aristotelian Society*, Supplementary Volume 62, 1-26.

Wright, C., 1992 *Truth and Objectivity*, London: Harvard University Press.

ALEXANDER MILLER
Rule-Following, Response-Dependence, and McDowell's Debate with Anti-Realism

1.

The *objectivity of meaning* has been characterised by Crispin Wright as the claim that "we can, by appropriately rigorous explanations and sufficiently distinctive paradigms, lay down so specific a content for a statement that its truth-value is settled quite independently of the result of any investigations which we may carry out to settle it; and any correspondence between the truth-value and our findings about it, if we bother to investigate, is utterly contingent on our capacity to keep track of our antecedent semantic obligations".[1] Elsewhere, Wright has characterised belief in the objectivity of meaning as the belief that "there is in our understanding of a concept a rigid, advance determination of what is to count as its correct application".[2] And elsewhere as the notion that "the meaning of a statement is a real constraint, to which we are bound, as it were, by contract, and to which verdicts about its truth-value may objectively conform, or fail to conform, quite independently of our considered opinion on the matter".[3] Wright equates belief in the objectivity of meaning with *platonism* about meaning. According to Wright, the later Wittgenstein's rule-following considerations contain the resources for the destruction of such platonism, and

1. Wright (1986a), p. 273
2. Wright (1980), p. 21.
3. Wright (1986b), p. 5.

hence also for the destruction of the view that meanings are, in the relevant sense, objective. John McDowell, on the other hand, sees the objectivity of meaning, thus defined, not as a component of an objectionable philosophical conception of meaning, but rather as an essential facet of the everyday notion of meaning: "the idea of ratification independence is itself just part of the idea of meaning's normative reach".[4] So McDowell thinks that the objectivity of meaning can be discarded only on pain of discarding our intuitive notion of meaning and its normative reach. But McDowell also describes himself as rejecting platonism about meaning. So he cannot identify platonism about meaning (which he wishes to reject) with the objectivity of meaning (which he wishes to retain):

> Understanding is a grasp of patterns that extend to new cases independently of our ratification, as required for meaning to be other than an illusion (and - not incidentally - for the intuitive notion of objectivity to have a use); but the constraints imposed by our concepts do not have the platonistic autonomy with which they are credited in the picture of the super-rigid machinery.[5]

> It is wrong to suppose that platonism is implicit in the very idea that meaning and intention contain within themselves a determination of what counts as accord with them.[6]

But this is puzzling. What can the "platonistic autonomy" alluded to in Wittgenstein's picture of the "super-rigid rail" consist in, if not the objectivity of meaning as characterised by Wright? How, in other words, can McDowell reject platonism without thereby also rejecting the objectivity of meaning?

In this paper I want to do nothing more than sketch, in very bare outline, a framework within which an answer to this question might be given. By sketching an alternative to Wright's anti-realist construal of response-dependence, I will suggest that there is a notion of platonism about meaning which is, plausibly, the proper target of the rule-following considerations, but whose rejection nevertheless leaves scope for the retention of the objectivity of meaning.

---

4. McDowell (1992), p. 149.
5. McDowell (1984), p. 353.
6. McDowell (1991), p. 168.

2.

In order to do this, I want to look at a conception of what is necessary for the possibility of our cognitively accessing the facts about a certain subject matter. I'll do this by focussing on the notion of a *conceptually structured property*. The intuitive idea is that there is an appropriately close connection between the system of interrelationships among the things which may possess the property and our *concept* of that property, in the sense that there is a close connection between that system of interrelationships and our judgements *that the property is or is not instantiated*. This sort of structure can be called conceptual, because making the judgement necessarily requires the exercise of the concept of the property in question. What sort of appropriately close connection do I have in mind here? I'll speak of a property as being conceptually structured when there is an *a priori* and *non-trivial* connection between the facts about its instantiation and at least some of our judgements to the effect that the property is instantiated.

How can we read off this feature of properties from facts about the correctness conditions of the predicates which denote them? Intuitively, we would expect the correctness condition for a predicate "P" to have the form "*P*" *applies to x if and only if Fx*. Say that the property denoted by "P" is *conceptually structured* when and only when there is an *a priori* and *non-trivial* biconditional *Fx if and only if Gx*, where "P" is embedded in Gx within the scope of a content-specifying that-clause.

What can we say about the epistemology of properties which are conceptually structured? Let P be such a property. Suppose Smith forms the judgement *that a is P*. Suppose that a is P. Then one way to represent the situation is as follows. Smith's judgement *tracks*, or provides Smith with *cognitive access* to, the fact of a's being P; and this fact *confers* truth or falsity upon that judgement. But this might seem problematic. The notion of tracking or access intuitively carries with it an implication of *independence*: the thing tracked or accessed has to be independent of the tracker or accesser. (This is why you cannot *follow* your own shadow, though you can perfectly well follow the shadow of someone else). So, applying this intuition to the present case, when the tracker or accesser is a judgement, the fact tracked or accessed has to be independent of human judgement. But this independence is precisely what seems to fail in the present case: the fact that is putatively tracked or accessed is structured by the very concept which is necessarily implicated in the judgement that is the putative tracker or accesser. So where the property P is conceptually structured we cannot think of our judgement that a is P as tracking or accessing a fact which confers truth upon it. Conceptually structured properties thus require an epistemology couched fundamentally in terms other than those of tracking and cognitive access.

If you took this story about the epistemology of conceptually structured properties seriously, then you would be an adherent of what I shall call the *Sublimated Conception of Tracking and Cognitive Access*. The Sublimated Conception can be summed up as follows: *we can think of our judgements about the instantiation of a property as capable in principle of tracking or cognitively accessing the facts about its instantiation only if the property in question is conceptually unstructured.*

Why have I called this conception the *Sublimated* Conception of cognitive access? The idea is as follows. In our pre-theoretic, pre-philosophical thinking, we have a perfectly healthy desire for a degree of independence between our judgements and the facts which those judgements are capable of tracking. When we do philosophy, this healthy desire becomes sublimated into an *unhealthy philosophical conception* of what this independence has to consist in. So just as Gustav Mahler's perfectly healthy respect for women becomes sublimated into an unhealthy syndrome known as the Virgin Mary complex, our own perfectly healthy desire for a measure of independence between the knower and what is known becomes sublimated into the idea that the properties which the judgements of the knower cognitively access have to be conceptually unstructured.

What I'll suggest is that the proper target of the rule-following considerations is the Sublimated Conception of cognitive access. Of course, rejecting one conception of what cognitive access must consist in is not to reject the notion of cognitive access *tout court*. What I'll suggest is that the rule-following considerations are consistent with an alternative conception of cognitive access - what, following McDowell, I'll term the Humanized Platonist conception of cognitive access.[7] This alternative notion of cognitive access allows us to think of ourselves as tracking or cognitively accessing the facts about the instantiation of conceptually *structured* properties. In developing this alter-

---

7. The term "humanized platonism" is taken from the original version of McDowell's (1994): in the published version, he has replaced this with "naturalized platonism", for reasons I cannot go into here.

native conception of cognitive access we bring the unhealthy Sublimated Conception to consciousness in order to exorcize it. Just as Mahler's psychoanalyst displays to him that in order to have a healthy respect for women he needn't think of them in the way he would think of the Virgin Mary, we will suggest that we can have a healthy measure of independence between our judgements and the properties which they cognitively access, without requiring that the properties in question be conceptually unstructured.

To recap. The Sublimated conception sets down a necessary condition on the legitimacy of talk of tracking and cognitive access with respect to a given property: it says that in order for us to have the right to think of ourselves as tracking or cognitively accessing the facts about its instantiation, the property in question must be conceptually unstructured. My contention is that the proper conclusion to draw from the rule-following considerations is that the Sublimated Conception, in its application to the case of meaning, is useless.

3.

To see this, I'll characterise the notion of a *semantic predicate*. Just think of a semantic predicate as a predicate which ascribes guidance by a particular correctness condition to a given speaker. If we let "P" be a predicate, and let C stand for some correctness condition, we can represent the claim that Jones has his practice with "P" normatively constrained or guided at time t by C as "P"tC(Jones). So in general, "'P'tC" applies to a speaker if and only if he has his practice with the predicate "P", at time t, normatively constrained or guided by the correctness condition C. By a *semantic predicate*, then, I just mean a predicate like "'P'tC".

I'll describe as a *Platonic Conception of Meaning*, any conception according to which, *in the sense of tracking or cognitive access defined by the Sublimated Conception*, we can with propriety speak of our judgements about the instantiations of semantic properties as, in favourable cases, *tracking* the facts about their instantiation, or as allowing us to *cognitively access* those facts. I'll now sketch an argument to the effect that the correct moral to draw from Saul Kripke's interpretation of Wittgenstein's "rule-following considerations" is that the Platonic Conception of meaning, *thus defined*, is a failure.[8]

---

8. See Kripke (1982).

4.

Kripke claims that we can recover from the rule-following considerations an argument for what he calls the *sceptical paradox*: the view that there is really no such thing as meaning, that the notion of meaning, as he puts it, "vanishes into thin air", or, as we might put it, that *semantic predicates do not have correctness conditions*. What I want to suggest is that we are forced to this *irrealist* conception of meaning only if we accept the Sublimated Conception of cognitive access: what Kripke's Wittgenstein's arguments show is that if you accept the Sublimated Conception you cannot give an account of the correctness conditions of semantic predicates which is consistent with the thought that we are capable, in principle, of tracking or cognitively accessing the facts about the instantiation of semantic properties.

What constraints does a biconditional such as "*'P'tC*" applies to speaker s *if and only if Fs* have to satisfy in order to count as a correctness condition? I suggest that there are four such constraints:

(1) *The A Priority Constraint.* The biconditional must be a priori true: its truth must be available a priori to a subject who understands the predicate in the manner specified by that correctness condition.

(2) *The Non-Triviality Constraint:* The extension-determining property F (which appears on the right-hand side of the biconditional) must be specifiable in such a way that the biconditional is not merely trivially true. In other words, F must not be specified simply as that property which has "whatever it takes" to ensure that "'P'tC" is applicable to the speaker.

(3) *The Extensionality Constraint:* Let C* be a correctness condition which is incompatible with C in the sense that it generates, in at least some possible cases, an incompatible verdict concerning the applicability of the predicate "P" itself. Then the fact that Fs must provide us with a warrant for thinking that the subject s has his practice with "P" normatively constrained or guided by C, which warrant is stronger than any warrant we have for thinking that his practice with "P" is normatively constrained or guided by C*.

(4) *The Normativity Constraint:* the fact that Fs has to be able to *justify* the subject s in, or provide him with a reason for, his practice with the

predicate "'P'tC"; the extension-determining property has to be such that it can *tell* s how he *ought* to use the predicate "'P'tC" in his ongoing linguistic practice.

Now recall that the Sublimated Conception tells us that we can only think of our judgements as tracking the facts about the instantiation of the property which "P" denotes if the extension-determining state of affairs Fx sustains no non-trivial but a priori relationship to states of affairs whose description involves the embedding of "P" within a content-specifying that-clause. So in order to earn the right to use the locutions of tracking and cognitive access in a given case, we have to find an extension-determining property which is such that all of the relevant constraints on a correctness condition are satisfied. The proper way to interpret Kripke's Wittgenstein's conclusion is as a claim to the effect that this cannot be done: for semantic predicates, we cannot find, even under conditions of idealised epistemic access, an extension-determining property F, tailored according to the specifications of the Sublimated Conception, which is such that all of the intuitive constraints on the notion of a correctness condition can be satisfied.

The argument to this conclusion basically proceeds by elimination: we look at each platonistically respectable property F, and then argue that at least one of the intuitive constraints on the notion of a correctness condition fails to be satisfied. I only have time here to illustrate how the argument operates, and for brevity I'll show how it operates in the case of a strawman, the first of the dispositional responses which Kripke considers in response to the sceptical paradox.

5.

Let C be a correctness condition for "+" such that for all z, z=x+y if and only if z is the arithmetical *sum* - the result of performing *addition* on - the numbers x and y. Then what we require, in order to answer the sceptic who questions whether the subject s really means addition, is for a property F which can play the role of an extension-determining property: which is such that the biconditional "'+'tC" *is applicable to s if and only if Fs* satisfies each of the intuitive constraints on the notion of a correctness condition.

How does the Kripkean argument eliminate the *simple dispositional response* to the sceptical challenge? According to this response "the referent ø of 'f' is that unique binary function ø such that I am disposed, if queried about 'f(m,n)', where 'm' and 'n' are numerals denoting particular numbers m and n, to reply 'p', where 'p' is a numeral denoting ø(m,n)".[9] The suggestion is thus that the correctness condition for "'+'tC" is given by (SD): *"'+'tC" is applicable to s if and only if s is disposed, if queried about 'm+n', where 'm' and 'n' are numerals denoting particular numbers m and n, to reply 'p', where 'p' is a numeral denoting the sum of m and n.*

This suggestion violates the extensionality constraint. Let C* be a correctness condition which is such that for all z, "x+y" denotes z if and only if either (a) z is the arithmetical sum of the numbers denoted by "x" and "y" and s is disposed to answer "z" in response to the appropriate arithmetical query, *or* (b) the numerals involved are so large that s would die before he had a chance to hear the arithmetical query out, in which case z=0. According to the correctness condition C*, then, for values of x and y that are appropriately large, s ought to answer "0" in response to the query "x+y=?", if he is to accord with his understanding of the plus sign. The crucial point is that the extension-determining property proffered by the simple dispositionalist is unable to discriminate between s having his practice with the plus sign guided by C and s having his practice with the plus sign guided by C*. In other words, modulo s's dispositions, the following is as acceptable as the correctness condition (SD) given above (SD*): *"'+'tC*" is applicable to s if and only if s is disposed, if queried about "m+n", where "m" and "n" are numerals denoting particular numbers m and n, to reply "p", where "p" is a numeral denoting the sum of m and n.* That is to say, this is precisely the disposition we would expect s to have if his practice with the plus sign was in fact governed by a correctness condition along the lines of C*. So, if we let F be the property ascribed to s on the right-hand sides of the biconditionals (SD) and (SD*) above, then there is no way of discriminating between *"'+'tC" is applicable to s if and only if Fs* and *"'+'tC*" is applicable to s if and only if Fs.* The extensionality constraint is thus violated, so *neither* biconditional can be viewed as providing a correctness condition for the respective semantic predicates involved: the simple dispositional property cannot be viewed as a genuine extension-determining property.

There is also a problem concerning the *normativity* constraint. The extension-determining property has to be such that it can tell the speaker how he *ought* to use the expression concerned in his ongoing linguistic practice. But

---

9. Kripke (1982), p.26.

the property suggested by the simple dispositionalist will not be adequate to this task. We will only be able to read off from the fact that a speaker instantiates the simple dispositional property how he is *in fact* disposed to apply that expression, which falls short of how he *ought* to use it. As Kripke puts it:

> Suppose I do mean addition by "+". What is the relation of this supposition to the question how I will respond to the problem "68+57"? The dispositionalist gives a *descriptive* account of this relation: if "+" meant addition, then I will answer "125". But this is not the proper account of the relation, which is *normative*, not descriptive. The point is *not* that, if I meant addition by "+", I *will* answer "125", but rather that, if I intend to accord with my past meaning of "+", I *should* answer "125". Computational error, finiteness of my capacity, and other disturbing factors may lead me not to be *disposed* to respond as I *should*, but if so, I have not acted in accordance with my intentions. The relation of meaning and intention to future action is *normative*, not *descriptive*.[10]

So it seems that the simple dispositionalist satisfies neither the extensionality nor normativity constraints.

It is important to be clear about the nature of the extension-determining property that is proposed by the dispositionalist. The dispositional property offered as an extension-determining property is *conceptually unstructured*. The property possessed by s is not that he is disposed, in the face of an appropriate query, to say or judge or believe *that* the numeral denoted by "p" is the sum of m and n; rather, it is to be disposed to write the inscription, or utter the appropriate sequence of noises, corresponding to "p", whenever faced with the appropriate query (i.e. with another written inscription or sequence of noises). The behavioural performances which manifest the speaker's possession of this disposition are specifiable without embedding the semantic predicate within a content-specifying that-clause. Thus specified, the simple dispositional property fits exactly the rubric laid down by the Platonic Conception of meaning.

I think it is plausible that the same holds true of the more sophisticated version of dispositionalism that Kripke's Wittgenstein considers and rejects. It attempts to specify an extension-determining property in line with the Sublimated Conception of cognitive access, but the price it pays is an inability to satisfy all of the intuitive constraints on correctness conditions for seman-

---

10. Kripke (1982), p.37.

tic predicates. I won't try to show that now.[11] Instead, I'll move on to look at Kripke's Wittgenstein's objections to non-reductionist accounts of meaning.

6.

Kripke asks "Why not argue that meaning addition by '+' denotes an irreducible experience, with its own special quale, known directly to each of us by introspection? (Headaches, tickles, and nausea are examples of inner states with such qualia)".[12] That is, why not construe meaning as a unique, irreducible experience, with its own distinctive qualitative phenomenology?

The emphasis placed by Kripke here on qualia and qualitative phenomenology, and the examples he chooses to illustrate the idea, suggest that he takes the relevant sort of irreducible experience to satisfy the demands of the Sublimated Conception: the thought is that the ascription of the experience of nausea doesn't require recourse to states of affairs whose description involves embedding the predicate "nauseating" within the scope of a content-specifying that-clause. Feeling nausea doesn't require the exercise of the conceptual capacity corresponding to the concept *nausea*.

Kripke criticises this answer on two counts. First, the normativity constraint again goes unsatisfied. He asks "How on earth would this [irreducible experience] help me figure out whether I ought to answer '125' or '5' when asked about '68+57'?".[13] And secondly, there simply is no state which is available to introspection in the relevant way. This second point is familiar from Wittgenstein's own writings: there is no essential inner phenomenology of meaning or understanding.

The proposed answer thus errs on both factual and conceptual counts. The sort of state postulated does not exist, and even if it did it could not play the sort of normative and justificatory role demanded of meaning.

In response to these sorts of familiar considerations, Kripke wonders whether

> we may recoup, by arguing that meaning addition by '+' is a state even more sui generis than we have argued before. Perhaps it is simply a primitive state, not to be assimilated to sensations or headaches or any 'qualitative' states, nor to be assimilated to dispositions, but a state of a unique kind of its own.

---

11. I attempt this in my (1995), Chapter 1.
12. Kripke (1982), p.51.
13. Kripke (1982), p.42.

But this answer is criticised on the grounds that

> such a move may in a sense be irrefutable... [and] it seems desperate: it leaves the nature of this postulated primitive state - the primitive state of meaning addition by '+' - completely mysterious. It is not supposed to be an introspectible state, yet supposedly we are aware of it with some fair degree of certainty whenever it occurs.[14]

The suggestion countenanced here is thus that meaning is a unique non-introspectible state with no distinctive affective phenomenology, and the central criticism is that the postulation of such a state is irrefutable, and apt to leave the nature of the postulated state shrouded in mystery.

But note that the two proposals considered here by Kripke (that, on the one hand, the experience of meaning is irreducible, introspectible, and qualitative, and, on the other, that it is irreducible, non-introspectible and non-qualitative) are exhaustive only if the following assumption is obligatory: *that the range of inner states that are introspectible are limited to those possessed of a distinctive qualitative phenomenology.* But why should we make this assumption? Why cannot we conceive of understanding as irreducible, introspectible, and yet as possessing no distinctive qualitative phenomenology? The proposed account of cognitive access which I shall suggest as an alternative to the Sublimated Conception is designed, in its application to the inner, to make sense of this possibility, in a manner that avoids the charges of irrefutability and mystery mongering, as well as the other problems that beset the two non-reductionist solutions rejected by Kripke.

7.

If my suspicion is right, then, accepting both the Sublimated Conception and the thought that semantic predicates have correctness conditions leads to the conclusion that we could never, even in principle, cognitively access semantic properties. One way to try to live with this unpalatable sounding conclusion would be to combine a concession that semantic predicates do *not* have correctness conditions with an argument to the effect that semantic discourse can be viewed as playing some non fact-stating role. If this could be done satisfactorily, there would simply be no need to worry about the unavailability of cognitive access and tracking. But it is now generally accepted that this *semantic irrealist* option cannot be made out satis-

---

14. Kripke (1982), p. 51.

factorily.[15] By way of working towards the Humanized Platonist account of cognitive access, what I want to consider now is Wright's *anti-realist* solution to the sceptical paradox.[16] Rather than following the irrealist route of rejecting the factuality of semantic discourse, Wright's response *retains* the claim that semantic predicates do indeed have correctness conditions but attempts to neutralise the conclusion that semantic properties are rendered in principle cognitively inaccessible by rejecting the thought that the epistemology of meaning is to be couched fundamentally in terms of tracking and cognitive access. According to Wright's anti-realist, the conclusion that if there were semantic facts they would be in principle undetectable is nothing to worry about, not because semantic discourse can be given a satisfying non-factualist construal, but rather because such semantic facts as there are are susceptible to a fundamentally *non-detectivist* epistemology.

Wright's anti-realist response is non-reductionist, but he attempts to avoid Kripke's charges of desperation and mystery-mongering by explaining how there could be an inner state which is not introspectible, but which is such that its possessor can ordinarily be taken to have authoritative and non-inferential access to its content. Wright outlines his account with respect to self-ascriptions of intention, but the point is intended to carry over to the case of meaning.

What we find is that under certain conditions what a speaker says about the content of his intention, as it were, goes: under these conditions a speaker's first-person avowal of an intention is authoritative, in the sense that there is ordinarily no higher authority to which we can appeal in order to overthrow his judgement that he intends to so-and-so. What conditions are these? Wright spells them out as follows: the speaker must not be lying, or prey to self-deception, or making a slip of the tongue, he must have grasped the concepts necessary for the expression of the intention, and he must be adequately attentive to the question of the content of that intention. When these cognitively ideal conditions obtain, the subject's opinions about the content of his intentions, and the truth about the content of his intentions, match perfectly: the *provisional biconditional*

---

15. This is of course the route Kripke's Wittgenstein himself takes in the "sceptical solution" to his own sceptical challenge. For the reasons why it doesn't work, see Wright (1984), Boghossian (1989), and Hale (1997).
16. See especially Wright (1987), (1989a) and (1989b).

If C then (S believes that P if and only if P)

is *a priori* true, where "P" is a self-ascription of an intention. So how do we explain this covariance of truth and best opinions—opinions that are formed under the cognitively ideal C-conditions? Wright suggests that there are two ways in which we might seek to explain this. On the one hand, we might view the C-conditions as conditions in which we are ideally placed to *track* some species of independently constituted states of affairs which confer truth or falsity upon the appropriate avowals; getting into the C-conditions would amount to getting into conditions in which one was optimally placed to accomplish some substantial cognitive achievement. Taking this line would involve viewing first-person knowledge of intentions as the upshot of some "superlatively sure genre of detection"—the beliefs formed under the C-conditions at best *reflect* the independently determined extension of the truth predicate as it applies to first-person ascriptions of intention.

Alternatively, we might view the best opinions as playing an *extension-determining* role.[17] Here, best opinions are viewed, not as tracking independently constituted states of affairs which make it true that the subject has such and such intentions with such and such content, but as themselves *constitutively determining* the truth of the relevant first-person ascriptions: the fact that under the C-conditions, I judge that I intend to drink a pint or two constitutively determines the truth of "I intend to drink a pint or two".

In the case where we have an a priori covariance of the sort mentioned, how can we decide which sort of role to attribute to best opinions? Wright suggests that, in order to attribute an extension-determining role, the following four conditions have to be satisfied:

(A) *A Priority:* The provisional biconditional must be a priori true: there must be a priori covariance of best opinions and truth.

(B) *Non-triviality:* The C-conditions must be specified non-trivially: they cannot simply be described as conditions under which the subject has "whatever it takes" to form the right opinion.

---

17. When best opinions play such a role with respect to a predicate P, the concept of P can be described as *judgement-dependent*. The anti-realist story developed by Wright is thus one attempt at utilising the notion of a *response-dependent concept*. For a general exposition of Wright's notion of response-dependence, see the appendix to Chapter 3 of his (1992).

(C) *Independence:* Whether the C-conditions actually obtain in a given instance must be logically independent of the class of truths for which we are attempting to give an extension-determining account of best opinion. If we have to assume, say, certain facts about a subject's intentions in the specification of cognitively ideal conditions, then we cannot view best opinions as somehow constitutively determining the truth about what the subject intends, for specifying the conditions under which opinions were best would presuppose some conceptually *prior* determination of the very facts thought to be constitutively determined by best opinion.

(D) *Extremal:* There must be no better explanation of why (A) to (C) are satisfied than the claim that best opinion plays an extension-determining role.

Wright suggests that if each of the above four conditions is met, we can view best opinions as playing an extension-determining role.[18] And he makes out a case for thinking that, in the case of self-ascriptions of intention, each of the four conditions is actually met: a subject's best opinions about the contents of his intentions partially determine the extension of the truth-predicate as applied to his self-ascriptions of intention, since the provisional biconditional in the case of self-ascriptions of intention arguably satisfies all of these conditions.[19]

What are the payoffs if Wright's suggestion is correct? For one thing, a solution to the problem of the first-person epistemology of intention would appear to be in the offing: a subject's knowledge of the contents of his own intentions is non-inferential and authoritative because it is his own judgements about the contents of his intentions that constitutively determine the truth about what those contents are. We thus meet the charge of mystery mongering which Kripke levelled at non-reductionism, without sliding into the dubious semantic irrealism of the sceptical solution.

8.

Wright's proposal has received criticism in the literature on the

---

18. For a sophisticated attempt at developing a notion of response-dependence that imposes only conditions (A) and (B), see Pettit (1991).
19. For critical discussion of Wright's response-dependent account of intention, see Miller (1989), Edwards (1992), Holton (1993), and Miller and Divers (1994).

grounds that the independence condition (C) cannot be satisfied. I now want to briefly outline two such lines of criticism. I'll then suggest that Wright is forced to impose the independence condition in the first place only because he accepts the Sublimated Conception of cognitive access. This will then give us a route into an alternative conception of cognitive access. The two objections I have in mind have been raised by Paul Boghossian and Mark Johnston.

Consider the provisional biconditional central to Wright's account:

(2)   If C then (S believes that P if and only if P)

where P is some self-ascription of an intention or meaning. Boghossian's problem is this. We want to view S's beliefs on the left-hand side of the consequent of this biconditional as determining the extension of the truth-predicate as it applies to his self-ascriptions of content. But we cannot view S's best *beliefs* as playing an extension-determining role with respect to ascriptions of content because we have to take for granted, in order to get the account going, at least the content of the beliefs which figure in the consequent of the provisional biconditional. Best opinions *cannot* constitutively determine the extension of the truth-predicate as it applies to self-ascriptions of content, because we have to assume some prior determination of the content which these best opinions are themselves thought to possess. As Boghossian puts it:

> There is a serious difficulty seeing how facts about mental content could conceivably satisfy the stated requirements on judgement-dependence. For it is inconceivable, given what judgement-dependence amounts to, that the biconditionals in the case of mental content should satisfy the requirements that their left-hand sides be free of any assumptions about mental content. For at a minimum the *content of the judgements* said to fix the facts about mental content have to be presupposed. And that means that any such biconditional will always presuppose a constitution of mental content quite independent of constitution by best judgement.[20]

Boghossian's objection applies only to judgement-dependent accounts of content. Johnston, however, has raised an objection which applies to judgement-dependent accounts of any sort of concept whatsoever, and thus calls into question the intelligibility of Wright's way of drawing the distinction.

Johnston argues that there can be *no* cases in which Wright's independence condition is satisfied. He writes:

---

20. Boghossian (1989), p.547.

Wright's distinction turns on the directional idea of determination. But how can the extension of the proposition P be determined by anyone's belief under specified circumstances that P? Surely only if the belief that P already has some extension already associated with it. For if the belief that P has no extension and so no mode of determining an extension associated with it, then the belief that P will be devoid of content and so will not constrain anything at all.... As far as extension-determining goes, there seem to be just two live options. Either 'P' and 'Believes that P' have their extensions determined together, in which case talk of order of determination is out of place, or talk of order is in place and the order in question is the order exhibited in a standard compositional semantics.[21]

The upshot is that the independence condition, as it applies, not to the cognitively ideal conditions but to the judgemental *responses* that figure on the right-hand sides of the provisional equations, could never in fact be satisfied. For the independence condition rules out, in an account which purports to provide a story about how the extension of P gets determined, presupposing some logically prior determination of the extension of P. And Johnston's claim is that we *always do* have to make such a presupposition, because otherwise the very beliefs that are thought to do the work of determining the extension of P will be devoid of content and therefore unable to discharge that role.

9.

We could consider how Wright's anti-realist might try to respond to these objections.[22] But I'd rather think about why he finds himself facing them in the first place: why, that is, he feels it necessary to impose the independence condition at all. It is plainly because he takes the best judgements to be constitutively determining the extensions of the predicates concerned. And why does he assign best judgements such a role? Because the condition which the Sublimated Conception sets down as necessary for tracking and cognitive access has been violated: Wright's own story gives us a set of correctness conditions for semantic predicates, conditions which satisfy the intuitive constraints on the notion of a correctness condition, but only at the expense of embedding semantic predicates themselves within content-specifying that-clauses on the right hand sides of the correctness conditions. But the rule-following considerations have shown the Sublimated Conception to be untenable! So why do we need to take the fact that Wright's provisional bicon-

---

21. Johnston (1993), p.124.
22. See Wright (1992), appendix to Chapter 3, for Wright's own responses to these (and other) objections.

McDowell's Debate with Anti-Realism 191

ditionals are non-trivially a priori as forcing us to describe the situation as one in which the locutions of tracking and cognitive access have no place? Why can't we take the satisfaction of conditions (1) – (4) as actually *grounding* the claim that our judgements can cognitively access or track the relevant facts? *Humanized Platonism* is just the view that we can take the mere satisfaction of (1) – (4) as so grounding the applicability of the locutions of cognitive access and tracking. Once we realise that the rule-following considerations have destroyed the Sublimated Conception, the only thing preventing us from saying this seems to be the thought that the mere satisfaction of conditions (1) to (4) doesn't give the judgements which do the tracking a sufficient degree of independence from the facts which they track. Recall that our claim about the Sublimated Conception was that it changed a perfectly healthy desire for a degree of independence between our judgements and the facts which they track into a philosophically objectionable conception of what such independence has to consist in. But I also claimed that the Humanized Platonist conception of cognitive access could show how the healthy desire for independence could be satisfied without taking on the unwanted philosophical baggage. How is this to be done? In what sense, according to Humanized Platonism, are our judgements *independent* of the facts which they track or cognitively access? Here we can appeal to some remarks which John Campbell makes in a recent paper:

> We have to appreciate how fundamental in our thinking is our grasp of a simple theory of perception. This provides us with the idea that our perceptions are caused by a pair of factors: by the way things are in the environment, and by one's meeting the enabling conditions of perception - being in the right place at the right time, suitably receptive, and so on. It is this simple theory that makes it intelligible to us that our perceptions concern a world of objects which are there independent of us. The independence of the particulars is grasped once the subject understands that perception requires not just their existence, but the meeting of further, enabling conditions of perception. The existence and character of the particulars is quite independent of whether the further conditions are met.[23]

It is unlikely that anything essential here turns on the talk of perceptions as opposed to talk of judgements. Consider the following biconditional for "red": *"red" applies to x if and only if suitable subjects in suitable conditions would judge that x is red*, with suitability cashed out in the familiar way in terms of typical visual functioning and conditions of illumination. Then the

---

23. Campbell (1993), p. 260.

"independence" which Campbell speaks of can be cashed out as follows: the judgement that an object is red is independent of the fact that the object is red in the sense that it can *fail* to track or cognitively access that fact when the enabling conditions—concerning either the state of the judging agent or the conditions that obtain in the world when the judgement is made—fail to be met. Because of the inclusion of enabling conditions, judgement and fact can come apart. The judgement that x is red is independent of the fact that x is red because it is possible for that judgement to occur in the absence of the fact.

Someone might object as follows. The above claim is, strictly speaking, false. For even though non-C-conditioned judgement can occur in the absence of the relevant fact, so that the suggestion secures the independence of less than best judgements from the facts which they are capable of tracking, the same claim is manifestly not applicable to best judgement: for it is acknowledged that it is non-trivially a priori true that best judgement and the facts covary. Best judgement and the facts are not even *modally* independent, so that whatever degree of independence Campbell's suggestion secures for judgement that is less than best, it is not available for best judgement itself.

This argument is a non-sequitur. Judgements are individuated by *content*, not by whether or not they are best. The judgement that the pillar box is red, made in the dark, has the same content as the judgement that the pillar box is red, made out of doors on a lightly cloudy summers afternoon: namely, *that the pillar box is red*. So the judgement that the pillar box is red, made in the dark, is identical to the judgement that the pillar box is red, made out of doors on the summer afternoon. So even when a judgement is made under ideal conditions, that very same judgement can be made under conditions that are less than ideal, in which the relevant fact is absent. So a judgement which is formed under conditions which are best is indeed modally independent of the facts in the sense required by our suggestion.

My suggestion is that this modal independence of judgement and fact is all that is required to justify talk of tracking and cognitive access. This means that we can take Wright's own account of how best opinion and facts covary in the case of meaning as grounding the thought that those best opinions are capable of cognitively accessing or tracking the facts about meaning. And when we do this, the *motivation* for imposing the problematic independence condition simply vanishes. On the anti-realist story, when best opinions play an extension-determining role, they themselves constrain, rather than merely track, the facts about the applicability of the predicate. Given this, it is obligatory to demand, with the anti-realist, that in the specification of the C-conditions themselves, we include no ingredients whose satisfaction presupposes some mode of constraint *prior* to that which is supposed to be imposed by best beliefs themselves. And this type of presupposition is precisely what is ruled out by the independence condition: the relevant concepts are to be involved in the formulation of the C-conditions only in ways which allow the satisfaction of those conditions to be logically independent of the details of the extensions of those concepts. But on the Humanized Platonist conception of tracking, we deliberately separate the idea that best-opinions play an extension-determining role from the idea that they constrain rather than track the facts about the extension of the relevant predicate: in Humanized Platonism we view best beliefs as playing a constraining role with respect to the applicability of a predicate *only in virtue of the fact that they infallibly track its extension*. If we view the extension-determining role of best beliefs as essentially constraining in a manner that derives from sources other than the capacity of such beliefs to infallibly track the facts, then it is indeed necessary to rule out presuppositions about logically prior constraints from the specifications of the ideal conditions. But since, in Humanized Platonism, the best beliefs don't play a constraining role *in that sort of way*, there is simply no *need* to rule out the implication of prior presuppositions about such constraining features, and hence no need for the anti-realist's independence condition.

Given this, the objections from Boghossian and Johnston simply cannot get a grip on Humanized Platonism, for Humanized Platonism doesn't impose anything like the independence condition.

10.

One might worry that this non-reductive aspect of Humanized Platonism leaves it open to Kripke's charge that it is "in a sense... irrefutable... it leaves the nature of this postulated primitive state [of meaning such and such] completely mysterious". But these charges of *irrefutability* and *mystery* can be dispelled. The claim that we are tracking or detecting, in the sense defined by Humanized Platonism, a given species of irreducible fact, *can indeed be refuted*, by the provision of an argument to the effect that one or more of the intuitive constraints on the notion of a correctness condition is not satisfied. And the worry about mystery can be assuaged by noting that, in showing that Humanized Platonism is applicable in any given case, we shall have given a concrete account of the epistemology associated with the predicate under consideration. For example, in the case of semantic predicates, we will have given a detailed account of what sort of position one has to be in to track or cognitively access the facts about the instantiation of semantic properties. The level of *detail* that we are likely to have to go into in arguing that the various intuitive constraints are indeed satisfied should be enough to stave off the charge of mystery mongering.

In addition, we can now see why the two non-reductionist proposals considered by Kripke were not exhaustive. Recall that the first of these was the idea that the experience of meaning is irreducible, introspectible, and qualitative, while the second was the idea that the experience of meaning is irreducible, non-introspectible, and non-qualitative. But if Humanized Platonism can indeed be applied to e.g. semantic properties, then we shall have an account of meaning as irreducible, and which sees meanings as introspectible (for we are applying the notion of cognitive access, inwards, as it were), but which does not invoke the idea that the experience of meaning has a distinctive affective phenomenology. So if Humanized Platonism can be defended, the assumption that the range of inner states that are introspectible is limited to those with a distinctive qualitative phenomenology will have been shown to be non-obligatory.[24]

---

24. In this regard, see the very interesting remarks on p. 542 of Boghossian (1989): "It is interesting to note that one of the more striking examples of the introspective discernment of a non-qualitative mental feature is provided by, of all things, an experiential phenomenon. I have in mind the phenomenon, much discussed by Wittgenstein himself, of seeing-as. We see the duck-rabbit now as a duck, now as a rabbit; we see the Necker cube now with one face forward, now with another. And we know immediately precisely how we are seeing these objects as, when we see them now in one way, now in another. But this change of 'aspect', although manifestly introspectible, is nevertheless not a change in something qualitative, for the qualitative character of the visual experience remains thesame even as the aspect changes". Our discussion here is intended to throw light upon, as well as gain sustenance from, the discussion in McDowell (1991), which culminates (p.150) in the claim: "Wittgenstein is not concerned to dispel everything that is intentional from the province of introspective self-consciousness. The idea that he is involves a misconception of the province of introspective self-consciousness which is itself part of Wittgenstein's target".

11.

I want now to finish by going back to the puzzle with which we began. What does the "platonistic autonomy" in Wittgenstein's picture of the "super-rigid rail" consist in if not the objectivity of meaning as characterised by Wright? How can we reject platonism without thereby also rejecting the objectivity of meaning? With our distinction between the Humanized Platonist and Sublimated Conceptions of cognitive access we are now perhaps in a position to explain why this identification of "platonistic autonomy" with the objectivity of meaning in Wright's sense is not mandatory. The key to understanding this lies in the two notions of independence that I used to characterise the Humanized and Sublimated Conceptions respectively. "Independence" is just another word for "autonomy", and the basic idea is that in rejecting the "platonistic autonomy" of the super-rigid rail we are rejecting the notion of independence that is at the heart of the Sublimated Conception. But rejecting this notion of independence leaves the notion of independence central to the Humanized Platonist account intact. This notion of independence can then be invoked to save the objectivity of meaning. *Rejecting the "platonistic autonomy" of the super-rigid rail does not involve rejecting the objectivity of meaning because the two positions should be characterised in terms of two different conceptions of independence.* To explain further, rejecting the platonistic autonomy of the rule-as-rail consists in rejecting the idea that we track or cognitively access the requirements of rules, where those requirements are conceived of as independent of human judgement in the sense of independence constitutive of the Sublimated Conception: the fact about the applicability of the relevant semantic predicate sustains no non-trivial but a priori relationship with idealised human judgement concerning its applicability. However, rejection of this idea does not involve rejection of the idea that we track or cognitively access the requirements of rules, where those requirements are independent of human judgement in the sense of independence central to Humanized Platonism: our judgements about the applicability of the semantic predicate which encapsulates the imposed requirement can still come apart from the fact of that semantic predicate's applicability when the non-trivially specified ideal conditions do not obtain. We can thus still see ourselves as sometimes tracking or cognitively accessing the requirements of rules that reach ahead to separate as yet unactualised behavioural episodes into those that do, and those that do not, normatively accord with the relevant rule. This explains how the objectivity of meaning can be retained, even while the spurious autonomy of the super-rigid rule-as-rail is consciously rejected.[25]

Department of Philosophy
University of Birmingham
Edgbaston, Birmingham B15 2TT
United Kingdom
a.miller@bham.ac.uk

References

Boghossian, P. 1989 "The Rule-Following Considerations", *Mind* Vol.98, pp. 507–549.

Campbell, J. 1993 "A Simple View of Colour", in J. Haldane and C. Wright, eds., *Reality, Representation, and Projection*, Oxford: Oxford University Press, 257–268.

Edwards, J. 1992 "Best Opinion and Intentional States", *Philosophical Quarterly* Vol. 42, pp. 23–33.

Hale, B. 1997 "Rule-Following, Objectivity, and Meaning", in B. Hale and C. Wright, eds., *A Companion to the Philosophy of Language*, Oxford: Blackwell, 369–396.

Holton, R. 1993 "Intention-Detecting", *Philosophical Quarterly* Vol.43, 298–318.

Johnston, M. 1993 "Objectivity Refigured: Pragmatism Without Verificationism", in J. Haldane and C. Wright, eds., *Reality, Representation, and Projection*, Oxford: Oxford University Press, 85–130.

Kripke, S. 1982 *Wittgenstein on Rules and Private Language*, Cambridge, Mass.: Harvard University Press.

McDowell, J. 1984 "Wittgenstein on Following a Rule", *Synthese* Vol. 58. 325–363.

McDowell, J. 1991 "Intentionality and Interiority in Wittgenstein", in K.Puhl, ed., *Meaning Scepticism*, Berlin: De Gruyter, 148–149.

McDowell, J. 1992 "Meaning and Intentionality in Wittgenstein's Later Philosophy", *Midwest Studies in Philosophy* Vol. XVII, 40–52.

---

25. A version of this paper was read at the staff seminar at the University of Birmingham in February 1995: my thanks to all those present for their comments, especially Greg McCulloch and Jose Zalabardo. Thanks also to the Editors and to an anonymous referee. Special thanks to Jim Stuart for very useful written comments.

McDowell, J. 1994 *Mind and World*, Cambridge, Mass.: Harvard University Press.

Miller, A. 1989 "An Objection to Wright's Treatment of Intention", *Analysis* Vol. 49, 169–173.

Miller, A., Divers, J., 1994 "Best Opinion, Analytic Functionalism, and Intention Detecting", *Philosophical Quarterly* Vol. 44, 239–245.

Miller, A. 1995 *Sublimation, Realism, and Rule-Following*, PhD Dissertation, University of Michigan, Ann Arbor.

Pettit, P. 1991 "Realism and Response-Dependence", *Mind* Vol. 100, 587–626.

Wright, C. 1980 *Wittgenstein on the Foundations of Mathematics*, London: Duckworth.

Wright, C. 1984 "Kripke's Account of the Argument against Private Language", *Journal of Philosophy* Vol. LXXXI, 759–78.

Wright, C. 1986a "Rule-Following, Meaning, and Constructivism" in C.Travis, ed, *Meaning and Interpretation*, Oxford: Basil Blackwell, 271–297.

Wright, C. 1986b *Realism, Meaning, and Truth*, Oxford: Blackwell.

Wright, C. 1987 "On Making Up One's Mind: Wittgenstein on Intention", in Weingartner and Schutz, eds, *Logic, Science, and Epistemology*, Vienna: Hölder-Pichler-Tempsky, 391–404.

Wright, C. 1989a Critical Notice of Colin McGinn *Wittgenstein on Meaning*, *Mind* Vol.98, 289–305.

Wright, C. 1989b "Wittgenstein's Rule-Following Considerations and the Central Project of Theoretical Linguistics", in A.George, ed, *Reflections on Chomsky*, Oxford: Blackwell, 233–264.

Wright, C. 1992 *Truth and Objectivity*, Cambridge, Mass.: Harvard University Press.

ALEX BYRNE
Interpretivism

1. Interpretivism introduced

In the writings of Daniel Dennett and Donald Davidson we find something like the following bold conjecture: it is an a priori truth that there is no gap between our *best judgements* of a subject's beliefs and desires and the *truth* about the subject's beliefs and desires. Under ideal conditions a subject's belief-box and desire-box become transparent.

To make this picture more vivid, let us introduce the familiar device of the *Ideal Interpreter*: an idealisation of a human being. The Ideal Interpreter, according to the bold conjecture we are considering, is capable of discovering exactly what you believe and desire. For now, let's be silent on the details of the Interpreter's knowledge and powers—with the following exception. The Interpreter's stipulated initial stock of knowledge had better not include knowledge of your propositional attitudes, else the conjecture will be trivialised.

Is this a kind of behaviourism? It does not have to be. For it may be that we wish to make our Interpreter take into account various non-behavioural facts when determining what someone believes or desires. For example, perhaps the discovery that someone is a hollow shell controlled from Mars would lead us to reject the hypothesis that he is a believer and desirer, no matter how convincing his behaviour. Very well, if there are such defeaters of the hypothesis that someone is a believer and desirer (or any other relevant inner facts), we can let our Interpreter know if any of them obtain in a particular case.[1] But both Dennett and Davidson think that the Interpreter does not need to open up the subject's head, and I shall not dispute this.

This intriguing picture of the mind—that, as an a priori matter, the facts about mental content are precisely captured by the judgements of some Ideal Interpreter—I shall call *interpretivism*.[2]

It is important to note that the Ideal Interpreter's presence (equivalently, the reference to our best judgements) is an indispensable component of interpretivism. Suppose it is (implausibly!) claimed that believing that snow is white is a priori equivalent to being disposed to produce the string 'snow

---

1. The Mars example is taken from Peacocke 1983, p. 205. Peacocke imagines "The Body"—a debrained human body controlled by a computer from Mars which "has been given the vast but finite number of conditionals specifying what a typical human would do with given past history and current stimulation; so it can cause The Body to behave in any circumstances exactly as a human being would" (p. 205). Peacocke's Body, according to him, "does not have propositional attitudes at all: it is just a Martian marionette" (p. 205). I think Peacocke's verdict on the case debatable, but the important point is that even if Peacocke is correct, this does not spell disaster for the view which is the topic of this paper. It *would* spell disaster if the Martian puppeteers, with their evil intentions, were an essential component of Peacocke's example. For then any Ideal Interpreter would need to know whether her subject was controlled by *thinking* puppeteers, and this means that the Interpreter's database includes intentional facts. This problem cannot be avoided by taking the Interpreter to deliver the facts, with no intentional initial data, about whether the subject is controlled by thinking beings. The Interpreter might then be off on an infinite regress: the Martians themselves might appear to be Venusian marionettes, who in turn might appear to be Plutonian marionettes, and so on. In such a case, the Interpreter can have no final opinion whether the Martians are genuine thinkers, unless she knows whether the Venusians are genuine thinkers, and she cannot know *that* unless she knows whether the Plutonians are genuine thinkers...

    Fortunately, the Martians with their evil intentions, and even the fact that the computer is distant from The Body, are surely dispensable (and misleading) parts of Peacocke's story. If the computer is shrunk to the size of a human brain, and placed in The Body, this *ought* to make no difference to our considered opinion about The Body's mental life. Or so I think.

2. I borrow the term from Johnston 1993b. Interpretivism should be distinguished from what Dennett calls *interpretationism*, which "likens the question of whether a person has a particular belief to the question of whether a person is immoral, or has style, or talent, or would make a good wife" (1979, p. 15). Dennett takes interpretationism (avowedly not his own position) to involve some sort of relativism.

is white' (and likewise for other beliefs). This theory could be expressed to sound superficially like interpretivism, using an Ideal Interpreter who has as initial data the subject's dispositions to produce strings of symbols, and the relevant alleged a priori equivalencies. But here the Interpreter is otiose: she could be eliminated if desired, and so this theory is not a version of interpretivism.

It is worth noting that interpretivism holds the promise of elegantly vindicating the supervenience of intentional states on matters physical, with no reductionist assumptions. No commitment to reduction, because the Interpreter (a believer and desirer herself) is an essential part of the story. But a vindication of supervenience, because surely the Interpreter would not interpret differently without a physical difference in the subject of interpretation, or a physical difference in the subject's environment.[3] And as the Interpreter delivers the *facts*, this means there could be no difference in beliefs or desires without a physical difference. (This argument for supervenience should not be attributed to either Dennett or Davidson.)

Fodor and Lepore have, unfortunately, appropriated 'interpretivism' to label the thesis that "[t]here is an 'element of interpretation' in content ascription" (1992, p. 259). (The phrase 'element of interpretation' is taken from Dennett 1987b, p. 342.) But this is so imperspicuous as to be hardly worth naming.

After this paper was completed, I discovered that William Child (1994) discusses at length something similar to interpretivism as I formulate it (he calls it 'interpretationism'). But Child's interpretationist—who comes in a bewildering variety of guises—never quite becomes my interpretivist. The reader should consult Child's book for a different and more sympathetic way of approaching these issues.

3. Both Dennett (e.g., 1987a, p. 41) and Davidson (e.g., 1979) accept versions of Quine's indeterminacy thesis. They hold (at least) that it is sometimes indeterminate exactly what a subject believes or desires. Consider two physical doppelgangers S_1 and S_2, in physically identical environments. Given indeterminacy, might not an Interpreter permissibly interpret S_1 as believing that p, and S_2 as not believing that p? If so, it's wrong to say that the Interpreter would not interpret differently without a physical difference. However, the answer to the question is "no". What we should say instead is that the Interpreter interprets *both* S_1 and S_2 as indeterminately believing that p. Hence, even given indeterminacy, S_1 and S_2 are interpreted alike, and the argument for supervenience goes through as before. (NB: for simplicity, in what follows I shall assume that there are no cases of indeterminacy.)

2. Textual evidence

I suggested that Daniel Dennett and Donald Davidson are both interpretivists. More cautiously, there is a strong dark thread of interpretivism running through their views. Let us briefly survey the textual evidence.

As is well known, Dennett distinguishes three "stances", or predictive strategies, one might adopt towards some system—a chess-playing computer, to take Dennett's example.[4] First, we might adopt the *design stance*, and predict the computer's behaviour on the basis of what we know about its design. Second, we might adopt the *physical stance*, and base our predictions on the physical makeup of the machine. However, as Dennett observes, when it comes to predicting the moves a chess-playing computer will make, neither one of these stances will be of much use in practice—such machines are far too complicated.

There is a third predictive strategy: one may view the machine "rather like an intelligent opponent" (1971, p. 5), treating the system *as if* it had propositional attitudes. And certainly, whether or not it is a mere *façon de parler*, the language of beliefs and desires becomes almost irresistible in such cases. For instance, it might be said of the computer that it thinks it ought to get its queen out early (to use an example of Dennett's that is now something of a cliché in the philosophy of mind[5]) and no one would find such mentalistic talk at all odd. This third predictive strategy is the famous *intentional stance*.

It is somewhat obscure, to me at least, just what Dennett's claim was in the 1971 paper, "Intentional Systems". There were hints that it was merely convenient to assume that certain complex systems (including ourselves) had beliefs and desires, even though, strictly speaking, this assumption is mistaken. But in any event, Dennett's position has clarified and developed, and by 1978 we find him saying:

x believes that $p \equiv x$ can be predictively attributed the belief that p[6]

This schema is elaborated in the 1979 paper "True Believers", which, Dennett says, has replaced "Intentional Systems" "as the flagship expression of my position" (1987, p. 3). There he makes the following self-styled "perverse claim":

---

4. In the classic paper "Intentional Systems" (1971).
5. The example occurs in Dennett 1977.
6. Dennett 1978, p. 67. See also Dennett 1981, p. xvii.

> [a]ll there is to being a true believer is being a system whose behaviour is reliably predictable via the intentional strategy, and hence *all there is* to really and truly believing that *p* (for any proposition *p*) is being an intentional system for which *p* occurs as a belief in the best (most predictive) interpretation (p. 29).

Both this "perverse claim" and the earlier one appear to be clear statements of interpretivism. Dennett shows absolutely no sign of wanting to show how talk of interpretations, interpreters, the intentional stance, and so on, is a mere heuristic device, in principle eliminable from his theory. The failure of reductions in general has in any case been one of his major themes.

As to Davidson, one quotation will suffice. In "A Coherence Theory of Truth and Knowledge", he says:

> What a fully informed interpreter could know about what a speaker means is all there is to learn; the same goes for what the speaker believes (1986, p. 315).

It is plain that this is intended as a statement of interpretivism, for two reasons.

First, Davidson is not making an empty claim. "[F]ully informed" is not an abbreviation for "fully informed about all a speaker's meanings and beliefs". He here has in mind his "Radical Interpreter" (Davidson 1973), of whom more anon.

Second, although Davidson's remark is consistent with the idea that some of a speaker's beliefs and meanings are not knowable by an Interpreter, because they are completely hidden, and so unlearnable, and so no part of "all there is to learn", this is not Davidson's intent. For one thing, it is implicit throughout the paper from which the quotation is taken that "[w]hat a fully informed interpreter could know" includes all a speaker's beliefs.

But now, in order to make the thesis of interpretivism more precise, we need to take a short detour.

3. Judgement-dependent concepts

In recent work, Crispin Wright (1988, 1989, 1992, 1993) and Mark Johnston (1993a, 1993b) have separately investigated *judgement-dependent concepts* (Johnston's terminology).[7] The idea is this. Take some

---

7. Definitional epicycles aside, a concept *C* is judgement-dependent (Johnston) just in case judgements that something falls under *C* are "extension-determining" (Wright). Judgement-dependence is a species of what Johnston calls "response-dependence".

concept *C*. There is its extension, on the one hand, and our *best opinion* as to its extension, on the other. The two may coincide—either because we are lucky or skillful, or because their coincidence is an a priori matter. In the latter case—where it is an a priori truth that *C*'s extension coincides with our best opinion of its extension—we say that *C* is judgement-dependent. Of course, we must avoid, to use Crispin Wright's phrase, trivializing "whatever it takes" specifications of "our best opinion": if our best opinion is characterised as the *true* opinion, then trivially all concepts will turn out to be judgement-dependent.

Let us have an example. There is something fishy, many would say, in the idea that the moral facts could outrun our idealised dispositions to make moral judgements. There couldn't be moral facts that we are forever unable to discover. So perhaps something like the following biconditional is a priori:

> A state of affairs *A* is morally good iff the Impartial Observer would be disposed to judge that *A* is morally good.

This—understanding the Impartial Observer to be an idealised impartial human being—is a judgement-dependent account of moral goodness. If the Impartial Observer would not judge two states of affairs differently unless they differed descriptively—which seems plausible—then it follows that the moral supervenes on the descriptive.

Note three features of judgement-dependent accounts. First, they are not reductive: the concept in question—moral goodness in this case—appears on both sides of the biconditional (although a judgement-dependent account might be used as a stepping stone to a genuinely reductive account[8]). Second, a judgement-dependent account of '*x* is *F*' is not happily formulated as an account of *what makes it true* that *x* is *F*, or of what *constitutes* the fact that *x* is *F*. We have a biconditional, for one thing, and no obvious motivation for taking one side of it to be any more basic than the other.[9] Third, judgement-dependent accounts are not necessarily relativistic. To

---

8. That is, a reductive account *of the concept C*. Take it as a stipulation on judgement-dependent accounts that the idealisations of ourselves mentioned in the biconditionals cannot themselves be reduced away.
9. I here draw on Appendix 3 to Johnston 1993a. Dennett himself mistakenly takes a judgement-dependent account of qualia to imply that they are "*logical constructs* out of subjects' qualia judgements" and so "akin to theorists' fictions" (1988, p. 55).

take the above example: if some other moral observer—perhaps from a society quite different from ours—disagrees with the Impartial Observer, then he is, according to the account, simply mistaken. And by understanding the Impartial Observer to be an idealisation of human beings as they *actually* are, we can say that even if our moral judgements had been different, the moral facts would have remained the same.

Interpretivism in general is the thesis that mental content is judgement-dependent: the facts about what propositional attitudes someone has are exactly captured by the (potential) judgements of some Ideal Interpreter (or Interpreters).[10]

Dennett's and Davidson's versions of interpretivism are *third-personal*: the Interpreter is someone who interprets someone *else*. But there are also *first-personal* accounts, where the Interpreter is taken to be the subject of interpretation, perhaps made ideally introspective.[11] But such accounts will not be our concern here.[12]

We now need an initial formulation of interpretivism that at least captures the spirit of Dennett's and Davidson's claims. Although the Interpreter is supposed to have knowledge of the contents of all your attitudes, for definiteness let us concentrate on belief. Let our initial formulation be the thesis that all biconditionals of the following form are a priori:

> x believes that p iff if there were an appropriately informed Ideal Interpreter, she would be disposed to attribute to x the belief that p.

where Wright's strictures against a trivializing "whatever it takes" reading of the right hand side apply (so we do not, for instance, take the Ideal Interpreter by stipulation to be omniscient and infallible with respect to x's beliefs). We will fill in some gaps a little later. For now, there is one unique feature of interpretivism to note—not only does the *concept* expressed by 'believes that p' occur on the right hand side, but *facts* about belief are expressed by both sides. For in appealing to the Interpreter's *judgements*, we

---

10. As Johnston puts it: "the truth about meaning or content cannot outrun our idealized dispositions to grasp that truth" (1993a, p. 126).
11. For an example of a first-personal account, applied to intention, see Wright 1989.
12. For criticism of Wright's first-personal account (see above note), see Holton 1993; for a response to Holton, see Divers and Miller 1994.

are assuming that the Interpreter has beliefs. Interpretivism *presupposes* facts about mental content: namely facts about what an Interpreter would believe or, equivalently, facts about what *we* would believe under ideal conditions. So we have a reason specific to interpretivism (as opposed to general considerations about judgement-dependent accounts) to deny that it is a metaphysical thesis concerning what *constitutes* facts about content.

4. Interpretivism evaluated

We are now in a position critically to examine interpretivism. Our initial formulation was this:

> *x* believes that *p* iff if there were an appropriately informed Ideal Interpreter, she would be disposed to attribute to *x* the belief that *p*.

We now cannot put off the question of the Interpreter's knowledge and powers any longer. Who is Dennett's Ideal Interpreter, and is Davidson's Interpreter significantly different?

Well, despite Dennett's attempt (1987b) to reconcile his views with Davidson's, it seems to me that they have substantial disagreements.[13] Dennett's Interpreter employs the intentional stance—and so do we, although not as well. Dennett's Interpreter employs whatever tacit methodology we

---

13. Here is as good a place as any to mention two other philosophers who have made use of the device of an Interpreter (or something like it)—Quine and David Lewis. Lewis is certainly not an interpretivist. As he puts it, "my problem of radical interpretation is not any real-life task of finding out about Karl's beliefs, desires, and meanings. I am not really asking how we could determine these facts. Rather, how do *the facts* determine these facts?" (1974, p. 110). Quine's relation to interpretivism is more complex. Quine's (1960) device of the radical translator is supposed to show that facts about meanings are not determined by facts about behavioural dispositions, and since Quine thinks that meaning-facts must supervene on behavioural dispositions, he concludes that there are no meaning-facts (see Van Cleve 1992). However, Quine need not appeal to some a priori connection between the deliverances of an idealised human translator and facts about synonymy to reach his conclusion. The radical translator could be God, and the argument would be unaffected. (And if the radical translator is God, Quine is simply asking how "*the facts* determine these facts".) But there is a taint of interpretivism in Quine's reason—namely, verificationism—for thinking that behavioural dispositions are the only candidates for the meaning-determining facts.

employ when determining what someone believes. We can think of her as an invisible onlooker, carefully observing your movements, your interactions with your environment, and so on, and following the interpretive practices—whatever they may be—that we human beings follow when deciding what someone believes. Let's call her the *Homely* Interpreter.[14] Unlike most of us, however, the Homely Interpreter never misapplies the tacit rules of interpretation, has unlimited concentration, is not perceptually defective, is never mistaken about the non-intentional facts, and so on. Anything which ordinary folk would take to be (non-intentional) evidence relevant to discovering what you believe, is part of the Homely Interpreter's database. A reminder: we can't allow the Interpreter *by stipulation* to have knowledge of all your thoughts, or beliefs, or actions (intentionally described), and the like. The Homely Interpreter is supposed to *find out* exactly what your propositional attitudes are, not be handed them on a definitional plate. But if sweating, reddening of the ears, blinking, whether you are drinking H_2O or XYZ, or whatever, are deemed relevant by the folk, then we will let the Homely Interpreter know these facts. We could think of the Homely Interpreter aided in her task by hidden high resolution cameras, shooting you from all angles; the Interpreter then views the resulting films in the comfort of her own home, aided by her compendious memory of what she saw herself.

Davidson's Ideal Interpreter is quite different, however: she is a *Radical* Interpreter, employing a methodology alien to the one we use in everyday life when determining what someone believes (Davidson 1973).[15] Such an Interpreter is one who begins the task of interpretation as might a scientifi-

---

14. Not to be confused with Blackburn's "homely interpreter", whom he contrasts with the "bleak interpreter". The former uses the "principle of humanity"—roughly, maximise intelligibility when interpreting; the latter, the "principle of charity"—roughly, maximise truth when interpreting (1984, pp. 277-81). This distinction is independent of the one being made in the text.
15. What about children learning their first language? Are they—according to Davidson—approximations to Radical Interpreters? Even if they are, it remains true that we who have learnt language do not employ the methodology of radical interpretation in our ordinary interactions with others. However, Davidson's position appears to be, not that children are Radical Interpreters, but rather that any Radical Interpreter would learn just what a child learns, given the same initial data (see Davidson 1994, p. 124). For more on language learning, see the Third Objection in section 4 below.

cally-minded visitor to an utterly strange land. The Radical Interpreter's data will be of this austere kind: system *K* produced the inscription 'es regnet' in circumstances of precipitation.

(Here, for three paragraphs, I interpolate a tricky question of Davidson exegesis, that I shall for the most part set aside in what follows.

The Radical Interpreter's official data includes, according to Davidson's 1973 and elsewhere, *intentional* facts—concerning what uninterpreted sentences the subject "holds true". But since Davidson's interpretivism seems to be at least in part motivated by Wittgensteinian "publicity" considerations—see the Third Objection below—he ought to hold that the Radical Interpreter's official data, at least in the final analysis, is purely *non*-intentional. For Davidson evidently thinks that it is not good enough, to answer worries about the public accessibility of meaning, to reply simply that we *directly observe* that someone believes that *p*, or utters a sentence that means that *q*. And he also evidently thinks that an *adequate* answer would be that by directly observing bodily movements, the production of certain sounds, and suchlike, we can recover just what a subject means and believes. But then Davidson ought not to rest content with "holdings true" as part of the Ideal Interpreter's initial database. Why should we find the intentional "holds true" epistemically unproblematic if belief contents and sentence meanings are disallowed as initial data? Surely these three categories should be in the same leaky boat.

But although I see no compelling reason to be this charitable, I will assume that "holdings true" are part of the Radical Interpreter's database.)

Bearing this exegetical digression in mind, let us return to the main thread. For our purposes, the important difference between the Homely and the Radical Interpreter is this: the Homely Interpreter needs to be in *perceptual* contact with the subject of interpretation (understanding this broadly enough to allow the Interpreter to use hidden cameras and similar devices). For there is little prospect of characterising, in non-intentional terms, information sufficient to enable us—*without the benefit of perception*, and using *our ordinary methods*—to work out what someone believes. That would be rather like giving a person a description of the distribution of color patches on a canvas, and expecting him to tell us whether the description is of a beautiful painting. Using ordinary methods of art appreciation, she will be at a loss: she needs to be *confronted* with the painting itself, not a description of it.[16] And similarly in the case of interpreting others: we can only say that, *confronted* with some subject, we manage (here might follow a detailed account) to come to an opinion about what he believes.

But the Radical Interpreter, although Davidson normally situates her in the field, observing the subject with notebook in hand, need not be there. For there *is* supposed to be some complete characterisation of the Radical Interpreter's initial data, and hence we could simply take the Radical Interpreter simply to be supplied with it, never leaving her laboratory at all. Indeed, we can even take the Radical Interpreter to be entirely alone, off in some other possible world. (At any rate, I will assume that the preceding part of this paragraph is correct. As I shall go on to raise a problem for any version of interpretivism that requires the Interpreter to be in perceptual contact with the subject of interpretation, this assumption is a concession to Davidson.[17])

Before we get on to some objections, two minor and two major preliminary points. The minor points: let us take the necessary reference to the time period during which the subject has a particular belief to be implicit, and let us not fuss about the alleged influence of the subject's social milieu on his mental content (see Burge 1979).

The major points. First, although placing *some* knowledge of the subject's beliefs and desires, or knowledge of a theory of meaning for his language, in the Interpreter's initial endowment would not thereby trivialise interpretivism, I shall not consider these possibilities. Insofar as Davidson and Dennett are interpretivists, their interpretivism is of the stronger, more

---

16. Well, no doubt being confronted with a physical duplicate of the painting would be sufficient, which she might construct from a description. Similarly, the Homely Interpreter would not be impaired if she were confronted with a physical duplicate of the subject of interpretation (in a duplicate environment). So, strictly speaking, the Homely Interpreter need not be in perceptual contact with the *subject* of interpretation, just in perceptual contact with a *duplicate* of the subject of interpretation. But this qualification does not affect any of my objections, and so I will ignore it henceforth.
17. And in fact it seems that even if Davidson would accept the concession that the Radical Interpreter does not need to be in perceptual contact with the subject of interpretation, he thinks that *someone* must be. In his 1992 he gives what amounts to a transcendental deduction of the existence of next-door neighbours. He argues that someone could not "satisfy all the conditions for being interpretable—without actually being interpreted" (p. 260).

exciting kind. Second, a point that I have already touched on, and which cannot be stressed enough. *None* of my objections will assume the falsity of, or be objections to, supervenient behaviourism: the metaphysical thesis that facts about a subject's mental states supervene on facts about his behavioural dispositions. Interpretivism is the target, not behaviourism.

Here, then, are three objections to interpretivism. The first is only an objection to taking the Interpreter to be *Homely*. The other two are objections to interpretivism *simpliciter*. When we are through with these, I shall briefly examine whether a weakened version of interpretivism might fare any better.

First Objection: the curious case of the strange believers

The following examples are related to some that are familiar from secondary quality accounts of color (they are more readily dealt with in the color case, however).[18]

His argument for this truly extraordinary conclusion runs as follows. Suppose we interpret a child's use of 'table' as referring to tables. How do we do that? We need to find the salient cause of the child's utterance of 'table'. And "[i]t is the common cause of our response and the child's response" (p. 263).

[This] kind of triangulation...while not *sufficient* to establish that a creature has a concept of a particular object or kind of object, is *necessary* if there is to be any answer at all to the question of what its concepts are concepts of. If we consider a single creature by itself, its responses, no matter how complex, cannot show that it is reacting to, or thinking about, events a certain distance away, rather than, say, on its skin.

The problem is not, I should stress, one of verifying what objects or events a creature is responding to; the problem is that without a second creature responding to the first, there can be no answer to this question...So we can say...that if anyone is to speak a language, there must be another creature interacting with the speaker (p. 263).

If I understand this argument, a corollary of it is that if no one ever overhears me saying 'chair', then there can be "no answer" to the question of what I use this word to refer to. To reply that this is mistaken, because if an interpreter *had* been interacting with me, then he *would* have believed that 'chair' in my mouth refers to chairs, is obviously to undercut the entire argument.

18. See Johnston 1992, to which I am indebted. The present objection convicts our initial formulation of interpretivism of the "conditional fallacy" (Shope 1978).

First, there might be a believer who emitted rays capable of confusing any Homely Interpreter in the vicinity. The Homely Interpreter will then be ignorant of (many of) the subject's beliefs. Could we not say that the Interpreter interprets the believer as he would have been had he not produced the rays? Not obviously: the believer might live in a world where, as a matter of law, the rays are produced by certain *beliefs*. So if the believer had not produced the rays, he would have had different beliefs, if he had beliefs at all. Or perhaps one such believer believes on good evidence that he does produce these rays. And if the believer had not produced the rays, he would not have had this belief.[19]

Second, there might be an unobservable believer: perhaps invisible, perhaps of sub-microscopic size, or perhaps so large that only small parts of him can be observed. Again, the Homely Interpreter will be ignorant of (many of) the subject's beliefs. Could we not idealise the Homely Interpreter so that she has astonishing perceptual powers, sufficient to observe such believers? Perhaps. But the Homely Interpreter is a believer too, and once we allow believers to have astonishing perceptual powers, the following third problem arises.

There might be a believer, with astonishing perceptual powers, who believes on the basis of overwhelming evidence that he is not being perceived, and hence not interpreted by any Homely Interpreter. If a Homely Interpreter were to interpret him, no matter how subtly, he would no longer believe he was not being interpreted. So this believer has a belief that no Homely Interpreter can discover.

These problems are of no force against Davidson's vision of the Ideal Interpreter.[20] But they appear to raise serious difficulties for Dennett's account.

It might be suggested that these problems can be overcome by reformulating interpretivism in the style of Wright's "provisional equations", yielding:

> If there were an Ideal Interpreter appropriately informed vis-à-vis x, then: x would believe that p iff the Interpreter would be disposed to attribute to x the belief that p.[21]

---

19. The counterpart of this character in the case of color is "killer-yellow", due to Saul Kripke in lectures.
20. Under my concessive assumptions, anyway. But cf. note 17 above.
21. See Wright 1992, p. 119, 1993. Here I am indebted to an anonymous referee.

Here the idea is that the Interpreter now only delivers a verdict on the subject's beliefs as they would be when he is being interpreted. Hence if the process of interpretation itself affects the subject's beliefs—as is the case in the last problem mentioned above—this does not matter. There are two obvious points to be made in response. First, as Wright notes[22], this kind of thesis lacks generality: nothing is said about the beliefs of a subject who is not being interpreted. Second, the reformulation does not help with the problem of the believer who induces confusion in the Interpreter. If there were an Ideal Interpreter appropriately informed vis-à-vis one of these believers then she would be disposed to judge mistakenly.

Second Objection: the problem of actuality

Suppose you are out walking alone. On a path through a forest, you glimpse a rabbit ahead, motionless in some tall grass. You think to yourself: Lo, a rabbit. You believe, at that moment, that there is a rabbit ahead. Preoccupied with your ruminations on *Word and Object*, before the end of your walk you completely forget about the rabbit. You definitely believed at the time (t, say) that there was a rabbit ahead. There is nothing unusual about this sort of case—it is utterly commonplace. But how do we get the Ideal Interpreter to deliver the right result?

We can suppose that the rabbit is not clearly visible to you, and although you look straight at it, you give no visible sign that you see the animal (you have seen enough rabbits to last a lifetime). To the Interpreter, you behave in just the way you would have had the rabbit slipped your gaze.

So if the Interpreter just knows of your *actual* movements, at best she will be of two minds about whether you have this belief (or perhaps two acceptable choices of Interpreter will disagree about whether you have it). This will then be a case of indeterminacy. At worst, she might be of one mind, and just not affirm that you have this belief—for perhaps you sincerely say later that your walk was entirely rabbit-free. In which case, according to interpretivism, you definitely do not have this belief.

Will going inside the head help? Not necessarily. For suppose the Interpreter knew that there was a rabbit-image on your retina at t, and even that a light-bulb marked 'rabbit' illuminated in your brain at that time, and such-

---

22. Wright 1992, p. 120.

like. Whether or not in fact this guarantees that you have the rabbit-belief, it is surely not an a priori matter that an Interpreter with access to such actual inner goings-on will be able to find out just what you believe (remember that an a priori reduction of beliefs to, say, inner light-bulbs, is not an option in the present context: reduction renders the Interpreter redundant).

This result—the missing rabbit-belief—is not acceptable. You definitely had that belief, if only for the reason that it might have influenced your action (although in fact it did not). Suppose you have a helpful disposition, and dislike rabbits. Had you met a rabbit hunter on the path a little after time t, you would have reported the rabbit sighting. The point here could apply equally to your ruminations on *Word and Object*—perhaps you come to believe during your walk that Quine is seriously mistaken, and out of embarrassment never give any indication then or later that this is what you believe.

Our initial formulation of interpretivism cannot be correct. The Interpreter must know, or be able to know, what the subject *would* have done, not just what he *actually* did.

Clearly, what *would* have happened had you met a rabbit hunter is relevant here. Could we perhaps equip our Interpreter with knowledge of a vast set of counterfactuals of the form: if so-and-so had happened, then you would have done such-and-such?

There are two immediate problems with this suggestion, apart from the obvious difficulty of specifying just what counterfactuals are supposed to count.

First, we cannot allow the counterfactuals to be couched in terms of belief and desire. It is sufficient to note that this suggestion is quite unmotivated—why should we allow the Interpreter to freely help herself to beliefs you *would* have had, but not to beliefs you *do* have? It is often *harder* to divine a subject's *counterfactual* beliefs than to find out what he *actually* believes.

Second, irrespective of the vocabulary in which the counterfactuals are supposed to be couched, giving the Interpreter such knowledge is to firmly distance her from all examples of the process of interpretation that are given in the literature. Note that problem of actuality arises because knowledge of how the subject *actually* behaves—both inside and outside the head—will not deliver the right results. Therefore we have to give the Interpreter knowledge of counterfactuals that *cannot* be known on the basis of how the subject actually behaves. But the ordinary person adopting the intentional stance, or the anthropologist approaching a totally alien tribe, are simply not in possession of enormous quantities of counterfactual knowledge that cannot be gleaned from actual observation of the subject.

Now I have been unable to find a clear argument for interpretivism in the writings of either Dennett or Davidson. Their many insights concerning the mind can all be, and should all be, sharply divorced from this epistemological thesis. Be this as it may, *if* the literature contains any arguments for interpretivism, it seems fair to suppose that they depart either from the premise that the Interpreter is an idealisation of an ordinary person adopting the intentional stance, or from the premise that the Interpreter is an idealised anthropologist. But the problem of actuality shows that interpretivism, if the Interpreter wears either of these hats, is false. Therefore *if* there are any arguments for interpretivism in the literature, they are mistaken.

Third Objection: the problem of language

Language-using believers do not all use the same language, of course, and this poses an immediate problem for Dennett. For any Interpreter has got to understand the language of those she interprets, and directly building this into the Interpreter's powers amounts to smuggling in facts about the subject's beliefs. But it is quite unclear how else we are to give the Homely Interpreter (who, recall, interprets his subjects as you might interpret me) the resources she requires. There would appear to be little hope of arguing that some idealised version of myself, transplanted to China, *must* be capable, using *everyday* interpretive methods, of learning Chinese. Here Davidson is evidently on firmer ground, so let us examine how the Radical Interpreter might fare.

Davidson apparently has some general line of thought leading to the conclusion that the Radical Interpreter must be able to learn exactly what a subject's language means. But what this line of thought is, I find very hard to discover. The places in Davidson's writings where the methodology of radical interpretation receives most discussion (1973, 1974b) do not, as far as I can see, contain it. However, in "The Structure and Content of Truth" (1990), Davidson writes:

> As Ludwig Wittgenstein, not to mention Dewey, G.H. Mead, Quine, and many others have insisted, language is intrinsically social. This does not entail that truth and meaning can be defined in terms of observable behaviour, or that it is "nothing but" observable behaviour; but it does imply that meaning is entirely

determined by observable behaviour, even readily observable behaviour. That meanings are decipherable is not a matter of luck; public availability is a constitutive aspect of language (p. 314).

The argument is a little terse.[23] It does, however, hint at an explicit argument along these lines:

Premise

(1) As Wittgenstein showed, there can be no "private languages". That is, if S speaks some language L, it must be possible for others to come to know (a) that S speaks L, and (b) all truths of the form 'sentence s means (in L) that p'.

Premise

(2) Our reasons for thinking we have understood a speaker are ultimately based on observation (of him, or those others who speak his language).

Premise

(3) When we observe a speaker, what we observe is behaviour.

Therefore:

(4) Any language can be learnt by observing some speaker of that language.

Premise

(5) If observable behaviour did not determine meaning, then we could not learn a language by observing some speaker of it.

Therefore:

(6) The meaning of any language is determined by the observable behaviour of some speaker of that language.

(4) gives the desired conclusion about radical interpretation, which is just as well, because the move from (4) to (6) is unwarranted. (5) is clearly false. If the condition which it states were imposed generally, most learning

---

23. It bears comparison with Dummett's arguments for anti-realism (see e.g. Dummett 1973). For some discussion, see Craig 1982 and Devitt 1991, chapter 14.

would be impossible. We have learnt much about the world that is not "determined" by what we have learnt it from.

Turn now to the argument for (4). Let us grant the first premise, for the sake of the argument (for what I take to be the correct rebuttal to—what is usually regarded as—the "private language argument", see Craig 1982). Now suppose you and I are both speakers of L. It would seem that I can have good reason to think that this is so, through our complex social interaction (how does it work this well if we speak different languages?). It is, perhaps, harmless to take this reason, as (2) declares, to be "ultimately based on observation". Turn now to the meaning of 'behaviour' in (3). Is this "behaviour described in folk psychological and semantic terms"? It can't be, on pain of giving the Interpreter knowledge of the subject's beliefs and desires from the start. But then (3) is highly contentious. For (3), in conjunction with (2), requires that my reasons for thinking that you speak L are "ultimately based" on observation of mere bodily movements plus "holdings true". That is hardly obvious. When we observe others, we do not only observe "raw behaviour" or that they hold certain symbol strings true—we also observe them *acting*, or *stating something*, and so forth. And it is these *folk psychologically/semantically described* deliverances of observation on which my reasons for thinking that you speak L are "ultimately based". At any rate, no considerations have been offered to make us doubt this natural way of describing matters.

Even if the first three premises are granted, (4) does not follow. (4) says that any language can be learnt by observing some speaker of that language. But the first three premises do not even imply *that language learning is possible*, let alone that all languages are learnable. The first premise, for instance, says that if A speaks L, then it must be possible for some other speaker B to know that A speaks L, and to know what is stated by the translation manual for L. Of course, to do the latter, B must understand L himself. However, there is no obvious reason why B, or anyone else, should have *learnt L*, or be capable of doing so. And it is clear at a glance that the second and third premises are equally unconnected with language learning. To be sure, we humans learn the languages we speak, but this seems to be an empirical fact, not one discoverable a priori.

In any case, (4) is too weak. (4) could at most support: for any language L, L must be learnable by the methodology of radical interpretation. But it does not follow from this that, given any speaker, S, of L, L must be learnable by radically interpreting *S*. Yet that strong conclusion seems to be what Davidson needs. For take some speaker of *L*, *S*, whose language cannot be learnt by radically interpreting *S* (perhaps because conversation is not *S*'s strong suit). The Radical Interpreter must be able to discover that *S* speaks *L*, if she is to find out what *S* believes. The reconstructed argument, even if sound, won't allow us to conclude that the Radical Interpreter can find out that *S* speaks *L*.

The line of argument suggested by Davidson's remarks, therefore, does not appear promising; the "problem of language" remains.[24,25]

5. Interpretivism weakened

I took interpretivism to be the a priori thesis that:

x believes that *p* iff if there were an appropriately informed Ideal Interpreter, she would be disposed to attribute to *x* the belief that *p*.

The Ideal Interpreter, according to Dennett, is a *Homely* Interpreter; according to Davidson, she is a *Radical* Interpreter. I raised a number of difficulties for both versions of interpretivism. Jointly, I think them conclusive. But it might be that there is a weaker kind of third-personal interpretivism about mental content, substantial enough to be of philosophical interest, yet immune to the previous objections. That is what I shall now examine.

---

24. A fourth problem might be called the "problem of anthropocentrism". The Ideal Interpreter, recall, is an idealisation of a *human being*. And if the reference to a human being is taken seriously, then it would seem interpretivism implies that there could not be believers who spoke a language uninterpretable by human beings. And Davidson, of course, has explicitly argued that, indeed, there could not be such believers ("On the Very Idea of a Conceptual Scheme", 1974a). However, I believe that Davidson's paper contains materials which point to the very opposite conclusion (a rare vindication of deconstruction!). (Mark Johnston has expressed similar views in a seminar—see Hurley 1992.) So here we have a potential *reductio* of Davidson-style interpretivism.
25. In his 1994, a reply to Fodor and Lepore 1994, Davidson for the most part says things quite compatible with interpretivism. But there is one glaringly recalcitrant passage. Davidson denies he has "ever argued for the claim that radical interpretability is a condition of interpretability" and says that he has "never argued that every language is radically interpretable". "I do not think", he continues, "that radical interpretation of natural languages *must* be possible; I have only argued that it *is* possible" (p. 122). If I understand these remarks correctly, Davidson is claiming simply that, as a matter of contingent empirical fact, human natural languages are radically interpretable.

With one exception to be consigned to a footnote, my objections to interpretivism were directed at the claim that the interpretivist's biconditionals provide *necessary* conditions for a subject to believe that p.[26] For example, I complained (the Third Objection) that there is no a priori guarantee that the Interpreter could learn the subject's language, and so no a priori guarantee that the Interpreter could find out all the subject's beliefs (in particular, those that are linguistically expressed). But that only shows that the Interpreter might fail to recognise a subject's belief, not that she might be wrong in making a positive belief attribution. So let us weaken interpretivism to provide merely *sufficient* conditions, as follows:

> x believes that p if the following conditional holds: if there were an appropriately informed Ideal Interpreter, she would be disposed to attribute to x the belief that p.

Here we are allowing that the Interpreter might miss some beliefs, in her final report of what a subject believes. But, if a belief attribution appears in the report, then (according to the weakened thesis), the subject definitely has it.

However, there is a fundamental difficulty, afflicting both Dennett and Davidson alike, which can be extracted from the problem of actuality (the Second Objection). Our attributions of belief are, for the most part, defeasible. If we observe what someone actually does, and ascribe beliefs to him on

---

But this is inconsistent, it seems to me, with some of Davidson's other writings. For example, in his 1986, he argues against scepticism roughly as follows. First, he claims that a Radical Interpreter would find the subject of interpretation as holding mostly true beliefs, by the Interpreter's lights. Then he claims that "an interpreter who is omniscient about the world" (p. 317) is one permissible choice of Radical Interpreter. Hence we (possible subjects of an Omniscient Interpreter) have mostly true beliefs by the Omniscient Interpreter's lights, which is to say mostly true beliefs *simpliciter*. I do not understand how this argument against the sceptic could get off the ground if it requires a contingent empirical premise about natural languages.

26. The exception is the last problem considered under the First Objection. That example concerned a subject who believes that he is *not* being interpreted, but who would change his mind if he were being interpreted. Supposing that the Interpreter would interpret the subject as believing that he *was* being interpreted, the initial formulation of interpretivism gives the result that the Interpreter's judgement is mistaken. Hence the Interpreter's judging that the subject believes that p is not sufficient for the subject to believe that p. But this problem can be overcome, as I discuss, by appeal to Wright's "provisional equations". I ignore this complication in the text below.

this basis, we must be prepared to revise our opinion if certain new evidence comes to light. For example, suppose that someone is looking in good light at a cup on a table, affirms that there is a cup on the table, reaches out for it when the tea is ready to pour, and so on. Clearly he believes that there is a cup on the table! But not necessarily. He may take himself to be the victim of some crafty cup-illusion, and not wish to give the impression that he is wise to the trick. Admittedly, this hypothesis is a little wild. But as it is a conceivable explanation of the subject's actual behaviour, the Interpreter must be able to rule it out, if her opinion that the subject believes that there is a cup on the table is guaranteed to be correct. If the hypothesis can be conclusively ruled out at all, the Interpreter will have to know what the subject *would* have done in various circumstances, not merely what he *actually* does. But this is the problem of actuality all over again. Therefore, either we restrict the Interpreter's knowledge to the subject's actual behaviour, in which case the Interpreter's firm opinions—if she has any—will be scant indeed, or else we squarely face the problem of actuality. But I do not see how that problem can be solved.[27]

In "A Study in Scarlet", Dr. Watson reported his reaction to an article written, as he later discovered, by Sherlock Holmes, as follows:

> It struck me as a remarkable mixture of shrewdness and absurdity. The reasoning was close and intense, but the deductions appeared to me to be far fetched and exaggerated. The writer claimed by a momentary expression, a twitch of a muscle or a glance of an eye, to fathom a man's innermost thoughts. Deceit, according to

---

27. There is a final corner into which an interpretivist might retreat, following the failure of the merely sufficient conditions proposal. Take the Interpreter now simply to have an unimpeachable positive opinion that the subject of interpretation has a mind—not whether he believes that *p*, or desires that *q*, but simply whether he has beliefs and desires at all. That is:

    x is a thinking being if the following conditional holds: if there were an appropriately informed Ideal Interpreter, she would be disposed to judge that *x* is a thinking being.

    Arguably, the Interpreter would give the same judgements in the same physical circumstances, so this proposal would—if true—vindicate a supervenience claim: that the physical facts are at least metaphysically *sufficient* for the existence of minds. The proposal also has the merit of solving the problem of other minds (a virtue shared by the stronger versions of interpretivism). For I think it reasonable that an idealised version of myself would continue to *judge* that you have a mind, and therefore I can reasonably conclude, if the present version of interpretivism is correct, that you *have* a mind.

him, was an impossibility in the case of one trained to observation and analysis. His conclusions were as infallible as so many propositions of Euclid.

Interpretivism—at least in the versions we have considered here—is indeed, to borrow Watson's phrase, "far fetched and exaggerated". There is a certain irony in the fact that Dennett, and also Davidson, are prone to see Cartesianism as the root of all error in the philosophy of mind. They rightly repudiate the Cartesian picture of the mental as an inner stage to which the subject has complete and infallible access. But it seems to me that the picture still lingers on: the audience of one has been expanded, but the view of the stage remains as clear as ever. In denying that the Cartesian theatre is essentially private, interpretivism simply opens it up to the public.[28]

The present version is closely connected with the well-known Turing test. In "Computing Machinery and Intelligence" (1950) Alan Turing proposed, roughly, that if some entity could *convince* a human interrogator via a teleprinter that it was thinking, then it *was* thinking. In other words, passing the "Turing test" (not Turing's phrase) is sufficient for having a mind. This characterisation *is* a little rough. In the first place, Turing proposed to "replace" the question "Can a machine think?"—which he found "too meaningless to deserve discussion" (p. 49)—with the question "Can a machine pass the Turing test?" And in the second place, the machine had to do more than convince the interrogator that it was thinking. For Turing's actual proposal was that the machine must fool the interrogator into taking it to be a *human being*. But there is no obvious reason why it should have to do *that*—why is simply convincing the interrogator that he is talking to a thinking thing not sufficient? This unnecessary restriction on what counts as passing the test led Turing to consider objections of the form: a machine can't fall in love or be telepathic, etc., but human beings can. These objections are irrelevant to the question of whether a machine could pass the Turing test conceived of as a test for *thinking*, rather than as a test for humanity. All this is a little ironic, since the Turing test has been widely criticised for being too *easy*, not too *hard*.

Now in fact I think that this etiolated form of interpretivism can be made very hard to refute, in the sense that there are no convincing counterexamples. But I suspect that its appeal is precisely the appeal of the notorious "paradigm case argument", much discussed in the heyday of linguistic philosophy. "Surely *you* are a *paradigm case* of another mind. Therefore there *are* other minds." The difficulties with this are well-known.

28. Thanks to Fiona Cowie, Mark Johnston, David Lewis, Jim Pryor, Gideon Rosen, Mark Sainsbury, Mike Thau, Ralph Wedgwood, and two anonymous referees for the *European Review of Philosophy*. I am also grateful to a number of audiences who had the misfortune to hear earlier versions.

Department of Linguistics & Philosophy
Massachusetts Institute of Technology
77 Massachusetts Avenue
Cambridge, MA 02139-4307
USA
abyrne@mit.edu

References

Blackburn, S. 1984 *Spreading the Word*, Oxford: Oxford University Press.

Burge, T. 1979 "Individualism and the Mental," in P. French, T. Uehling, and H. Wettstein, eds., *Midwest Studies in Philosophy* 4, Minneapolis: University of Minnesota Press, 74–121.

Child, W. 1994 *Causality, Interpretation and the Mind*, Oxford: Oxford University Press.

Craig, E. 1982 "Meaning, Use, and Privacy," *Mind* 41, 541–64.

Davidson, D. 1973 "Radical Interpretation," Reprinted in Davidson 1985, 125–39.

Davidson, D. 1974a "On the Very Idea of a Conceptual Scheme," Reprinted in Davidson 1985, 183–98.

Davidson, D. 1974b "Belief and the Basis of Meaning," Reprinted in Davidson 1985, 141–54.

Davidson, D. 1979 "The Inscrutability of Reference," Reprinted in Davidson 1985, 227–41.

Davidson, D. 1985 *Inquiries into Truth and Interpretation*, Oxford: Oxford University Press.

Davidson, D. 1986 "A Coherence Theory of Truth and Knowledge," in E. Lepore, ed., *Truth and Interpretation: perspectives on the philosophy of Donald Davidson*, Oxford: Basil Blackwell, 307–19.

Davidson, D. 1990 "The Structure and Content of Truth," *Journal of Philosophy* 68, 279–328.

Davidson, D. 1992 "The Second Person," in P. French, T. Uehling, and H. Wettstein, eds., *Midwest Studies in Philosophy* 17, Minneapolis: University of Minnesota Press, 255–67.

Davidson, D. 1994 "Radical Interpretation Interpreted," in J. Tomberlin, ed., *Philosophical Perspectives* 8, Atascadero, Ca.: Ridgeview Press, 121–28.

Dennett, D. C. 1971 "Intentional Systems," Reprinted in Dennett 1981, 3–22.

Dennett, D. C. 1977 "A Cure for the Common Code?" Reprinted in Dennett 1981, 90–108.

Dennett, D. C. 1978 "Three Kinds of Intentional Psychology," Reprinted in Dennett 1987, 43–68.

Dennett, D. C. 1979 "True Believers," Reprinted in Dennett 1987, 13–35.

Dennett, D. C. 1981 *Brainstorms*, Brighton, England: The Harvester Press.

Dennett, D. C. 1987 *The Intentional Stance*, Cambridge, Mass.: MIT Press.

Dennett, D. C. 1987a "Evolution, Error, and Intentionality," in Dennett 1987. 287–321.

Dennett, D. C. 1987b "Mid–Term Examination: Compare and Contrast," in Dennett 1987.

Dennett, D. C. 1988 "Quining Qualia," in A. J. Marcel and E. Bisiach, eds. *Consciousness in Contemporary Science*, Oxford: Oxford University Press, 42–77.

Devitt, M. 1991 *Realism and Truth*, second edition, Oxford: Basil Blackwell.

Divers, J., and A. Miller 1994 "Best Opinion, Intention-Detecting and Analytic Functionalism," *Philosophical Quarterly* 44, 239–45.

Dummett, M. A. E. 1973 "The Philosophical Basis of Intuitionistic Logic," Reprinted in Dummett 1978, 215–47.

Dummett, M. A. E. 1978 *Truth and Other Enigmas*, London: Duckworth.

Fodor, J. A., and E. Lepore 1992 *Holism: a shopper's guide*, Oxford: Basil Blackwell.

Fodor, J. A., and E. Lepore 1994 "Is Radical Interpretation Possible?" in J. Tomberlin, ed., *Philosophical Perspectives* 8, Atascadero, Ca.: Ridgeview Press, 101–19.

Holton, R. 1993 "Intention Detecting," *Philosophical Quarterly* 43, 298–318.

Hurley, S. L. 1992 "Intelligibility, Imperialism, and Conceptual Scheme," in P. French, T. Uehling, and H. Wettstein, eds., *Midwest Studies in Philosophy* 17, Minneapolis: University of Minnesota Press, 89–108.

Johnston, M. 1992 "How To Speak of the Colors," *Philosophical Studies* 68, 221–63.

Johnston, M. 1993a "Objectivity Refigured: Pragmatism Without Verificationism," in J. Haldane and C. Wright, eds., *Reality, Representation, and Projection*, Oxford: Oxford University Press, 85–130.

Johnston, M. 1993b "The Missing Explanation Argument and Its Impact On Subjectivism," Ms.

Lewis, D. K. 1974 "Radical Interpretation," Reprinted in his *Philosophical Papers*, vol. 1, Oxford: Oxford University Press, 1983, 108–18.

Peacocke, C. 1983 *Sense and Content*, Oxford: Oxford University Press.

Quine, W. V. O. 1960 *Word and Object*, Cambridge, Mass.: MIT Press.

Shope, R. K. 1978 "The Conditional Fallacy in Contemporary Philosophy," *Journal of Philosophy* 75, 397–413.

Turing, A. M. 1950 "Computing Machinery and Intelligence," Reprinted in M. A. Boden, ed., *The Philosophy of Artificial Intelligence*, Oxford: Oxford University Press, 1990, 40–66.

Van Cleve, J. 1992 "Semantic Supervenience and Referential Indeterminacy," *Journal of Philosophy* 89, 344–61.

Wright, C. 1988 "Moral Values, Projection and Secondary Qualities," *Aristotelian Society Supplementary Volume* 62, 1–26.

Wright, C. 1989 "Wittgenstein's Rule-Following Considerations and the Central Project of Theoretical Linguistics," in A. George, ed., *Reflections on Chomsky*, Oxford: Basil Blackwell, 233–64.

Wright, C. 1992 *Truth and Objectivity*, Cambridge, Mass.: Harvard University Press.

Wright, C. 1993 "Realism: The Contemporary Debate—W(h)ither Now?" in J. Haldane and C. Wright, eds., *Reality, Representation, and Projection*, Oxford: Oxford University Press, 63–84.

ALISON DENHAM-SAJOVIC
Metaphor and Judgements of Experience

'...It is not true that whenever we hear a piece of music or a line of poetry which impresses us greatly, we say: 'This is indescribable'. But it is true that again and again we do feel inclined to say: 'I can't describe my experience.'...

Suppose we said that we cannot describe in words the expression of God in Michelangelo's 'Adam'. But this is only a matter of technique, because if we drew a latticework over his face, numbered, I would just write down numbers and you might say: 'My God! It's grand.'

It wouldn't be any description. You wouldn't say such a thing at all. It would only be a description if you could paint (act?) according to this picture, which, of course, is conceivable. But this would show that you can't at all transmit the impression by words, but you'd have again to paint.'

—Ludwig Wittgenstein, *Lectures on Aesthetics*

Introduction

Experience can indeed be difficult to describe. Our attempts to 'transmit the impression by words', as Wittgenstein says, often fail to convey all that is conveyed by experience itself. In such cases it is not uncommon for us to advert to figurative devices—to metaphor, simile and the rest. But why should figurative language sometimes succeed where literal language has failed? While I cannot set out my answer to that question here, what I have to say forms one part of that answer. And a background commitment of my discussion is that figurative language *does* sometimes succeed in this way; that is, I take it that in some sense and on some occasions figurative language succeeds in representing aspects of experience which resist characterisation in literal terms.

My present topic is the use of specifically *metaphorical* expressions in the representation of experience. Metaphors are sometimes dispensable, and dispensing with them often profits both our cognitive and communicative ambitions. I will argue that this is not always so, however, and that among the exceptions are certain metaphorical descriptions of phenomenologically characterised psychological states. I have in mind, first, those states marked by a distinctive affective character (such as sorrow or anxiety or elation) and, second, those experiential states bearing a distinctive sensational character, including those both of inner sense (such as pains and tickles) and of outer sense (typically, the perceptual deliverances of seeing, hearing, touching, smelling, and tasting). There is a reasonably uncontroversial sense in which all of these possess a 'phenomenological character'. It is this: a subject in some such state can sensibly aim not only to describe what it is his experience is *of*— the objects of his experience, as it were—but to describe himself qua *subject* of that experience. So, for instance, one may aim to describe the expression of God in Michaelangelo's 'Adam'; but one may equally aim to describe one's own condition as one gazes on that expression— how one's emotions are effected by the painting, or the specific, subjective character of one's visual experiences.[1] Whichever is one's project—to capture just what a given experience is an experience of, or to say what it is like for the subject whose experience it is—the fine grain of experience is often best captured metaphorically. Hence the special, initially metaphorical, vocabularies marking the discourse of the wine-taster, the art critic, the musician, the decorator, the gourmet.

Why should this be so? Why should metaphors feature so prominently and pervasively in the representation of phenomenologically characterised states? Perhaps the answer is, first, that in these contexts metaphors sometimes say something meaningful and, second, that what they say can not be said in other terms. In short, the answer may be that metaphors are (sometimes) both cognitive and irreducible, and that one case in which this is (sometimes) so is in metaphorical descriptions of phenomenology. That is in any case the answer which I will propose here.

As a preliminary, we require some account of metaphorical meaning,

---

1. I do not wish to suggest, however, that perceptual phenomenology can be characterised independently of the objects of perception. Indeed, that phenomenology so commonly resists independent characterisation is part of what motivates our appeal to figurative descriptions.

for there are accounts of metaphor which would discount the possibility that they represent anything at all. Part 1 is concerned in the main with this preliminary. Parts 2 and 3 develop a particular account for the category of metaphor to which my question pertains.

1.

1.1 In classical rhetoric, metaphor is distinguished as that trope for which an unstated relation of resemblance or similarity obtains between the utterance topic and the extension of the figurative term or expression applied to it—what we may call, following Richards, its 'vehicle'. Quintilian, for instance, refers to metaphor as 'a shorter form of simile'; Cicero describes metaphor as a 'brief similitude'; Aristotle wrote that to be good at metaphor is 'a sign of natural genius, as to be good at metaphor is to perceive resemblances'. I too characterise metaphor in a way which reflects the idea that there is a tight connection between metaphor and judgements of similarity: *a metaphor is a contextually identified figurative use of language whereby one thing is spoken of in contra-indicated terms that are standardly appropriate to another and in which the relation obtaining between the two is an unstated relation of similarity.*[2]

I aim to defend the idea that at least some metaphors meet both of two conditions. The first condition is that they are cognitive—they express truth-

---

2. Less briefly, metaphors are (a) contextually identified, figurative expressions, (b) of variable length and complexity, (c) characterising one thing (or kind of thing) in contra-indicated terms which are standardly appropriate to another thing or kind of thing (that is, for some *a* or *a*-type and some distinct *b* or *b*-type, metaphors characterise *a* in terms that our descriptive and prescriptive linguistic norms standardly indicate as appropriate to *b*); further (d) metaphors present *a* and *b* as standing in a relation of similarity or resemblance and (e) in metaphors, unlike similes or figurative comparisons, the relation of similarity is not presented by being asserted; that relation is not explicitly signalled. This characterisation abjures assuming what arguably ought not to be assumed, namely that we have to hand a clear distinction between the literal and non-literal. It also locates metaphoricity as a property of *contextually* identified utterance types. This does not, however, consign it *a priori* to the arena of pragmatics rather than semantics. It is true that if 'semantics' is narrowly defined as concerned with null context or default context assignments of meaning to sentences in virtue of the signs they contain and the order they are in, then there are no specifically semantic features of utterance types that are sufficient to determine the status of an expression as

apt judgements of states of affairs. The second condition is that they are 'conceptually autonomous'— the contents they express are not reducible to literal paraphrase.[3] Not every theory of metaphor allows that metaphors meet both of these conditions. Indeed, with few exceptions, accounts of figurative discourse, and of metaphor in particular, endorse *either* condition at the expense of the other: that is, they claim *either* that figurative discourse and the judgements expressed within it are non-cognitive and conceptually autonomous *or* they claim that figurative discourse is cognitive and conceptually supervenient. For convenience I'll call the alternative types of account *Non-cognitivist* and *Reductionist* respectively. 'Non-cognitivism' is a traditional label in this context, and its most familiar classical representative is perhaps Plato's Socrates of the *Ion*; contemporary counterparts are Davidson, Rorty and David Cooper. 'Reductionism' is a label I apply (with some reservations) to a complex of old attempts; its most familiar classical representative is Aristotle, particularly Aristotle of the *Rhetoric*, and in modern theory it has been represented by Max Black, Robert Fogelin and John Searle, among others.[4]

I will briefly sketch each of these positions in turn.

1.2 Non-cognitivism typically denies that metaphors express judgements, and restricts candidacy for truth assignments to the arena of the literal. As one proponent of this sort of account put the point nearly thirty years ago: '[If a sentence] contains an irreducible metaphor, it follows at once that the sentence is devoid of cognitive meaning, that it is unintelligible, that it fails to make a genuine assertion.'[5] In contemporary non-cogni-

---

metaphorical. But semantics need not be so construed. (Mere relativisation to speaker, time and place will leave *semantics* largely silent on the status of sentence as figurative, while broader conceptions of semantically relevant features of context may not.)

3. The phrase 'conceptual autonomy' is, in this context, owed to Crispin Wright. The question of whether a discourse is conceptually autonomous is just the question of whether it is or is not possible to state the truth conditions of assertoric utterances within the discourse solely in terms of concepts extraneous to it. An alternative way of thinking about conceptual autonomy is this: A discourse *fails* to be conceptually autonomous if all intelligible disagreements about the truth of judgements expressible in the discourse finally depend on disagreements about the truth of judgements extraneous to it. If it fails in this way, we may say that it is *conceptually supervenient* (c.f. Wright, 1994).
4. Davidson (1978: 31–47); Rorty (1987); Cooper (1986); Black (1962); Fogelin (1988); Searle (1978).

tivist accounts, this restriction follows naturally from the view that such candidacy is established by conformity to certain prescriptive and descriptive linguistic norms, norms set by conventional use; as metaphors and other figures (by definition) transgress those norms they are *eo ipso* disqualified as truth-apt, and so disqualified as cognitive. To be sure, they may elicit all manner of responses from us, but they do so not by way of expressing any genuine contents or articulating any judgements or assertions. Whatever may count as a judgement proper must be stated in literal terms—for if words are to be meaningful at all, they must be used in accordance with recognised meaning-determining norms.

Davidson has endorsed something like this view, claiming that metaphors 'like a picture or a bump on the head, make us appreciate some fact, but not by standing for or expressing that fact'.[6] Likewise, Rorty has claimed that our ability to understand metaphors is like our ability to 'understand' bird-song or music; he describes figurative language as 'unpredictable stimuli', concluding that 'the genius who transcends the predictable thereby transcends the cognitive and the meaningful'.[7] Plato offered a similar suggestion in rather more poetic terms: 'The poet', he said, 'is a light and winged thing, and holy…and is never able to compose until…he is beside himself and reason is no longer in him'.[8]

With respect to the second condition mentioned above—the status of metaphors as conceptually autonomous—Non-cognitivism treats metaphorical discourse as irreducible, because there is nothing there to reduce: strictly speaking, there are no metaphorical judgements. Our practises of paraphrase, on this view, are not to be conceived as elucidating or interpreting metaphorical meanings, for there are no such meanings. Thus Davidson remarks that metaphors cannot be paraphrased, 'not because metaphors say something too novel for literal expression but because there is nothing there to paraphrase'. Paraphrases are *causally* rather than conceptually or rationally related to the metaphorical utterances they elucidate. Attempts to set out systematic conceptual connections between metaphorical and literal uses of terms, he says, 'mistake their goal. Where they think they provide a

---

5. Edwards (1965)
6. Davidson (1978).
7. Rorty (1987).
8. Plato, *Ion*.

method for deciphering an encoded content, they actually tell us...something about the effects metaphors have on us. The common error is to fasten on the contents of the thoughts a metaphor *provokes* and to read these contents into the metaphor itself'.[9]

1.3 Reductionist accounts, by contrast, propose to treat metaphors as, precisely, expressing encoded contents. These accounts vary greatly, with some of their most prominent exponents (such as Black) supposing themselves to be arguing *against* the possibility of translating the metaphorical into the literal. But they all have in common a commitment to the availability of something like an analysis of metaphorical content in literal terms, where an analysis amounts to a *non-circular specification of its truth conditions*. Such analyses typically fix upon the terms used figuratively, and treat them as labels for a complex of judgements which can be spelled out in literal terms. The Reductionist thus typically defends the claims of some metaphors to be at least minimally cognitive, but cognitivity is only won by elimination—that, is by translation into the literal. Let us say that a metaphor is cognitive just if speakers can avail themselves of principled, shared procedures for (a) determining what are its truth (or assertibility) conditions and (b) deciding, at least in principle, whether those conditions prevail. A Reductionist account takes (a) and (b) both to hold for those metaphors which submit successfully to paraphrastic analysis: if there *are* principled, shared procedures for setting out a metaphor's truth conditions in literal terms, and if, in turn, speakers are able in principle to determine whether they do or do not obtain, then the metaphor's claim to cognitivity is vindicated.[10]

The Reductionist's position with respect to the status of metaphors as conceptually autonomous should also now be obvious. Metaphorical discourse, if it is meaningful at all, is not conceptually autonomous, but parasitic or conceptually supervenient: all intelligible disagreements about the truth of judgements expressed metaphorically will thus depend on disagreements

---

9. Davidson (1978).
10. See, for example, Black's account in 'More about Metaphor', in *Metaphor and Thought*, ed. Ortony, A., Cambridge, 1978. Black takes himself to be resisting substitution and comparison views alike, and claims that the 'interactive' process by which metaphorical meaning emerges has the consequence that their meanings cannot be captured in literal terms. But he then proceeds to spell out procedures for doing precisely that. Black is attached to the *idea* of interaction, but it finds no genuine home in his account of metaphorical content.

about the truth of judgements expressed in non-figurative terms. (The Reductionist's position with respect to metaphor is in this respect analogous to that of some moral cognitivists who win cognitive standing for evaluative discourse by proposing to provide definitions of the concepts distinctive of it in naturalistic terms.)

If the metaphorical is conceptually supervenient on the literal, then any disagreement about a metaphorically expressed belief can *only* be made sense of by appealing to differences of other, independently (and literally) stated beliefs. Suppose, for instance, that two readers disagree about the truth of Lady Macbeth's remark that her husband's heart is 'lily white'. One reader says that (in the context of the play, and considering all that it offers about the King's actions and character) the remark is plainly true and supplies evidence of Lady Macbeth's firm grip on the vagaries of human psychology. The other reader, however, insists that it is false, and evidences nothing more than Lady Macbeth's perverse need to distort the facts about her husband's character. How can this dispute proceed intelligibly, given that it is clearly not the *colour* of the King's heart that is at issue? The Reductionist has a ready explanation. The disagreement can be made intelligible by abandoning the realm of the metaphorical and engaging in a bit of paraphrase. It transpires that one reader takes 'lily white' to be a remark on the King's moral purity, perhaps a purity won by his inability to silence the voice of his conscience. The other takes it to be a remark on his cowardice (and perhaps takes Lady Macbeth to have confused cowardice with appropriate remorse). On this account, each reader justifies his judgement of the truth or falsity of the claim that 'the King has a lily white heart' by appeal to other, literally expressed beliefs. One reader reasons: lilies are a conventional Christian symbol of purity and resurrection, and white is a conventional symbol of innocence, of freedom from corruption. The other reader reasons: lilies are a conventional symbol of bloodlessness, as well as femininity, and white is the conventional symbol of surrender—the coward's refusal to fight. And so on. Given the context of utterance and other knowledge about the actions and attitudes of the characters, the two readers translate the metaphor into two different judgements, yielding two different assignments of truth values. Retracing the justificatory route taken by each reader we can at least hope to understand the disagreement, and we may even hope to resolve it.

1.4 Certain virtues attach to the Non-cognitivist and the Reductionist approaches alike. But they both err in attempting to offer an account that will do for any and all metaphors.

Non-cognitivism, for example, has much to recommend it as a theory apt to capture our appreciation of some of the more obscure imagist and symbolists poets. (Trakl and Celan, for example, provide excellent candidates for an account which holds that the interest of metaphors lies not in some specific—and paraphrasable—truth-bearing content, but in the perlocutionary effects they have on feeling and imagination.) Nonetheless, can it really be that there are *no* systematic rational relations holding between metaphors and literal paraphrases in *any* cases? Non-cognitivists arguably purchase autonomy for metaphorical discourse at an inflated price. Our ability to understand a metaphorical expression surely does depend *somehow* on our grasp of the more ordinary or pedestrian or standard senses of the terms of which it is composed. Paraphrases are not miracles.

Likewise, Reductionist accounts have much to recommend them with respect to certain metaphors: they can easily set out the translation-procedures on which one might rely in understanding familiar (or nearly idiomatic) metaphors such as Black's 'Man is a wolf' or Searle's 'Sally is a block of ice'. But once we move beyond such simple cases, do we really wish to embrace the idea that if a metaphor says anything at all, the truth-relevant content of what it says could in principle be said otherwise? This is an improbable claim even for much (I think most) of literal language.

It is just a mistake—and a bad starting-place for a theory of metaphor—to suppose that there is some one theory of metaphorical meaning appropriate for the whole of the varied typology of metaphorical utterances. It is likewise a mistake to suppose that there are any intelligible and true answers to the questions 'Is *all* figurative language minimally cognitive?' and 'Is *all* figurative language conceptually supervenient on literal language?'.[11] These are bad questions, which too often have elicited bad answers. They are bad

---

11. The phrases 'minimally cognitive' and 'minimally truth-apt' are adaptations of Crispin Wright's conception of 'minimal truth': 'The notion of truth which…is neutral territory regulates any statement-making practice which displays [this] interlocking set of characteristics…: [It is] a practise which is disciplined by acknowledged standards of justication and justified criticism, which has the syntax to be subjugated to ordinary sentential logic, which sustains embeddings within propositional attitudes, and where ignorance and error are possible categories of explanation of aberrant performances by its practitioners'. Wright (1993:69)

questions because they are too general, and too insensitive to important distinctions *within* the domain of the metaphorical. In attempting to answer them, Non-cognitivism and Reductionism alike foreclose on other, more illuminating alternatives.

I wish to set out one particular such alternative which is, I think, of special interest. It is an account that applies only to a restricted category or kind of metaphor, a kind individuated (in part) by its role in articulating both experiences and certain experience-dependent properties (e.g., affective experience, secondary qualities and aesthetic properties). I will call these *phenomenological metaphors*. In Part 2 I will identify the distinguishing features of this category, and defend its claims to both cognitivity and autonomy.

2.

2.1 Phenomenological metaphors are better introduced by example than by definition, and Proust serves this end very well. Widely acknowledged as a master of metaphorical description, Proust is often concerned to describe the first-person perspective of a character's experiential phenomenology; he devotes a great many passages to the careful articulation of the specifics of various experience-types, surveying them as if from the perspective of the experiencing subject. Equally often, he focuses on the description of experience-dependent properties of *objects* of experience—those sensible properties traditionally characterised as their secondary qualities—odours, colours, tones, felt textures. Proust's efforts are especially impressive when the properties described are not easily labelled or named, and part of what most interests him are those aspects of the world which vigorously resist submitting to linguistic order. His descriptions of music, for instance, speak for themselves. We are told that in *Tristan* one finds

> insistent, fleeting themes which visit an act, recede only to return again and again, and, sometimes distant, dormant, almost detached, are at other moments, while remaining vague, so pressing and so close, so internal, so organic, so visceral, that they seem like the reprise not so much of a musical motif as of an attack of neuralgia[12]

and that Vinteuil's symphonic music is

> a ray of summer sunlight which the prism of the window decomposes before it enters a dark dining-room[13]

---

12. Proust (1992: 174)
13. Proust (1992: 287)

and that the same composer's orchestration

> guided [the listener], deriving, from the colours he had just hit upon, a wild joy which gave him the strength to discover...enraptured, quivering as though from the shock of an electric spark when the sublime came spontaneously to life at the clang of the brass, panting, intoxicate, unbridled, vertiginous, while he painted his great musical fresco, like Michelangelo strapped to his scaffold and from his upside-down position hurling tumultuous brush-strokes on to the ceiling of the Sistine Chapel.[14]

And so on.

Some readers may find Proust extravagant, of course, or have doubts for other reasons about the success or aptness of his descriptions. Be that as it may, to the extent that he does succeed his success depends in part on his skill in constructing expressions where no literal concepts would seem to serve—his skill in the use of metaphor and simile to characterise the fine phenomenological grain of experiential contents. To put the point differently, one might say that Proust was skilful in the construction of *surrogates* for concepts; in particular, he understood well how to construct surrogate 'experience dependent' or 'response-dependent' concepts.[15]

The phrase 'response-dependence' is a refinement of the more familiar notion of mind-dependence often invoked in dispositional accounts of secondary qualities. Response-dependent concepts are sometimes characterised in terms of the properties they pick out, viz., dispositional properties—properties that are (at least in part) identified and individuated by their disposition to elicit particular responses under type-specified conditions in

---

14. Proust (1992: 287)
15. In saying, as I have above, that some metaphorically applied terms and expressions function as *surrogate* response-dependent concepts, I do not wish to rule out the possibility that the metaphorical terms and expressions might count as concepts in their own right. But I will say little here about the specific qualifications for that credential. Any metaphorical terms or expressions that do qualify for it must, at the least, earn their right to do so, just as metaphorical assertions must earn their right to count as judgements—by meeting the requirements of minimal cognitivity. Even if they all fail in *that* regard (as I think they do not) they may nevertheless express subjects' *conceptions* of certain experience types and experienced properties, which conceptions may not be expressible by any terms or expressions offered by the literal lexicon of the natural language in which they occur.

type-specified subjects.[16] 'Red' and 'bitter' and 'acrid' are, on this account, candidate response-dependent concepts. 'Jealous' and 'elated' are others, for it is arguably true *a priori* that to be jealous or elated is indeed to be disposed to manifest certain requisite responses (which need not be behavioural) under type-specified standard conditions in type-specified suitable subjects. (If one is passionately jealous, and one is a subject of the specified kind, then under thus-and-such conditions one's responses will be thus-and-so.) I prefer, however, to characterise response-dependent concepts *independently* of any fixed commitment to the kinds of objects or properties they might pick out. This is in part because it seems that we can have response-dependent concepts which pick out objects and properties which are not themselves response-dispositional; that is, we can individuate objects and properties in a way which directly implicates our experiential and other responses without supposing that the availability of that way renders the object or property itself dispositional. We might have, for instance, a perfectly good public concept going of a certain substance which identified it in terms of its propensity to make us sneeze—e.g., the substance that is in fact pepper—without pepper itself being a response-dispositional kind.[17]

The category of response-dependent concepts has been refined and reformulated in a number of different directions. For our purposes, one of Mark Johnston's attempts will serve well enough. It is this:

> If the concept associated with the predicate 'is C' is a concept interdependent with or dependent upon concepts of certain subjects' responses under certain conditions, then something of the following form will hold *a priori* : x is C iff in conditions K, Ss are disposed to produce x-directed response R (or : x is such as to produce R is Ss under conditions K).[18]

We must append to this a requirement that specification of the conditions K, of the suitability of the subjects S and of the responses all must be *substantial* specifications; that is, they may not be filled out trivially so that they 'overtly or covertly specify as the conditions and subjects whatever conditions and whatever subjects are required to get it right'.[19] In short, we may not spec-

---

16. For arguments against such dispositional accounts, see Hacker (1987).
17. See Johnston (1993).
18. Johnston (1989).
19. Wright (1992: Ch.4); See also Wright (1993) for a related notion of 'extension-determining' concepts.

ify any of these conditions merely in terms of 'whatever it takes' to produce the others. What we require are rigidified specifications of what actually do count for us as standard conditions, suitable subjects and requisite responses.

Much more could be said, and has been said elsewhere, about the status and epistemology of response-dependent concepts.[20] But my present remit is to lend conviction to the idea that certain metaphors serve as proxy for concepts of this kind. This schematic account of response–dependence will be adequate to that end.

2.2 Now, I think that certain metaphors can be reasonably described as instances of *catechresis*—the introduction of a new use for an old concept, to fill a lexical gap.[21] Catechretic innovation often fills a gap in the literal lexicon of terms describing phenomenologically characterised experiences and phenomenologically individuated properties—and this occurrence is not restricted to literary contexts. Consider, for instance, the professional vocabularies of musicians and painters, or even the everyday innovations of the child voicing his feelings, the lover expressing his pleasure, the traveller exclaiming on the landscape. In all of these contexts we commonly find extensions of terms specifically aimed at broadening our repertoire. And so it is with the special class of metaphors with which I'm here concerned—phenomenological metaphors. Phenomenological metaphors, as I conceive of them, are distinguished by the following credentials: They (i) function catechretically and (ii) take on a representational role which would otherwise be fulfilled by a response-dependent concept, i.e., a role which would be filled by a response-dependent concept were one available in the speaker's lexicon; they are also (iii) minimally cognitive or minimally truth-apt, and (iv) conceptually autonomous.

So: *do* any metaphors possess the credentials of phenomenological metaphors, thus characterised? I think that many do; certainly such metaphors are not at all uncommon in the more interesting exercises of figurative language—exercises such as Proust's.

---

20. See also my discussion of 'E-concepts' in Denham (forthcoming: chapters 3 and 4).
21. Webster's Dictionary rather unhelpfully defines catachresis as 'the use of the *wrong* word for the context'. I'll forego both that definition and the temptation to comment on its prospects.

Metaphor and Judgements of Experience 237

2.3 My general definition of 'metaphor' holds that metaphors present relations of similarity between two or more things—between the utterance topic and the vehicle extension.[22] The case for the existence of phenomenological metaphors largely depends on how that similarity relation is understood. Now, many theorists have insisted that despite their close connection with simile, metaphors ought *not* to be treated as figurative similarity statements. It is certainly true that the force of a metaphor may be altered by reconstructing it in simile form. Shakespeare's nineteenth sonnet, for instance, begins, 'Devouring Time, blunt thou the lion's paws, and make the earth devour her own sweet brood'. He knew better than to offer us, instead, 'Time, like something devouring, blunt thou the lion's paws, and make the earth do something comparable to some female devouring her own brood, a brood that is like something sweet'. Moreover, it is not obvious how we should even go about reconstructing some metaphors in simile form. Once we move away from a simple subject-predicate syntax the difficulties of doing so are evident. Consider for example, Cummings famous image—'nobody, not even the rain, has such small hands'. This thought would not work at all expressed as 'you are like someone with small hands, hands smaller than anyone's, smaller even than some feature of the rain which feature is like its hands'. Nevertheless, we can acknowledge the special role played by *similarity relations* in the construction and comprehension of metaphor without suggesting that all metaphors can be *replaced by* similes without loss of, or alteration to, either force or intelligibility. That is, we can acknowledge that when

---

22. I use *topic* and *vehicle* in a manner similar to I.A. Richards' terms of *tenor* and *vehicle*. (There are more contemporary labels, but in my judgment they represent no advance on these.) Richards's use is not consistent, however; at times he speaks as if they referred to ideas or images expressed or conveyed by a figurative expression, at times as referring to the expression itself, and at times as referring to the states of affairs or conditions of the world which the expression may represent or describe. As I use *topic* and *vehicle*, the former picks out the actual or possible state of affairs represented or described by a figurative utterance and the latter picks out figurative expressions within that utterance. The topic of Black's metaphor 'Man is a wolf', for instance, is just the alleged wolfish characteristics of man (however those may be spelled out); the vehicle is the (here figurative) expression 'wolf'. The parallel here with the Fregean notions of reference and mode of presentation should be obvious. The parallel is not an exact one, however, and I will use the topic/vehicle terminology for the reference and mode of presentation of *figurative* utterances only.

a metaphor speaks of one thing in terms literally appropriate to another (or, as I say, when something is spoken of in conventionally *contra-indicated* terms) then there is an implicit suggestion that these two things are similar in some relevant respects; no one could grasp the meaning of a metaphor without appreciating that they stand in that relation.

It is by attention to the nature of similarity judgements, I believe, that we will find some support for the claims of phenomenological metaphor. The first thing to note is that the similarity relations indicated by most metaphors will themselves, if stated, yield *figurative* similarity claims—that is, they will propose likenesses relevant to the actual context of utterances which would be contra-indicated in a default context. They yield *similes*, not literal assertions of likeness or comparison. As philosophers are fond of pointing out, of course, all similes are trivially true because everything is like everything else in some or other respect. But this observation is in fact uninteresting, because it assumes that speakers and interpreters are relying on a null, default context for in producing truth-assignments. Were a null context appealed to by speakers and interpreters in everyday conversation, however, we would succeed in understanding one another even less often and less well than we now do. In actual utterance contexts, similes, like other assertions, are candidates for substantial rather than trivial truth, and are distinguished from literal similarity statements precisely because the *context-informed* interpretation of the figuratively used term(s)—typically the vehicle term(s)—must deviate from that appropriate to the default context. Ortony illustrates this point well with sentence-pairs such as the following:

(1) Encyclopaedias are like dictionaries.
(2) Encyclopaedias are like goldmines.

While both (1) and (2) state a relation of likeness, the acceptance conditions of the default context use of 'dictionaries' in (1) parallel those of its actual sentence-context meaning; in (2), however, they do not. Sentence (2) is a simile: if the word 'goldmines' is assigned a default context meaning it could be only trivially true; only an assignment sensitive to its sentence context will allow a thinker to identify the conditions under which (2) would be non-trivially true.

A second point to note is the difference between symmetrical and asymmetrical similarity claims. The traditional 'geometric' model of similarity conceived of similarity as a relation of distance between objects regarded as points in geometric space. One consequence of the geometric model was that people's *judgements* of similarity were described as *symmetrical*—just as the distance between any two points, A and B, in Euclidean space is the same whether one measures from A to B or from B to A. But our similarity judgements often do not exhibit this kind of symmetry: the judgement that an object A is figuratively like an object B and that B is figuratively like A are not symmetrical, for the degree of judged similarity (the 'distance' between the objects) is altered by the order of the terms.[23] Consider, for instance: Venice is like a whore, tedious arguments are like winding streets, minds are like mirrors, money like a modern god. All of these are instances of asymmetrical similes. (Venice may be very like a whore in certain respects, but most whores are not much like Venice; and those that are, are so, e.g., in virtue of being beautiful and wealthy, while it is clearly not in virtue of these properties that Wordsworth proposed the converse comparison.)

Now, I have characterised phenomenological metaphors as (a) minimally cognitive assertions in which the figurative terms or expressions are (b) conceptually autonomous and (c) function catechretically as (d) proxy for response-dependent concepts. I have also proposed that the assertoric content of a metaphor should be understood as implicitly proposing some unstated relation of similarity to obtain between its topic and the vehicle extension. All of this suggests that if any metaphors *are* of this kind, then their truth or assertibility conditions will consist in the obtaining of some relation of similarity that is (i) capable of yielding determinate truth-assignments, and (ii) cannot be expressed in non-figurative terms and (iii) is a property that would otherwise be identified by a response-dependent concept.[24]

So, *are* there any such similarity relations? Surely there are.

2.4 *Some* judgements of similarity, say of the form '*a* is similar to *b*', whether symmetrical or asymmetrical, can be justified or explained or vindicated by specifying some feature or features $S_1...S_n$ common to *a* and *b*. Let us call these 'common-feature' similarity judgements, and the model of the similarity relation to which they conform the common-feature

---

23. For further discussion of the psychology of similarity judgements, see Tversky (1977)
24. That is, it will be a relational property R obtaining between some *a* and some *b* such that the truth of '*aRb*' is determined by the actual responses to *a* and *b* of substantially specified suitable subjects under substantially specified, appropriate, actual conditions.

model. We might take it as a rule that for such similarity judgements, that if *a* is similar to *b*, then there must be some specifiable feature S such that both of them (literally) possess it (and that the thinker believes them to possess it). A common-feature model of similarity will hold the following: For any *a* and any *b* or any *a*-type and any *b*-type, *a* is similar to *b* iff there is some specifiable feature S such that both of them literally possess it. This rule can be used to pick out non-trivial similarities by imposing a contextual relevance requirement: for any token *a* and any token *b* or any *a*-type and any *b*-type, *a* is similar to *b* iff there is some specifiable and contextually relevant feature S such that both of them literally possess it. The contextual relevance requirement is indispensable if the rule is to be of any use in distinguishing true from false similarity judgements.[25]

As Hume observed, however, some similarity judgements are basic and unanalysable: 'Tis evident' he said, 'that even different simple ideas may have a similarity or resemblance to each other, nor is it necessary, that the point or circumstance of the resemblance should be distinct or separable from that in which they differ. Blue and green are different simple ideas, but are more resembling than blue and scarlet; though their perfect simplicity excludes all possibility of separation or distinction'.[26] Hume's examples here are of the observed similarities of perceptually presented objects, and his point is that some such judgements are unsupported by an appeal to commonalties of parts or features independent of those of which the similarity is claimed. We don't assert the similarity of blue and green, and the dissimilarity of blue and scarlet on the basis of some *further* property which blue and green have in common, and which scarlet lacks.

In *The Varieties of Reference*, Gareth Evans develops Hume's suggestion, defending a (broadly Humean) view of similarity judgements which abjures the common-feature model.[27] Evans's account invokes the notion of *non-conceptual*, information-based thought; very roughly, information deriving from the senses, whether as experience or sensation, counts as nonconceptual. Conceptual information, in Evans' use of the phrase, is always embodied in language. 'Information-based' thoughts are, accordingly, thoughts

---

25. For supporting considerations and examples, see Sperber and Wilson (1986: chapter 3) and Denham (forthcoming: chapter 7).
26. Hume (1888: 637).
27. Evans (1980).

based on sensory information for which we can trace a causal route back to the object or objects at which the thoughts in question aim.[28]

Evans argues that some of our similarity judgements are information-based thoughts in this sense, and appeals to the distinction between recognition and recall to illustrate his point. For many perceptually presented objects a thinker's recognitional abilities allow him to judge *on the basis of object's appearance* that it is an object he has encountered on another occasion or occasions. Such abilities are distinct from, and not reducible to, the ability to judge that something *satisfies a certain description*, or *matches a certain iconic image*. We should take the phrase 'on the basis of appearance' to suggest that, in response to the question 'Why do you judge this object (or object-type) to be an *a*?', a thinker could, at the least (and perhaps at the most), be able to respond that it *looks like* or *feels like* or *sounds like* an *a* (or *a*-type thing). If the judgement is recognition-based, the thinker need not rely on some independent identifying feature of a thing being *a*—a feature in terms of which he could offer a justification or explanation or vindication of its looking or feeling or sounding so. Recall-based judgements, by contrast, do require some such independent identification: the thinker there judges that the thing is *a* because he knows that it is $\psi_1...\psi_n$, and knows that *a*-things are also $\psi_1...\psi_n$ (where ψ is specified by either a description or some other type of representation, such as a mental image). The ability to make a recall-based identification is neither necessary nor sufficient for a recognition-based one. It is not necessary because one need not be able to *recall* some description or image-representation of a thing (say, a friend's face or voice) in order to be able to *recognise* it. As Evans says, 'We need not use *anything* to make an identification'.[29] And it is not sufficient, because one's ability to recall a representation does not guarantee that one will rec-

---

28. Many would not now be so ready to tie the conceptual to the linguistic. Evans's choice of terminology, however, is not of so much interest as the distinction he aims to draw to with it. That distinction may be expressed thus: We are capable of having thoughts about objects and properties which are represented in perceptual experience, which objects and properties fail to be individuated either by words specifying types, or words specifying tokens, or by any identifying description. In such cases our thoughts are 'information-based'. The answer to the question 'Of *which* one are you thinking?' would be offered in terms of an historical record of the perceptual presentation of the object or property.
29. Evans (1980: 288).

ognise it when one encounters it: As Evans remarks, '...Even when we can recall the object, what we recall is a fairly poor guide to which object we shall recognise'.[30] But what is it for something to seem like something else, if *not* for them to share some identifiable property, or to both satisfy some specific predicate?

Consider an example. Suppose a musician were so skilled at aural score-transcription that he could listen to a piano sonata and—on that basis alone—were able to construct a highly detailed representation that uniquely identified it : suppose him to be capable of transcribing the piece as a written score, note for note and beat for beat. (Accomplished musicians and composers often are capable of this.) Now suppose further that he is peculiarly defective—due to a neurological malfunction, he possesses only a quite short-term aural memory, so that if more than a few hours lapse since he last heard a piece of music it is to him as if he were hearing it for the first time. (This is not such a fantastic example as one might like to think.) Finally, suppose that he undertakes the score transcription exercise on two separate occasions. Now, when later reading the scores, he is certainly in a position to judge that they transcribe the same composition: he can judge that the piece he heard on, say, Tuesday is the same as that he heard on Wednesday. But is he in a position to judge that Tuesday's performance *sounds similar* to Wednesdays? He is not. It is true that he can infer that a suitable subject in suitable conditions probably *would* judge them to sound similar. But this is not a judgement *he* can make, for he is wholly unable to *perceive* the identity (or similarity) between the two performances *on the basis of their appearance*—as it were, to *recognise* the first one in the second.[31] He is like the unfortunate wine-buyer whose has lost his sense of taste, and must choose his wines in his laboratory by correlating their chemical components with a table of predicates such as 'robust', 'elegant', 'retiring' and so on.

---

30. *Ibid.*
31. The recognition/recall distinction concerns not just how a subject possibly *could* identify some object or object type, but the route of thought he actually *does* exercise. (It is not difficult to find cases in which one does have available an adequately distinguishing recalled representation—such as one's home address—but does not actually *make use* of it in identifying an object or object-type.)

Countless examples could be adduced to illustrate this point — the point that, whatever the sense modality in question, *common-feature judgements of similarity* based on knowledge of common properties are neither necessary nor sufficient for *judgements of similarity of appearance* of the form 'looks like', 'sounds like', 'feels like'. The latter are judgements which require a thinker to conceive of objects in a certain way, namely, by way of an experiential mode of presentation. And where that way is unavailable to him, so are the judgements which only it can yield.

Evans has argued in a similar vein, proposing that in such cases similarity can be thought of as a '…secondary relation—on analogy with the secondary qualities of traditional philosophy, which hold of objects in virtue of the effects they have upon human beings'.[32] Let us call these instances of 'austere' similarity: more precisely, I will say that austere similarity is *a relational property ascribed to two distinct things, x and y, and so ascribed on no other basis than the properties of those object to elicit common responses of an identifiable type in subjects who encounter them.*[33] Assertions expressing observations of austere similarity thus will be some variation on the predications 'seems similar' or 'appears similar'.

But can such assertions actually qualify as *judgements*? Arguably they can, in so far as they are held accountable to a stable standard of correctness; for example, a subject's judgement of some austere similarity may be accepted as true or rejected as false relative to the beliefs of others like himself; moreover, we might maintain that pairs of objects which all or almost all find similar in appearance (austerely similar) are, accordingly, 'objectively' so, and pairs which none or very few find similar are not. In short, assertions of austere similarity can count as expressions of genuine judgements in so far as they are, as Evans puts it, 'issued subject to the control of human agreement —when the speaker is prepared to acknowledge that he is

---

32. *Ibid.*
33. It is of course not necessary that a thinker who observes some such similarity respond in *all* ways to x as he does to y. As Evans observes, 'A baby can strike me as like his father, but I may have no tendency to respond to him as I do to his father: even on a brief presentation on a dark night, I will have no tendency to confuse them. But the baby will remind me of his father, even without my knowing the relationship; I take this to mean that he has a tendency to get me to think of his father, and this is certainly a similarity in the effect the baby and the father have upon me.' *Ibid.*

wrong by withdrawing his remark in the face of an incapacity to get others to agree with him, to see things his way.'[34]

To say that 'getting others to see things one's own way' confers this status on our observations of austere similarity need not imply a conception of objectivity as a matter of democratic legislation. We can do better than that, by supposing rather that the objectivity of this or that observed similarity is established only by the fact of it being sustained by our *best* opinions informed and supported by our clearest and most alert responses—by responses elicited under conditions ideal or nearly ideal for discerning the features in question. In short, we need only accept those judgements sustained by our best joint efforts to discern what is true. If, under such circumstances, we continue to judge that, say, the portrait looks like the sitter or the tenor sounds like Carreras or the perfume smells more like jasmine than rose, then it may be that the best explanation of our so judging is that the portrait *does* look like the sitter or the tenor *does* sound like Carreras or the perfume *does* smell like jasmine. And if that is so, we have all that we could want to grant the assertions recording our responses the status of truth-apt judgements. On this account judgements of austere similarities will make ineliminable use of concepts that are essentially experience-dependent or response-dependent, of course; but that dependency need not impugn their claims to truth.

It may be objected, of course, that one cannot say both that the predicate 'seems similar' applies (in the case of judgements) iff subjects agree that it applies *and* say that what explains that agreement is that things 'really are' similar in appearance. But this objection only has force if we take our similarity judgements to be on par with, e.g., judgements that some style of dress is *chic*, rather than on par with judgements that, e.g., some object is red. The sense in which something is *chic* because it elicits '*chic* responses' in normal subjects admits of no converse claim; that is, there is no sense in which something elicits the requisite response just *because* it is *chic*. In the case of red, however, sense *can* be given to the converse claim: something can be said to elicit the red-responses just because it is red. As Philip Pettit remarks in a related context,

---

34. In Evans's terms, 'something will objectively look like something else if it strikes people as like that other thing; or, rather more usefully, b is objectively more like a than is c if and only if b strikes people as more like a than c does', *op. cit.*, p. 292.

An eraser is elastic and bends. Does it bend because it is elastic, or is it elastic because it bends? In one sense...it is elastic because it bends: the capacity to bend is what marks off elastic things. In a parallel sense something is red because it looks red to normal observers: the capacity to look red to such observers is what marks off red things. But in another sense—... a causal sense—the eraser bends because it is elastic: the elasticity is responsible, in part, for the bending. And in a parallel sense something looks red to normal observers because it *is* red....[35]

We can think of the property of being red as a feature common to red things—the very features that guarantee that suitable viewers under suitable conditions will have a certain experience. In the case of 'seems like', as in the case of 'red', the 'because' can run in both directions: one conceptual and the other causal. The tenor sounds like Carreras because we respond to him as sounding like Carreras; and, conversely, we explain our responses by appeal to the fact that (we say that we have those responses because) he really does sound like Carreras.

3.

3.1 It is not, I hope, wholly obscure how one might appeal to the notion of austere similarity relations to render plausible the proposal that certain metaphors fulfil my credentials for 'Phenomenological metaphors'. Recall that this proposal relied on two controversial ideas. The first idea (supporting cognitivity) is that the norms governing our practises of figurative discourse are sufficiently disciplined to allow evaluation of at least some metaphors as candidates for the assignment of truth-values. The second idea (supporting conceptual autonomy) is that some metaphorical assertions admit of no non-circular analysis in non-figurative terms. (Elucidations of a *kind* may be available, but, in the case of phenomenological metaphors, these will fall short of being meaning-preserving analyses, and will often be cast in figurative terms). Ordinary, literal judgements of austere similarity (judgements typically expressed in terms of 'looks like', 'sounds like' etc.) often are, I've suggested, perfectly good candidates for truth assignments; at the same time, they are supported by (or justified by) nothing other than best opinion—that is, the convergence of responses of qualified subjects judging under suitable conditions. This latter fact will be reflected in the holding of a priori conditionals such as: x looks like y iff qualified subjects in specified suitable conditions judge that x looks like y.

---

35. Pettit (1991: 615)

The conditional is circular, but that is no mark against it so long as it does not present itself as an analysis or definition. Moreover, it is still informative, for the details of subjects qualifications and of what count as suitable conditions may make perspicuous certain a priori, conceptual relations of which we were not aware.

Now, I am *not* suggesting that phenomenological metaphors one and all express judgements of primitive perceived resemblances; that would yield a class of metaphors *so* restricted as to be of vanishing interest. What I do claim is that the relations of similarity expressed in certain phenomenological metaphors are *like* those expressed in judgements of austere similarity in so far as they too have a good prospect of counting as cognitive and conceptually autonomous. When we assent to a metaphorical description, we may have *no* reason for doing so save the fact that it presents two things which elicit from us certain common responses; we needn't explain or justify the commonality of response by pointing to some property they both possess *independently* of those responses. It may be reassuring and interesting, of course, if we are subsequently able to identify some causal ground for the experienced similarity—as, for instance, we can (to a point) with respect to similarities in surface colours. But it isn't necessary that we be able to do so for the metaphor to be both intelligible and true.

This parallel between the similarity relations expressed in phenomenological metaphors and those expressed in judgements of austere similarity is not accidental. It derives from the fact that in both cases subjects' judgements rely on and issue from their acquaintance with the phenomenological character associated with the objects or properties in question. In both cases they are asked to assent to a judgement that is, either implicitly or explicitly, of the form "*a seems like* (looks like, feels like, sounds like) *b*". And in both cases, securing that assent turns on their propensity to respond (in salient ways) to *a*s as they do to *b*s. There is, however, an important difference in the *way* in which the responsive propensities are elicited. In the case of a standard assessment of austere similarity—say, Hume's assessment of blue, green and scarlet colour patches—the subject is asked to compare two or more perceptually presented samples. But perceptual comparison of independent samples is not, or is not typically, what underpins the comprehension of metaphors, and nor do we normally read them to be simply *pointing out* that one thing is like another. (Neither do we read similes so, for that matter.) Rather, there is a sense in which the metaphor *brings it about* that they are experienced as similar. Consider, for instance, another passage from Proust: this time he is describing M. Swann's terrible jealousy, and the effect on him of overheard remarks concerning Odette de Crecy:

> So often had it happened to him, when chatting with chance acquaintances to whom he was hardly listening, to hear certain detached sentences (as, for instance, 'I saw Mme de Crecy yesterday with a man I didn't know'), sentences which dropped into his heart and turned at once into a solid state, grew hard as stalagmites, and seared and tore him while they lay there, irremovable, that the words 'She didn't know a soul, she never spoke to a soul' were, by way of contrast, a soothing balm. How freely they coursed through him, how fluid they were, how vaporous, how easy to breathe![36]

It would be silly to suppose that Proust is just interested here in noting that stalagmites and jealousy typically elicit some of the same responses (or even, as we might more naturally say, carry some of the same 'associations'). No small part of the point of introducing the image of the stalagmite is to draw attention to aspects of the topic—Swann's jealousy in this case—which one might *not* otherwise discern. Likewise, Proust's characterisation of Swann's immense relief on hearing that Odette had not 'spoken to soul', doesn't simply point out that some of the responses one might have to a balm, or to having one's constricted breathing freed, figure among the responses felt by Swann. Rather Proust's metaphor *introduces* the reader to the specific character of Swann's emotions by provoking him to conceive of those words *as* a balm, as freed breathing.

But what is to conceive of one thing as another in such a way? That is a difficult question to which I cannot do full justice here. I can, however, say something to elucidate the key idea. To conceive of one thing as another, in the sense relevant here, is in part a mater of *actually* responding in some ways to the former (or to the thought of the former) as one does, or would do, to the latter—say, to actually respond to the thought of Swann's relief as one might to a balm. This is not quite the same as noting that there are responses elicited by the first that are also elicited by the second. (It is one thing to think of a green patch that it has a blue-ish hue—*to experience it as blue-ish*—and another to judge that is more similar to the blue patch than the red.) Neither is it sufficient for conceiving one thing as another simply to observe that, under thus-and-such conditions, the two things *would* elicit

---

36. Proust (1992: 381).

certain common responses. Consider a familiar example: Jastrow's duck-rabbit. To see the Jastrow figure as a duck and not a rabbit is not a matter of judging that thus and such line *would* count as a bill, rather than as some ears. No; to see it as a duck, rather than a rabbit, is also to *experience* those lines as bill-like rather than ear-like. Indeed, a subject could learn in considerable detail how the different parts of the figure would be labeled by one who saw it as a duck without being able to so see it oneself at all. Seeing the figure as a duck-picture requires that one's perceptual experience of the whole figure is organised by one's conception of it *as* a duck-picture. And this is not the same as being able to identify individual, discrete points of similarity between the figure and a duck's profile. The latter is neither necessary nor sufficient for the former.

Likewise, phenomenological metaphors do more than simply provoke the reader (or writer for that matter) to identify certain points of similarity; they do more, too, than provoke him to highlight certain features of the topic *by way of* getting him to search for points of similarity. Their special interest and special efficacy lies rather in the fact that they elicit in the reader a response to the topic (e.g., Swann's relief), a response which includes some of the actual responses he would have were he presented with the things in terms of which the topic is metaphorically described (e.g., a 'soothing balm'). We might say that such metaphors, if successful, provoke a subject to *simulate* encountering the topic thus characterised—say, to simulate feeling as Swann feels—just as in seeing Jastrow's figure *as* a duck-picture we are in part simulating seeing a duck.

I have developed these suggestions in greater detail elsewhere, and will not pursue them here. For present purposes, it is the affinities, rather than the differences, that matter in considering the relation between judgements of austere similarity and those expressed in phenomenological metaphors. I have proposed that phenomenological metaphors express observations of a relation (or relations) of austere similarity, and as such admit of no non-circular analysis or elucidation in non-figurative terms. That many metaphors evidently do *more* than express such relations—for instance, that they may also provoke us to conceive of one thing as another in the sense suggested above—does nothing to undermine this claim.

3.2 What account of speakers' understanding and judgement of phenomenological metaphors follows from this conception of their content?

Here is a somewhat idealised sketch.

Standardly competent speakers confronted with Proust's description will be acquainted with certain general communicative principles (e.g., Gricean co-operative principles) as well as more specific conventions governing the introduction of non-literal or non-standard uses, conventions signalling a figurative use and suggesting an appropriate interpretative strategy.[37] These readers should also be attributed an attitude of interpretative charity; that is to say, they will advert to such interpretative strategies as may maximise the truth of Proust's sentences. Doing what they can to maximise truth, they respond to the deviant and unfamiliar language by '[altering] their theories, entering hypotheses about new names, altering the interpretation of familiar predicates and revising past interpretations of particular utterances in the light of new evidence.'[38] In short, they will naturally and flexibly pursue an interpretation which is sensitive to the context and responsive to the speaker's aims. Having come this far, Proust's readers will need now to arrive at a conception of the conditions under which his metaphors would be true. Now let us suppose that those conditions include the obtaining of austere similarity relations: suppose that some *part* of Proust's description of certain sentences as 'stalagmites [which] seared and tore' him expresses an assertion of an austere similarity.[39] Need this debar the reader from grasping the conditions under which that description would be true? Is he thereby prohibited from identifying the experience-type it represents? Surely not. But it *will* debar him from exhaustively specifying those conditions solely in literal terms. It may even debar him (in an extreme case) from doing much more than recording the proposed similarity in the very same terms as the metaphor, merely making explicit that the relation is one of similarity by insert-

---

37. In this connection Searle proposes a list of conventions which, he argues, allow us to identify an utterance as metaphorical (Searle 1979). A more sophisticated (and empirically informed) attempt to provide a taxonomy of such conventions is Sperber and Wilson (1986).
38. Davidson (1986: 157–75).
39. Although I will not develop the point here, it should at least be noted that a single metaphorical expression need not represent only *one* observation of similarity for it to count as representing austere similarity or similarities. A number of similarity relations, all of them austere, may be captured in a single metaphor. What matters is that each such relation should resist analysis in non-circular, literal terms.

ing the requisite 'like' or 'as'. Even if the reader is able to proffer some non-circular elucidation, that elucidation may fail to be given in wholly *non-figurative* terms—it may be that his best prospects lie in offering further metaphors and further (figurative) similarity claims as elaborations of the target one. For example, the overheard sentences are experienced by Swann as 'sharp' and 'rough'; he feels 'stricken' by them; his heart is 'wounded' by the thoughts they provoke; his feelings are painfully 'torn' in all directions; as he recalls the incident the words seem to grow as stalagmites grow, ever harder and more penetrating. And so on. None of *these* elucidatory suggestions, however dull or apt, offer us an analysis of the metaphor in terms wholly extraneous to the similarity introduced by the metaphor itself, much less wholly extraneous to the domain of figurative discourse.

Why should we think, however, that the metaphor possesses any cognitive content at all? One possible response is that the best opinions of the most careful readers converge in their judgement of the truth of Proust's description (*'Sometimes jealousy really does feel like that...'*). And what could explain that convergence is the obtaining of the austere similarities the metaphor proposes. On this view, the convergence in judgement of linguistically competent readers—readers who bring to bear appropriate attention, imagination and, not least, an appropriate background of common experience and shared sensibilities—may be explained by the fact that the experience of intense jealousy sometimes *just is* as Proust says. Or more precisely: it may be explained by the fact that one aspect of the experience of intense jealousy is that, for a subject in its grip, one thing ('certain detached sentences') *seems like* another (stalagmites which sear and tear). Here we should bear in mind that if the similarity in question is an austere one, the 'seems like' just means we are aware that both things in question have a propensity to elicit certain responses of an identifiable type in those who encounter them—these distinguishable things (or types of thing) have a commonality of effect on us, and we are aware of that commonality.

It may be objected, however, that such convergence in opinion is often not forthcoming; indeed, many of the best and richest literary metaphors are precisely those about which disagreement is most likely, and for which re-interpretations and new construals seem to be most plentiful. Thus, while we may allow that we do advert to metaphors to serve proxy for response-dependent concepts and to compensate for lacunae in our lexicons, and while we may acknowledge that some of those metaphors are conceptually autonomous in the sense that no other words will do, in *practise* there may be very few that also count as apt candidates for truth. This kind of objection is already familiar from disputes concerning moral (and aesthetic) discourse, arenas in which parallel questions of cognitivity and autonomy are also held to be in question. It may be useful, by way of a closing response to the objection, to note a few further points of parallel, for some of the considerations which mitigate the spectre of disagreement in evaluative discourse apply as well, I believe, to metaphorical discourse.

I have proposed that at least some metaphors possess a kind of objectivity that is strong enough to permit a basis of successful communication. The fact that certain of these metaphors function as proxy for response-dependent concepts does nothing to undercut that prospect. Likewise, in the case of evaluative concepts, it has often been suggested that only such objectivity is needed as may explain the possibility of successful adjudication, and again, their response-dependent nature need present no obstacle to that aim. It is true that the adjudication of competing moral judgements does not often promise to satisfy every aspect of every competitor's evaluative perspective; it may only offer to deliver a judgement informed by a range of such perspectives. And so it is with contested interpretations of difficult and obscure metaphors: different attempts to evaluate their truth often reveal different aspects of the similarities they propose, and not every one of these attempts will be compatible with every other. But might not each attempt inform our understanding, corroborating or subverting available alternatives, showing us more of the similarities that are there to be seen? To the extent that we approach a settled and common understanding of these alternatives, we can claim a common understanding of a metaphor's content, and we can sensibly ask of it, 'Are matters as it says they are? Is it true or false?'. With care and attention we sometimes can and do converge in our answers. However, as with moral judgements (and other judgement types making use of response-dependent concepts), that answer will depend in part on whether and how we are equipped to discern all that matters to their truth. Some of us will be too inexperienced or too biased or too unimaginative to respond in ways that merit others' agreement, and even those who are more astute will sometimes be unable to reconcile certain aspects of their competing views. But this will seem more natural and less alarming if we remind ourselves that, as with other response-dependent concepts, what we are attempting to light upon is a *possible* object of experience, one which comes better into view as we progressively equip and attune ourselves to see it. That moral and metaphorical judgements alike invite disagreement does not imply that disputes in either domain are finally no more than conflicts of feeling and will. It need only suggest that truth in these domains is difficult to discern, and that our successive approximations to it ought to be taken as provisional resting places along a path that is not entirely certain. But in literary art and morality alike, is this not as it should be?

© A. E. Denham-Sajovic
St. Anne's College, Oxford
Oxford OX2 6HS
England
alison.denham@st-annes.oxford.ac.uk

References

Black, M. 1978 'More about Metaphor', in A. Ortony, A., ed. *Metaphor and Thought*, Cambridge: Cambridge University Press, 19–45.

Black, M. 1962 *Models and Metaphor*, Ithaca: Cornell University Press.

Cooper, D. 1986 *Metaphor*, Oxford: Oxford University Press.

Davidson, D. 1978 'What Metaphors Mean', *Critical Inquiry*, 5, 31–47; reprinted in his *Inquiries into Truth and Interpretation*, Oxford, Clarendon Press, 1986, 245–64.

Davidson, D. 1986 'A Nice Derangement of Epitaphs', in R. Grandy and R. Warner, eds., *Philosophical Grounds of Rationality: Intentions, Categories, Ends*, Oxford: Oxford University Press, 157–174.

Denham, A.E. forthcoming, *Metaphor and Moral Experience*, Oxford: Oxford University Press.

Edwards, P. 1965 'Professor Tillich's Confusions', *Mind* 74, 192–214.

Evans, G. 1980 *The Varieties of Reference*, ed. J. McDowell, Oxford: Oxford University Press.

Fogelin, R. J. 1988 *Figuratively Speaking*, Yale: Yale University Press.

Hacker, P.M.S. 1987 *Appearance and Reality*, Oxford: Blackwell.

Hume, D. 1888 *A Treatise of Human Nature*, ed. L.A.Selby-Bigge, Oxford: Clarendon.

Johnston, M. 1993 'Objectivity Refigured', in J. Haldane and C. Wright, eds. *Reality, Representation and Projection*, Oxford: Oxford University Press, 85–132.

Johnston, M. 1989 'Dispositional Theories of Value', *Procedings of the Aristotelian Society*, Supplementary Volume 63, 139–74.

Pettit, P. 1991 'Realism and Response–Dependence', *Mind* 100, 587–626.

Plato 1892 *Ion*, in *The Dialogues of Plato*, trans. B. Jowett, 3rd edition, Oxford: Oxford University Press, 1892.

Proust, M. 1992 *In Search of Lost Time*, trans. Mayor and Kilmartin, London: Chatto 1992.

Quintilian 1921 *Institutio Oratoria*, trans. H.E. Butler, London: Heinemann.

Rorty, R. 1987 'Unfamiliar Noises: Hesse and Davidson on Metaphor', *Proceedings of the Aristotelian Society*, Supplementary Volume 61, 283–296.

Searle, J. 1979 'Metaphor' in *Expression and Meaning*, Cambridge: Cambridge University Press.

Sperber, D. and Wilson, D. 1986 *Relevance*, Oxford: Blackwell.

Tversky, A. 1977 'Features of similarity', *Psychological Review*, 86, 327–352.

Wright, C. 1988 'Moral Values, Projection and Secondary Qualities', *Proceedings of the Aristotelian Society*, Supplementary Volume 62, 1–26.

Wright, C. 1982 *Truth and Objectivity*, Oxford: Oxford University Press.

Wright, C. 1993 'Realism: the Contemporary Debate – W(h)ither now?' in J. Haldane and C. Wright, eds., *Reality, Representation and Projection*, Oxford: Oxford University Press, 63–84.

PETER MENZIES
Possibility and Conceivability: A Response-Dependent Account of Their Connections[1]

1. Introduction

In the history of modern philosophy systematic connections were assumed to hold between the modal concepts of logical possibility and necessity and the concept of conceivability. Descartes, Berkeley, and Hume, for example, all thought that conceivability was the mark of the possible. They assumed that it is permissible to draw conclusions about what is possible and necessary from premises about what is conceivable and what is not. In recent years, however, contemporary philosophers have repudiated this earlier tradition of linking the modal concepts with the concept of conceivability. (See Yablo 1993.)

In the eyes of many contemporary philosophers, insuperable objections face any attempt to analyse the modal concepts in terms of conceivability. For example, it is objected that the notion of conceivability cannot form an

---

1. This paper is a descendant of a paper I delivered at the 1992 ANU Metaphysics Conference. I am grateful to Brian Garrett for the invitation to speak at the conference and to John Bigelow, David Braddon-Mitchell, Richard Holton, and Rae Langton for helpful comments on the version of the paper delivered at the conference. I am also indebted to Kevin Mulligan for discussions that helped to clarify a number of issues in my mind. I owe a special debt to Philip Pettit with whom I discussed issues to do with modality and response-dependence over a long period; many of the ideas in this paper derive from those fruitful discussions.

adequate basis for an analysis of logical possibility: if it is identified with sensory imaginability, it is too narrow a notion to encompass all the logical possibilities and if it is identified with supposability, it is too broad a notion to select out only the logical possibilities. It is also objected that any analysis of possibility in terms of conceivability must be circular and so vacuous, since the concept of conceivability—as the concept of that which *can* be conceived—is itself a modal concept. Again, it is said that there are logical possibilities which cannot be conceived by any human subject so that the notion of conceivability to be equated with logical possibility has to be understood as idealised conceivability. But it is impossible, it is objected, to explain this idealised notion of conceivability without appealing to the modal concepts themselves.

These are, indeed, powerful objections to the project of reductive analysis, the project of analysing the modal concepts exhaustively in terms of non-modal concepts. However, it is important to keep in mind that a philosophical explanation of modality does not inevitably have to take the form of a reductive analysis. Recent work on response-dependent concepts (Johnston 1989, 1995; Wright 1992; Pettit 1991, 1992) offers a model of how to provide a non-reductive, philosophical explanation of a concept such as logical possibility in terms of a human response such as conceivability. The sort of response-dependent account I have in mind is one that attempts to explain a concept, not in terms of the conditions under which the concept is applied, but in terms of the conditions that are essential to possession of the concept. (See Peacocke 1992.) This sort of explanation does not purport to characterise a concept in terms of concepts available to possessors of the concept, but rather in terms of concepts available to a theoretician surveying the practices of those possessors.

In this paper I attempt to provide a response-dependent account of the modal concepts in terms of conceivability along the lines of the non-reductive model just adumbrated. Section 3 of the paper is devoted to sketching such an account. In section 4 I attempt to show that this kind of explanation of modality obviates many of the objections that have been brought against reductive analyses of the modal concepts in terms of conceivability.

Before turning to these matters, I consider the issue whether accounts of the modal concepts in terms of possible worlds are satisfactory. The essential feature of these accounts is that they analyse modal locutions in terms of quantification over possible worlds. In section 2 I examine one well worked-out theory of possible worlds—that of David Lewis (1986a)—and argue that, whatever its other virtues, it fails in its aim of providing a reductive analysis of modality. This failure is symptomatic of the inadequacy of possible worlds analyses of modality in general. In view of the failure of these analyses, I argue that there is room left in the space of philosophical explanations for a non-reductive, response-dependent explanation of modality in terms of conceivability.

2. Possible Worlds Analyses of Modality

Possible worlds semantics have been remarkably successful in illuminating the logical properties of various modal locutions. For example, it clarifies the logic of the modal operators 'Possibly' and 'Necessarily' by taking them to be quantifiers over possible worlds. 'Possibly p' is analysed as 'At some possible world, p holds' and 'Necessarily p' is analysed as 'At every possible world, p holds'. Modal inferences are then explained by assimilation to the familiar patterns of quantificational reasoning. But is the quantification over possible worlds to be taken seriously?

Non-actualists about possible worlds answer this question affirmatively, arguing that the possible worlds quantified over are non-actual but real entities. The most famous exponent of non-actualism about possible worlds is, of course, David Lewis (1986a). His modal realism, as he calls his non-actualist position, states that reality consists of a plurality of worlds or universes. One of these worlds is what we ordinarily call *the* universe. The other worlds are things of the same kind: systems of objects, many of them concrete, connected by a network of external relations like the spatiotemporal relations that connect objects in our universe (pp. 74–6). Each world is isolated from the other worlds in the sense that there are no causal or spatiotemporal relations between constituents of different worlds (p. 78). The totality of worlds is closed under a principle of recombination which goes roughly: for any collection of objects from any number of worlds, there is a single world containing any number of duplicates of each, provided there is a spacetime large enough to hold them (pp. 87–90). Finally, Lewis holds that there are no arbitrary limits on the plenitude of worlds (p. 103).

Because of its ontological extravagance in other respects, it is easy to overlook the fact that Lewis's theory has, as one of its aims, the simplication of ontology by the elimination of modal facts. The reduction proposed by the theory proceeds in two stages. The first stage involves reducing modal facts, in the manner already discussed, to quantified facts about worlds; the second stage of the reduction involves providing a systematic theory of these worlds. It is essential to the goal of reduction that the theory should characterise worlds in completely non-modal terms; if the theory is to effect a reduction of what *might be* to what *is*, it must characterise the worlds in terms which do not involve any circular appeal to modality. Does Lewis's theory manage to do this? Does it succeed in eliminating modal facts completely?

To answer these questions it is necessary to consider an aspect of Lewis's theory left undescribed to this point. As a way of introducing this aspect, it is important to observe that the theory of worlds, so far described, is compatible with actualism, as Rosen (1990) points out. An actualist could embrace the theory if, for example, he held the eccentric cosmological view that actuality consists of not just one universe, but a vast sea of 'island universes', all causally and spatiotemporally isolated from each other. To be sure, this hypothesis would not sit well with the spirit of ontological austerity that usually motivates actualism. But it would be a consistent view. And it would be a consistent view precisely because Lewis's theory of worlds does not ascribe any modal properties to the worlds, and so does not exclude the actualist construal of their existence and nature.

Something must be added to Lewis's characterisation of worlds to exclude the actualist interpretation. Intuitively, what is needed is a supplementation that makes it clear that the universes are possible worlds that are genuine alternatives to the actual one, not just parts of the actual world. So, if it is stipulated that the universe of which we are part is the *actual* world and the rest of the universes in the plurality are *merely possible* worlds, that will exclude the actualist construal. The theory will then imply something that no actualist could accept: viz. that some things—the possible worlds and their occupants—exist but are not actual.

It would seem to be a consequence of this supplementation, however, that the theory of possible worlds loses its claim to modal innocence. Does not the fact that it makes essential use of the concepts of the *actual* world and the merely *possible* worlds mean that it forfeits its claim to be a reductive account of modality? These consequences do not, however, follow if the concepts of the actual world and the merely possible worlds can be defined in non-modal terms. And this is where the undescribed aspect of Lewis's theory comes in. For the theory does in fact offer non-modal definitions of these concepts. Thus, Lewis defines the *actual* world to be the system of objects that are *our worldmates*; that are, in other words, *spatiotemporally connected to us*. The *merely possible* worlds are those systems of objects that are not actual. There are two notable features of these definitions. First, the definitions bear out Lewis's claim that 'actual' is a locative indexical and so relational in character: what is actual to us is merely possible to the inhabitants of a different world and what is actual to them is merely possible to us. Secondly, and more relevantly, the definitions proceed in terms of the non-modal concept of worldmates, or objects spatiotemporally connected to each other, and so support the claims of the theory to provide a reductive account of modality.

But the question is whether these definitions are satisfactory. Even setting aside the issue of the indexicality of 'actual', one can see that the definitions imply some counterintuitive results. For one thing, they imply that if there were systems of objects spatiotemporally isolated from us, they would be possible worlds to us. But the actualist hypothesis of a plurality of 'island universes', spatiotemporally isolated from each other but all part of the actual world, seems coherent. Indeed, for all we know, this hypothesis might really be true of the actual world: for the general theory of relativity allows space-time of many different topologies, including ones with disconnected regions. In any case, Lewis (1992) himself allows that there could be a possible world containing regions which are almost isolated, regions which are connected by only a few wormholes. It does not take much, as Bigelow and Pargetter (1990, pp.189-92) point out, to get from this to the hypothesis that there could be a world consisting of completely isolated 'islands'. If, as seems likely, the existence of the wormholes in this possible world depends on what happens in the regions, then it would be true that if things were a little different in these regions, the wormholes would not exist, in which case we would then have a possible world containing completely isolated 'islands'.

The intuition that there could be a world of 'island universes' is quite powerful and hard to resist. Contrary to what Lewis says (1986a, pp.71-2), this is not a case of 'spoils to the victor'. How could Lewis modify his theory to handle it? He could simply posit as primitive the notion of an actual world and define the merely possible worlds accordingly. Or, in order to preserve his indexical account of 'actual' he might take the notion of worldmates as primitive, defining, as before, the actual world to be the system of objects that are our worldmates. Given such definitions, he could allow that the 'island universes' could be worldmates with us in the actual world, even though they are spatiotemporally isolated from us. But it is important to recognise that this notion of worldmates is a barely disguised modal concept: to say that two objects are worldmates is simply to say that they are compossible. Consequently, in either case, Lewis's theory must adopt a modal primitive of some kind if it is to offer a satisfactory answer to this objection.

The utility of possible worlds semantics in philosophy does not depend on construing them in Lewis's non-actualist fashion. There are other conceptions of possible worlds which are equally serviceable in the semantics but belong to a family of actualist views Lewis has labelled *ersatz modal realism*. These conceptions of possible worlds are ontologically less extravagant than Lewis's modal realist conception. However, they also fail to provide successful reductions of modal concepts for much the same reason that Lewis's fails—they appeal at some point or other to primitive modal concepts. For reasons of space I shall not pursue this line of argument here.

In summary then: Lewis's attempt to eliminate modal facts from his ontology depends crucially on whether he can offer a non-modal characterisation of possible worlds. The theory of possible worlds he advances does in fact succeed in characterising them non-modally, but at the cost of employing defective definitions of the actual and merely possible worlds, a fact brought out by the 'island universes' objection. To remedy the defects in the definitions Lewis must appeal to modal primitives at some point or other, either at the very beginning by positing primitive notions of actual and possible worlds, or in the characterisation of the actual world by positing a primitive worldmates relation. Whichever way he goes, it would appear that the invocation of modal primitives undermines the reductive ambitions of the theory.

Was it plausible in any case to think that one can eliminate modal facts from ontology; to think that one can derive modal conclusions—statements about what *might* be and *must* be—from non-modal premises—statements about what *is*? Echoing Hume's views on the fact-value distinction, I would maintain that it is impossible to derive a *must* from an *is*. Modal concepts cannot be analysed exhaustively in terms of non-modal concepts: some modal concepts must be taken as primitive, so that the programme of eliminating modality from one's ontology is bound to be a fruitless philosophical enterprise.

If this is so, is there any point to the possible worlds paraphrases of modal claims? It is hard to deny that the paraphrases do represent genuine *a priori* truths; that, for example, 'Possibly *p*' is legitimately paraphrased as 'At some possible world, *p* holds'. However, I suggest that the correct way to read these paraphrases is not from right-to-left as explanations of modal discourse, but rather from left-to-right as explanations of possible worlds discourse. On this proposal, statements such as 'Possibly *p*' are taken to be basic, unanalysable expressions, and the possible worlds talk is to be construed as an ontologically harmless but colourful way of expressing these modal statements. A claim that there is a possible world in which *p* holds is to be read as a *façon de parler*, as a more vivid way of saying that it is possible that *p*. So read, possible worlds talk does not entail a commitment to the existence of a plurality of real or ersatz possible worlds. Rather such talk carries the same ontological commitments as straightforward modal claims; and in my view these commitments are to the modal facts—the facts about possibilities and necessities—that serve as their truthmakers.

Philosophers have been wary of this way of proceeding because it has seemed explanatorily unsatisfactory simply to posit primitive modal concepts and positively mystery-mongering to invoke a realm of primitive modal facts. But I shall attempt to show that these worries are misplaced. The postulation of primitive modal concepts does not mean that no further philosophical explanation can be given of them, nor does the invocation of primitive modal facts as truthmakers for modal claims necessarily entail a violation of actualism.

3. A Response-Dependent Explanation of Modality

As remarked earlier, there are systematic connections between the concepts of possibility and conceivability, connections that were recognised by most of the prominent figures in the history of philosophy. Exactly how are these connections to be understood? Can they furnish the basis of a philosophical understanding of the nature of the modal concepts?

I think they can. The connections between the concepts of possibility and conceivability point, in my view, to the response-dependent character of the modal concepts. To say that a concept is response-dependent is to say, roughly, that the concept implicates a human response in the manner of a secondary quality concept. More precisely, the concept of a property C is *response-dependent* just in case there is some response R_C—sensory, affective, or cognitive—such that a biconditional of the following kind holds true *a priori*: *x* is *C* if and only *x* is disposed to elicit response R_C in suitable subjects in suitable conditions (Johnston 1989, 1995; Wright 1992). So, for example, the concept of colour, under a traditional representation of it as a secondary quality, is the paradigm of a response-dependent concept: for the traditional representation takes it to be true *a priori* that *x* is red if and only *x* is disposed to look red to a normal observer in normal conditions. I shall argue that the modal concepts turn out to be response-dependent too, since they conform to an appropriate modification of the definition. The important point to note is that the biconditionals that mark out a concept as response-dependent cannot be—and, invariably, are not taken to be—reductive analyses of the concepts, for the reason that the right-hand side of the biconditional employs the concept in question, or some cognate concept.

If the biconditionals do not represent reductive analyses, what purpose do they serve? Two kinds of answer to this question can be distinguished. One kind of answer (Johnston 1989, 1992) is that the biconditionals, despite their circularity, are useful summaries of the interdependences between concepts, in particular between concepts of things in the world and concepts of subjective responses. On this approach, the biconditionals do not state the application conditions for the response-dependent concepts (they cannot because they refer to the concepts themselves); nonetheless they are entailed by the application conditions of these concepts, taken in conjunction with those of the other concepts mentioned in the biconditionals. Thus, anyone who has a proper grasp of the concepts involved in the biconditional for the colour red, say, will be in a position to recognise the truth of that biconditional; that is, anyone who knows the application conditions of 'red', 'is disposed to look red', 'normal observer', 'normal conditions' will be in a position to know *a priori* that something is red if and only if it is disposed to look red to normal observers in normal conditions. Thus, a proper understanding of the application conditions of the concepts involved is sufficient for an appreciation of the response-dependent character of the concept.

The other kind of answer to the question about the purpose of the non-reductive biconditionals (Pettit 1991, 1992) proceeds in terms of the possession conditions of concepts, rather than their application conditions or the entailments thereof. (See Peacocke 1992 for the concept of possession conditions.) The possession conditions for a concept are those aspects of the practice of subjects possessing the concept that are essential to their competence with the concept. The possession conditions for the colour concepts, for instance, include the fact that ordinary subjects experience colour sensations, which form their primary criteria for applying colour concepts. They also include the fact that ordinary subjects do not always take colour sensations to be authoritative about colours and that they engage in corrective practices when intertemporal and interpersonal discrepancies arise, discounting some perceivers or perceptual conditions as abnormal. The response-dependent biconditionals governing the colour concepts, then, provide a summary of these possession conditions. Rather than offering an analysis of the concepts, they encapsulate in short-hand form the features of the response and of the corrective practices that are essential to competence in the concepts.

A significant feature of a response-dependent biconditional, according to this second answer, is that it is not necessarily accessible to the subjects whose conceptual competence is being explained: it is furnished by *us* in our role as *theorists* of their conceptual competence. Accordingly, the biconditional may be couched in terms of notions not possessed by the subjects themselves and may also present the response-dependent concept in a light that is unfamiliar to them. The response-dependent explanation of the colour concepts does not credit ordinary subjects with the concepts of 'normal observers' and 'normal conditions', nor does it impute a conception of colours as secondary qualities to ordinary subjects. In these respects, it differs from the account in terms of application conditions; and it is arguable that it is superior in these respects to that account. For it is plausible to think that ordinary subjects, untutored in philosophy or science, can possess an adequate mastery of the colour concepts without knowing what normal observers or conditions are, and without necessarily thinking of them as secondary qualities tied essentially to sensory experience. For these reasons this second kind of answer is, in my view, a much more plausible kind of explanation of the purpose of the non-reductive biconditionals.

Can a response-dependent explanation, parallel to that for the colour concepts, be given for the modal concepts? Can possession conditions be stated for the modal concepts of a kind with those stated for the colour concepts? The answer to these questions is 'Yes'. For the modal concepts have possession conditions that fit the pattern of the colour concepts' possession conditions: first, we experience a certain primitive response—that of conceiving something to be the case—which forms our primary criterion for applying modal concepts; and secondly, we engage in corrective practices whereby we refine the responses that count as veridical indicators of modality. In the following I attempt to expand these brief remarks into a full response-dependent explanation of the modal concepts.

It is uncontroversial that the primary criterion we use in applying modal concepts to things is the imaginability or conceivability of those things. In everyday reasoning it is assumed that if something can be imagined or conceived to be the case, that is a reason for thinking that it is possible; and equally, if something cannot be conceived to be the case, that is a reason for thinking that it is impossible. These assumptions are also made in more sophisticated reasoning. For example, philosophers try to establish the possibility of some state of affairs by constructing detailed imaginary scenarios illustrating the phenomenon, and in doing so reveal their presupposition that the imaginability of the phenomenon indicates its possibility. In a similar fashion, physicists take their thought experiments to shed light on physical processes, which they could not do unless they pointed to the possibility of the processes in question.

A remark is called for here about the way imagination is to be understood. There is a way of thinking of the imagination that takes it be a quasi-sensory faculty (Hart 1976, 1988; Peacocke 1985). On this view, there are modes of imagination corresponding to the five senses: perhaps the olfactory, gustatory, and tactual dimensions are not well developed, but the visual and the auditory dimensions are. This view is often invoked to motivate an analogy: just as we arrive at our beliefs about the actual on the basis of sensory experience, so we arrive at our beliefs about the possible on the basis of sensory imagination. Nevertheless, this view about the nature of the imagination is mistaken: while the imagination certainly originates in the sensory, it is not necessarily restricted to it. There are many things which can imagined intellectually, but not sensorily. For example, one can imagine, but not visualise, that there is an additional primary colour, that space has an extra dimension, that particles are waves, that space-time has a shape (Blackburn 1986; Craig 1985). Sometimes, the term 'conceive' is used to encompass this kind of intellectual imagining, a usage that goes back at least to Descartes (Williams 1978). It is clearly imaginability in this broad sense of conceivability that must be taken to be criterial of possibility.

What exactly is conceivability? What does the mental ability to conceive something consist in? Some have denied that we have any such mental ability (Hart 1988, p.15). To be sure, if conceivability is to be criterial of possibility, conceiving something to be the case cannot be identified with supposing it to be the case: for one can entertain a supposition which is later proved to be impossible, as in *reductio ad absurdum* proofs. Nonetheless, there is, I maintain, an intimate link between conceiving and supposing. We usually take it to be a reason for thinking that some state of affairs is possible that we can suppose that the state of affairs holds and that we can do so without generating an absurdity or contradiction. Consider, for example, the way in which philosophers go about establishing the possibility of backwards causation or disembodied minds. Typically, they describe a scenario involving the existence of backwards causation or disembodied minds and then attempt to show that this scenario does not give rise to any contradiction. If they are successful in these attempts, that is taken to be warrant for believing in the possibility of backwards causation, disembodied minds, or whatever. This is a defeasible warrant, of course, because it may turn out on closer examination that the scenario in question does after all give rise to a contradiction. The point is, however, that our reflective habits of thinking, as evidenced by the practices of philosophers, is to take the fact that some state of affairs can be supposed to hold without absurdity as *prima facie* grounds for accepting the possibility of that state of affairs.

Under this construal, the mental ability to conceive of something is really a complex ability, consisting in the ability to suppose that the state of affairs holds without being able to reduce this supposition to absurdity. Clearly, this complex ability presupposes a number of other more basic abilities: first, the ability to entertain suppositions; and secondly, the ability to infer other propositions, in particular absurd propositions, from suppositions. Is it possible to possess these capacities independently of the possession of the modal concepts? This is an important question in the context of the response-dependent explanation of the modal concepts, because it assumes that acts of conceiving can stand as criteria for the modal concepts and so it presupposes that the abilities involved in acts of conceiving can be possessed independently of the possession of modal concepts. But is this the case? Is not the concept of an absurdity the concept of a proposition which *cannot* be true? And is not the concept of a valid inference the concept of a transition from premisses to conclusion such that the former *cannot* be true without the latter being true?

To be sure, the most natural explanations of the concepts of an absurd proposition and of a valid inference may appeal to modal concepts. But this by itself does not establish that subjects who can entertain suppositions and draw inferences from them must possess these concepts: these may be primitive capacities, or at least capacities that are possessed independently of any grasp of the concept of an absurd proposition or a valid inference. Indeed, there seems to be some reason to think that human subjects have the ability to entertain suppositions and to infer propositions from these suppositions before they acquire any modal concepts. The ability to suppose something to be the case is an ability children possess early in their conceptual development, as is evident from the way in which they engage in games of make-belief from an early age. For example, in make-believing that there are indians behind the bushes, a child is entertaining the kind of supposition that in sophisticated practices forms the basis of *reductio* arguments. Again, children possess early in their conceptual development the ability to make inferences from suppositions, as evident once more from the way in which they readily draw inferences in their games of make-believe. In reasoning, for example, that there must be at least two indians behind the bushes from the make-believe supposition that there is an indian behind each of two bushes, the child demonstrates in rudimentary form the kind of reasoning from suppositions that achieves its most elaborate and sophisticated form in mathematical proofs. There seems some reason to believe, then, that children can possess these abilities well before they acquire any modal concepts, or any concepts such as those of an absurd proposition or of a valid inference that are explained in terms of modal concepts.

As remarked above, conceivability is merely a defeasible criterion of possibility. In this respect conceiving something to be the case is like perceiving something to be coloured: just as we acknowledge the possibility of colour illusions, so we acknowledge the possibility of modal illusions, of things seeming to be conceivable when they are not and inconceivable when they are. Built into our practice is a recognition that conceivability is a defeasible criterion for real possibility in the same way that colour appearance is a defeasible criterion of real colour. That imaginability or conceivability is not always an accurate guide to possibility is a familiar point with many illustrations. One of the best is provided by Lewis:

> We can imagine the impossible, provided we do not imagine it in perfect detail and all at once. We cannot imagine the possible in perfect detail and all at once, not if it is at all complicated. It is impossible to construct a regular polygon of nineteen sides with ruler and compass; it is possible but very complicated to construct one with seventeen sides. In whatever sense I can imagine the possible construction, I can imagine the impossible construction just as well. In both cases, I imagine a texture of arcs and lines with the polygon in the middle. I do not imagine it arc by arc and line by line, just as I don't imagine the speckled hen speckle by speckle—which is how I fail to notice the impossibility. (1986a, p. 90)

The traditional way of dealing with such cases was to distinguish proper acts of conceiving from improper acts of conceiving. Descartes, Berkeley, and Hume were all clear that not just any old act of conceiving is relevant to determining modality, only those acts of conceiving involving clear and distinct ideas were to count. But surely the point of Lewis's example is that it is not possible to distinguish purely phenomenologically, in terms of the clarity and distinctness of the ideas involved, between the two kinds of imaginary constructions. To deal with modal illusions of this kind the response-dependent explanation of modality must look beyond the internal phenomenological character of the acts of conceiving. This is not surprising if it is to be anything like the response-dependent explanation of colour: for that explanation does not distinguish a non-veridical from a veridical colour sensation in terms of a phenomenological feature of the sensation, but rather in terms of some feature of the observer or the conditions. Similarly, it must be some feature of the conceiver or his circumstances which marks out a case as one of non-veridical conceiving.

In this regard, it is important to take into account the public character of our practice of justifying modal claims on the basis of acts of conceiving. In claiming that something is possible because we can conceive it to be the case, we are expected to be able to offer a recipe whereby others can also conceive it to be the case. If our practice did not have this requirement of publicity, the conceivable would be infected with extreme subjectivity so that what *seemed* conceivable would *actually* count as conceivable. To meet the requirement of public justification it may be necessary, at least in the cases of complicated claims of conceivability, to appeal to certain 'aids to the imagination'—such things as geometrical constructions, proofs, and computer simulations. These enable the mind to take in the fine details of a situation too complicated to imagine in a casual, unaided way. Consequently, they play an essential role in the process of public justification, the process of explaining to others how to conceive what we have conceived.

Interpreted in this light, Lewis's example simply points to the fact that the unaided visual imagination sometimes has difficulty in distinguishing the possible from the impossible. Perhaps an attempt to visualise the construction of a nineteen-sided regular polygon produces much the same impressions as an attempt to visualise the construction of a seventeen-sided one. But that does not establish that these cases are the same with respect to conceivability. A geometer who tried to demonstrate the constructibility of these figures would soon recognise the difference between the cases. She would discover that the methods she used to construct a regular polygon with seventeen sides failed, or were frustrated, in the construction of one with nineteen sides. The lesson this points to is that the kind of act of conceiving that is a true indicator of possibility is not the casual, off-hand act of visual imagination, but the careful, attentive act of conceiving that can be given a public justification.

Under what circumstances do our corrective practices discount acts of conceiving as not being veridical indicators of possibility? The answer is simple: when they suffer from one kind of cognitive limitation or another. In Lewis's example, the act of conceiving the construction of a nineteen-sided regular polygon is discounted because it is based on inadequate reasoning: in particular, it is not based on the kind of reasoning required of a publicly justified demonstration of the constructibility of such a figure. There are, of course, many other kinds of limitation recognised in our practice—limitations due to inadequate critical reflection, limitations due to lack of concentration and attention, limitations due to external interference, limitations due to insufficient memory, and so on. The list is open-ended, as there is a potentially infinite number of kinds of cognitive incapacities or deficiencies which our practice regards as discounting factors. It is important to observe in this connection that it is not necessary to explain why these limitations are discounted by adverting to modal considerations. It is not that one justifies the preference for acts of conceiving based on critical reflection, say, on the grounds that they are more reliable guides to modal reality. The justification can proceed simply in terms of the fact that a person who has critically reflected on some supposition possesses information and abilities possessed by a person who has not critically reflected on it *and more besides*. As a person critically reflects more and more on some imaginary supposition, she thinks of more inferential strategies to probe the supposition for inconsistencies; she notices more relationships of coherence or incoherence between different parts of supposition; she comes to possess greater insight into the complexities of the supposition. In some cases the reverse may happen. But, by and large, the process of increasing critical reflection goes hand-in-hand with increasing powers of conceiving.

A number of kinds of limitations that can affect a person's powers of conceiving have been discussed. They have been characterised by way of their role in our corrective practices: they are those limitations registered in our corrective practice as sufficient grounds for discounting an act of conceiving. The possibility of this description permits the introduction of the theoretical concept of *an ideal conceiver*. Let us call a subject who does not suffer any of the limitations recognised in our practice as discounting acts of conceiving *an ideal conceiver*. The concept of ideal conceiver allows for the precise formulation of the connection between conceivability and possibility. As we have seen, not any old kind of conceivability is taken to be sufficient and necessary for possibility. Even when one can conceive something to be the case and can give instructions others can follow to duplicate one's experience, that does not establish conclusively the possibility of the thing in question. It could be that there is some flaw in one's conceiving that is concealed from everyone. Conversely, one's failure to conceive of something does not constitute a conclusive reason for its impossibility, for one's failure could simply be due to some limitation in one's powers of conceiving. It is a coherent supposition that there could be a possibility so complicated and involved that it is beyond the powers of any actual person to envisage it in actual conditions. But we need not entertain these reservations about the powers of an ideal conceiver: since the powers of this being do not suffer any of the limitations discounted by our practice, we can take the conceivings of this being to limn the boundaries between the possible and impossible.

These reflections suggest a response-dependent biconditional of the following kind for the concept of possibility: it is possible that p if and only if an ideal conceiver could conceive that p. In keeping with the fact that necessity is the dual of possibility, the following biconditional for the concept of necessity suggests itself: it is necessary that p if and only if an ideal conceiver could not conceive that not-p.

It needs emphasising that these biconditionals are not supposed to state the application conditions of the concepts of possibility and necessity.

Rather their point is to encapsulate the possession conditions of these concepts—those features of our practice that we take to be essential conditions of competent possession of the concepts. Thus, one possession condition is that conceivability is a criterion of possibility; and another possession condition is that this criterion is defeated in cases where the conceiver suffers some limitation of cognitive powers—a limitation of reasoning, of memory, of attention, or what-have-you. With the introduction of the notion of an ideal conceiver, the possession conditions can be encapsulated in the form of biconditionals. These biconditionals cannot be read as stating application conditions of the modal concepts, if only because they appeal to the notion of an ideal conceiver, a notion unfamiliar to most participants in modal discourse. Still, the truth of the biconditionals can be recognised by us in our role as theorists about modal discourse, even if not by ordinary participants in that discourse. Indeed, anyone who has followed the response-dependent explanation of the possession conditions of the modal concepts—and in particular the explanation of an ideal conceiver—should be able to see that the biconditionals are *a priori* truths; and so that the modal concepts are proper response-dependent concepts.

This characterisation of the biconditionals helps to clarify some of their features. One feature that requires further discussion is their use of the modal 'could': the biconditionals link the modal concepts, not just with what an ideal conceiver *actually* conceives, but with what such a being *could* conceive. If these biconditionals were intended to state reductive analyses of the modal concepts, this feature would count against them because of the vicious circularity it would induce. But as I have said, the biconditionals are intended to state possession conditions rather than application conditions. In this guise, it is entirely in order for them to employ the modal concepts of disposition and ability to articulate the relevant possession conditions. There is no circularity here since the modal talk of disposition and ability takes place at the level of the response-dependent explanation—the meta-level, so to speak, from which we survey our first-order practices with modal concepts. Certainly, at this theoretical level we must be able to understand the modal talk of disposition and ability in order to formulate the response-dependent explanation. But that does not mean that we have to presuppose what is to be explained, since what is to be explained are our practices, *qua* participants in ordinary modal discourse, not *qua* theoreticians about this discourse.

4. Some Common Objections Answered

As remarked earlier, few contemporary philosophers endorse the early tradition in the history of modern philosophy of linking the modal concepts with the concept of conceivability. So the present response-dependent explanation of the modal concepts is bound to provoke many objections. In this section I consider just three objections against the account that will appear to be the most pressing to contemporary philosophers.

First Objection. The response-dependent biconditionals advanced for the modal concepts are trivial. The notion of an 'ideal conceiver' can be specified only in the 'whatever-it-takes' way (Wright 1992). For an ideal conceiver can only be characterised as that kind of being, whatever it may be, that is able to conceive all and only the possibilities. Clearly, on this understanding, the biconditionals may be *a priori* true, but they are also completely uninformative.

In response to this objection, I wish to maintain that the theoretical stance adopted in the present response-dependent explanation allows for a substantial definition of the notion of an ideal conceiver. (For the general point see Pettit 1991.) The notion was introduced by describing our practices of discounting the conceivings of some subjects on the grounds of their limitations; and an ideal conceiver was defined in a higher-level way as that kind of conceiver that does not suffer from any of the discounted limitations. To be sure, this definition does not specify the discounted limitations individually: it cannot do this in any case since they are open-ended. But it does specify them independently of any connection with modality, and it is this fact that establishes that the definition is not a 'whatever-it-takes' definition. Correspondingly, it can be seen that the biconditionals, framed in terms of an ideal conceiver, are substantial ones. The biconditional for possibility, for example, does not say that something is possible if and only if it is conceivable by some subject who can conceive all and only the possibilities. Rather it says that something is possible if and only if it is conceivable by someone recognised to be ideal by our practices of correction.

Second Objection. The theory, proceeding as it does in terms of an ideal conceiver, faces an epistemological problem as serious as that facing Lewis's modal realism. Lewis's epistemological problem is the problem of explaining how the canonical kinds of evidence for modal claims—evidence in the form of acts of conceiving—can bear on modal claims, when these claims are construed to be about causally inaccessible possible worlds. The epistemological problem facing this response-dependent account is the problem of explaining how our ordinary modal claims are ever justified, given that these claims are tied to what an ideal conceiver can conceive. Since we are never in ideal conditions, or at least could never know that we were, how do we ever come by justified modal beliefs?

It is indeed true that we can never be certain that we are in ideal conditions: no matter how hard we try to overcome of our cognitive limitations, we can never be certain that we have succeeded. All the same, in many cases we can be reasonably confident that we are in conditions that are close to ideal, or close enough for the purposes at hand. For example, suppose you carry out a simple thought experiment in which you suppose that you pursued a different career; and on the basis of this thought experiment, you arrive at the conclusion that it is possible that you pursued a different career. You can be reasonably confident of your modal conclusion in a case like this, because you can be reasonably confident that you do not have any of the limitations that would discredit a claim to have successfully conceived this situation. For example, you can be assured that your inferential skills are adequate to the task of detecting any inconsistency in such a simple imaginary scenario. The other idealisations that are called for in other kinds of thought experiment are not relevant to this case and so can be safely ignored. Your confidence in the modal conclusion would be reinforced if increasing critical reflection on the imagined scenario continued to issue in the verdict that it does not generate any absurdity. It would also be reinforced if you were able to set out instructions whereby others could carry out the same thought experiment and also conclude that it does not give rise to absurdity.

Moreover, in contrast to Lewis's modal realism, the present account can provide a plausible explanation of the internal connection that exists between acts of the conceiving and beliefs about modality. It is generally agreed that the canonical method for finding out whether some state of affairs p is possible is to conduct a thought experiment. On the present account, success in carrying out the thought experiment constitutes *prima facie* evidence for the possibility of p. Of course, it will be fallible evidence, but, subject to reconsideration in the light of new evidence, it will be enough to be going on with. So it will be reasonable to believe that it is possible that p. The story that Lewis gives is very similar, except that he interpolates a step in the middle. He says that success in carrying out the thought experiment that envisages p is *prima facie* evidence that p holds in some causally inaccessible possible world so that it will be reasonable to believe that p is possible. But what is the justification for this intermediate step? It is a complete mystery why one's acts of conceiving should be taken to be a guide to the domain of causally inaccessible objects.

Third Objection. Kripke (1980) has shown that some sentences describing contingent truths are *a priori* and so cannot be conceived to be false. For example, suppose that the reference of the term 'metre' is fixed by the description 'the length of the stick S'. Then the sentence 'The stick S is one metre long' can be known *a priori* to be true and so cannot be conceived to be false. Yet the sentence records a contingent fact: the stick S might have had a different length if it had been heated, say. Kripke's example shows, then, that it is not permissible to equate possibility with conceivability. Kripke has also shown the converse: that it is not permissible to equate impossibility with inconceivability. For he has shown that some sentences recording impossible states of affairs are *a posteriori* and so can be conceived to be true. For example, the sentence 'Water is not H_2O' represents an impossible state of affairs and yet, in virtue of its *a posteriori* nature, can be conceived to be true.

This objection raises the issue: what kind of knowledge do we hold fixed in our acts of supposing? The objection presupposes that in trying to conceive some state of affairs—in entertaining the supposition that the state of affairs obtains—we are allowed to hold fixed only *a priori* truths. If this were so, it would follow that the falsehood of any *a priori* truth, even a contingent one, would be inconceivable and the truth of any *a posteriori* falsehood, even an impossible one, would be conceivable. These consequences would certainly confound any attempt to identify the possible with the conceivable and the impossible with the inconceivable.

It is false, however, that the only kind of knowledge that we hold fixed in entertaining suppositions is *a priori* knowledge. We can see this by considering the way in which our acts of supposing seem to be governed by a certain principle of thought. In entertaining suppositions about imaginary situations, we suspend many of the constraints of actuality, but not all of them. In particular, we do not suspend constraints to do with the identity of the individuals and properties that enter into the imagined situations. An important principle governing the mental activity of entertaining suppositions—I call it the *fixity principle*—is this: in supposing some imaginary scenario obtains, we hold fixed the identity of the constitutive objects, properties, and relations as far as they are know to us. For example, in conceiving whether there could be a talking donkey we hold fixed the properties of talking and being a donkey, as they are known to us, and ask whether they can be combined together in imaginative thought. On the basis of a commonsense understanding of them, it is reasonable to conclude that they can be combined together in the imagination.

The fact that our activity of entertaining suppositions is governed by the fixity principle explains several Kripkean observations about modality. One is Kripke's observation that transworld identity is stipulational in character—a thesis he uses to motivate his famous claim that proper names are rigid designators (1980). In criticising the opposing view, according to which transworld identity is established on the basis of qualitative similarities between individuals in different worlds, Kripke writes:

> Why can't it be part of the *description* of a possible world that it contains *Nixon* and that in that world *Nixon* didn't win the election?... 'Possible worlds' are *stipulated*, not *discovered* by powerful telescopes. There is no reason why we cannot stipulate that, in talking about what would have happened to Nixon in a certain counterfactual situation, we are talking about what would have happened to *him*. (1980, p. 44)

While Kripke talks in these passages of stipulating possible worlds, what is really being stipulated are the identities of the individuals, properties, and relations as they occur in counterfactual worlds or situations. He claims that, in talking about what would be true of certain actual objects or properties in counterfactual worlds, we simply stipulate that we are talking about the very same individuals and properties, not some qualitative counterparts. Kripke does not offer an explanation of this feature of our modal discourse; he simply presents it as an obvious datum. However, this datum is explained very naturally by the fixity principle, taken in conjunction with the proposed account of modality. For they imply that, in evaluating what would be true of some actual individual or property in a counterfactual situation, we hold fixed the identity of that individual or property and try to conceive what would hold true of it in the new scenario. The stipulational character of transworld identities follows straightforwardly from the fixity principle.

The other observation of Kripke's which the fixity principle illuminates is his observation, noted in the objection, that the distinction between necessary and contingent truths does not coincide with, but crosscuts, the distinction between truths known *a priori* and truths known *a posteriori*. Kripke argues that the distinction between necessary and contingent truths is a metaphysical distinction to do with whether things could have been different from the way they are, whereas the distinction between truths known *a priori* and those known *a posteriori* is an epistemic distinction to do with how knowledge of the truths is arrived at. He gives convincing examples of necessary truths that are known *a posteriori* and contingent truths that are known *a priori*.

Consider the way in which the fixity principle explains some of Kripke's examples of necessary *a posteriori* truths and contingent *a priori* truths. Given the fixity principle, it turns out, on the proposed account, to be necessary that water is H_2O because anyone who knew the identity of the property variously called 'water' and 'H_2O', and held it fixed in his acts of conceiving could not suppose that water is not H_2O without generating an absurdity. Nonetheless, knowledge of this truth's necessity is *a posteriori*, relying as it does on empirical findings about the identity of the property variously called 'water' and 'H_2O'. It also turns out, on the proposed account, to be contingent that the standard metre stick S is one metre long, even though the sentence 'The stick S is one metre long' can be known to be true *a priori*. This truth is merely contingent because a person, holding fixed the identity of the stick and the property of being one metre long, could consistently suppose the stick to lack the property—the stick might, after all, have had a different length if it had been heated. Nevertheless, the assumption that the reference of 'meter' is fixed by the description 'the length of the stick S' means that the truth of the sentence 'The stick S is one metre long' can be known *a priori* without investigation of the world.

5. Conclusion

In this paper I have sought to argue that, contrary to the common opinion of contemporary philosophers, it is possible to explain the modal concepts in terms of the concept of conceivability. To substantiate this claim it has been necessary to introduce some new ideas. First, it has been necessary to provide a new model of conceiving, a model that explains it, not in terms of the mental activity of sensorily imagining something, but in terms of the mental activity of entertaining a supposition that does not generate an absurdity. Secondly, it has been necessary to introduce a new kind of explanation—a response-dependent explanation. This kind of explanation does not state application conditions for the modal concepts of the sort required by a reductive analysis, but rather states the possession conditions for the concepts. The response-dependent explanation takes off from the idea that our modal concepts ultimately derive from the human response of conceiving or imagining something to be the case. It refines this idea into a response-dependent biconditional linking the modal concepts with the acts of the kind of conceiver recognised to be ideal by our practices of correction. When formulated in this way, the response-dependent explanation of the modal concepts sheds considerable light on modality (especially by way of the fixity principle) and obviates some of the standard objections to linking possibility with conceivability.

School of History, Philosophy, and Politics
Macquarie University
NSW 2109
AUSTRALIA
pmenzies@laurel.ocs.mq.edu.au

References

Bigelow, J. and Pargetter, R. 1990 *Science and Necessity*, Cambridge: Cambridge University Press.

Blackburn, S. 1986 "Morals and Modals" in G. Macdonald and C. Wright, eds, *Fact, Science and Morality*, Oxford: Basil Blackwell.

Craig, E. 1985 "Arithmetic and Fact", in I. Hacking, ed, *Exercises in Analysis*, Cambridge: Cambridge University Press.

Hart, W. 1976 "Imagination, Necessity, and Abstract Objects" in M. Schirn, ed, *Studies in Frege Vol I*, Stuttgart: Friedrich Frommann Verlag.

Hart, W. 1988 *The Engines of the Soul*, Cambridge: Cambridge University Press.

Johnston, M. 1989 "Dispositional Theories of Value" *Proceedings of Aristotelisan Society*, Supplementary Volume 63, 139–74.

Johnston, M. 1995 "Objectivity Refigured", in J. Haldane and C. Wright, eds, *Realism, Representation and Projection*, Oxford: Oxford University Press.

Kripke, S. 1980 *Naming and Necessity*, Oxford: Basil Blackwell.

Lewis, D. 1986a *The Plurality of Worlds*, Oxford: Basil Blackwell.

Lewis, D. 1986b *Philosophical Papers Vol 2*, Oxford: Oxford University Press.

Lewis, D 1992 "Review of Armstong 1989", *Australasian Journal of Philosophy*, 70, 211–224.

Menzies, P. 1992 "Review of Armstrong 1989", *Philosophy and Phenomenological Research*, 52, 731–34.

Peacocke, C. 1985 "Imagination, Experience, and Possibility: A Berkeleian View Defended" in J. Foster and H. Robinson, eds, *Essays on Berkeley*, Oxford: Oxford University Press.

Peacocke, C. 1992 *A Study of Concepts*, Cambridge, Mass: MIT Press.

Pettit, P 1991 "Realism and Response-dependence", *Mind*, 100, 587–626.

Pettit, P. 1992 *The Common Mind*, Oxford: Oxford University Press.

Rosen, G. 1990 "Modal Fictionalism", *Mind*, 99, 587–626.

Williams, B. 1978 *Descartes*, Harmondsworth: Penguin.

Wittgenstein, L. 1961 *Tractatus Logico-Philosophicus*, translation by D. Pears and B. McGuiness, London: Routledge and Kegan Paul.

Wright, C. 1992 "Order of Determination, Response-Dependence, and the Euthyphro Contrast", in *Truth and Objectivity*, Oxford: Blackwells.

Yablo, S. 1993 "Is Conceivability a Guide to Possibility?", *Philosophy and Phenomenological Research*, 53, 1–42.

Previous and forthcoming volumes of the European *Review* of Philosophy

Volume 1, *Philosophy of Mind*, 1994.
Edited by Gianfranco Soldati (University of Tübingen)
ISBN: 1-881526-38-0 Paper

The present volume contains a main thematical part with papers in the Philosophy of Mind addressing issues such as Self-Deception, Other Minds, Qualia, and Cognitive Science.

> Mario Alai, "Brains in the Vat and Their Minds: A Wrong Impossibility Proof", pp. 3–18.
> Alexander Bird, "Rationality and the Structure of Self-Deception", pp. 19–38.
> Alex Burri and Stephan Furrer, "Truth and Knowledge of Other Minds", pp. 39–43.
> Paul Castell, "Moore's Paradox and Partial Belief", pp. 45–53.
> Ronald L. Chrisley, "The Ontological Status of Computational States", pp. 55–75.
> Michael Louglin, "Against Qualia: Our Direct Perception of Physical Reality", pp. 77–88.
> Adriano P. Palma, "Hopes and Doubts", pp. 89–98.
> Daniel Seymour, "The De re/de dicto Distinction: A Plea for Cognitive Science", pp. 99–122.
> Francesco Orilia, "A Note on Gôdel's Ontological Argument", pp. 125–131.
> Murali Ramachandran, "Frege's Objection to the Metalinguistic View", pp. 133–141.
> Taylor Carman and Gianfranco Soldati, "Good Intentions. A Review of: David Bell, Husserl, London, 1990", pp. 243–159.

Volume 2, *Cognitive Dynamics*, 1997.
Edited by Jérôme Dokic (University of Geneva)
ISBN: 1-57576-072-4 Paper

> John Perry, "Rip van Winkle and Other Characters"
> François Recanati, "The Dynamics of Situations"
> Michael Luntley, "Dynamic Thoughts and Empty Minds"
> Maite Ezcurdia, "Dynamic and Coherent Thoughts"
> Christoph Hoerl, "Cognitive Dynamics: An Attempt at Changing

Your Mind"
Tobies Grimaltos and Carlos J. Moya, "Belief, Content, and Cause"
Alberto Voltolini, "Critical Notice of François Recanati's Direct Reference"

☞ Call for papers for Volume 4, *The Nature of Logic*.
Edited by Achille C. Varzi (Columbia University)

    This issue aims to offer a vivid, up-to-date indication of the contemporary debate on the nature of logic. The intended focus is on questions pertaining to the existence and individuation of clear boundaries delineating the concerns of logic: What is their distinctive character? What makes logic a subject of its own, separate from (and generally in the background of) the concerns of other disciplines? What is it that makes a logical theory a *logical* theory, as opposed to, for instance, a mathematical theory, or simply a theory about entities or relations of some specified sort? What is it for an expression to be a logical constant? Or, perhaps equivalently, what is it for an operation or a relation to be logical? Can these questions be addressed in a general setting, or are they intrinsically unanswerable except within specific frameworks of reference (e.g., a language, or a conceptual scheme)? How are they to be addressed? Are they semantic, syntactic, pragmatic? And how do semantics, syntax, or the theory of pragmatics contribute to our understanding of these questions? Are the answers fully captured by existent systems of logic?

    Submissions, two copies, double spaced, should reach the editor no later than 21st September 1997. Requests for blind refereeing will be respected. No manuscripts will be returned unless special provisions are made by the author. Please send submissions to the following address: Achille C. Varzi, ERP, Department of Philosophy, Columbia University, Philosophy Hall 708, 1150 Amsterdam Avenue, Mail Code 4971, New York NY 10027, USA. Email: av72@ columbia.edu

☞ Call for papers for Volume 5, *Normativity and A Priori Knowledge*.
Edited by Tom Stoneham (Merton College, Oxford)

    The issue will concentrate on questions raised by any aspect of the following familiar argument. 1. Meaning is normative. If a word has a meaning, then there are correct and incorrect uses of that word. Words are used to make judgments, ask questions, give orders, express wishes. (Parallel points can be made for conceptual content.) 2. Understanding a word (or possessing a concept) entails conforming usage to these standards of correctness (to some degree). 3. So, understanding involves knowing norms of use. 4. Norms of use alone determine the truth-values of some judgments. 5. So, the truth-values of some judgments are knowable merely on the basis of understanding, that is *a priori*. It is hoped that contributors will address themselves to such questions as: What determines the norms? Do the norms include more than just truth-conditions, such as whether a judgment is warranted in a given situation? To what extent, if any, might one misuse a word, as opposed to using it with a different meaning? Is the knowledge involved in understanding propositional knowledge or know-how? Must *a priori* knowledge be indubitable? Critical discussion of work on these topics by philosophers such as Wittgenstein, Quine, Davidson, Dummett, Burge and Millikan will also be welcome.

Submissions, two copies, double spaced, should reach the editor no later than 21st September 1998. Requests for blind refereeing will be respected. No manuscripts will be returned unless special provisions are made by the author. Please send submissions to the following address: TWC Stoneham, ERP, Merton College, Oxford OX1 4JD, UK. Email: tom.stoneham@ philosophy.oxford.ac.uk

☞ For further information about this review, cf. http://kan-pai.stanford.edu/publications/european.html

☞ Other titles of interest available from CSLI Publications

☞ *Self-Deception and Paradoxes of Rationality*
Edited by Jean-Pierre Dupuy (Ecole Polytechnique/Stanford University)

Can the notion that we are capable of deceiving ourselves, or susceptible to being self-deceived, be made philosophically and psycholgocially consistent? Much of the way Continental Philosophy currently apprehends the structure of consciousness, and Analytic Philosophy currently tackles the major problems in the philosophy of mind, depends on the answer given to that question. The present volume focuses on two distinct, although related, issues: the thorough questioning of the validity of Donald Davidson's "standard approach" to self-deception; and the role played by the concept of self-deception in the treatment of a series of paradoxes that jeopardize the foundations of the theory of Rational Choice.

Externalism and Self-Knowledge
Edited by Peter Ludlow (State University of New York, Stony Brook) and Norah Martin (University of Portland)

One of the most provocative projects in recent analytic philosophy has been the development of the doctrine of externalism, or, as it is often called, anti-individualism. While there is no agreement as to whether externalism is true or not, a number of recent investigations have begun to explore the question of what follows if it is true. One of the most interesting of these investigations thus far has been the question of whether externalism has consequences for the doctrine that we have authoritative, a priori self-knowledge of our mental states. The papers in this volume, some previously published, some new, are representative of this debate and open up new questions and issues for philosophical investigation, including the connection between externalism, self-knowledge, epistemic warrant, and memory.